# ETHICS AND VALUES IN SOCIAL RESEARCH

UNIVERSITY OF
GLOUCESTERSHIRE
at Cheltenham and Gloucester

# Ethics and Values in Social Research

*By Paul Ransome*

First published 2013 by
PALGRAVE MACMILLAN

Palgrave Macmillan in the UK is an imprint of Macmillan Publishers Limited, registered in England, company number 785998, of Houndmills, Basingstoke, Hampshire RG21 6XS.

Palgrave Macmillan in the US is a division of St Martin's Press LLC, 175 Fifth Avenue, New York, NY 10010.

Palgrave Macmillan is the global academic imprint of the above companies and has companies and representatives throughout the world.

Palgrave® and Macmillan® are registered trademarks in the United States, the United Kingdom, Europe and other countries.

ISBN 978–0–230–20220–7 hardback
ISBN 978–0–230–20221–4 paperback

This book is printed on paper suitable for recycling and made from fully managed and sustained forest sources. Logging, pulping and manufacturing processes are expected to conform to the environmental regulations of the country of origin.

A catalogue record for this book is available from the British Library.

A catalog record for this book is available from the Library of Congress.

10   9   8   7   6   5   4   3   2   1
22  21  20  19  18  17  16  15  14  13

# Contents

# List of Tables

# Preface

In writing this book I have tried to encourage the reader to think about social research 'in the round', rather than as a series of discrete steps or stages that merely have to be gone through in order to produce 'good social research'. As social researchers, we are in the business of constructing the objects of our analysis and thus enjoy a remarkably free hand in interpreting and conveying to others the meaning and significance of our findings. This freedom comes at a price, however, which is the responsibility of exercising our skills in an ethically robust manner. The burden of ethical responsibility has both intellectual and practical implications for social researchers, and a principal purpose of this book is to help the reader reflect on these issues and to consider ways in which they might be resolved.

The second underlying theme is to encourage the reader to treat the wider theoretical and epistemological debates underpinning social research as a valuable resource that can sometimes help simplify understanding of what the research is trying to achieve, what kind of data are required and therefore which research design would be most effective. Theoretical issues, in other words, are not peripheral to social research but are central to it in a very practical sense.

Questions of ethical responsibility, and issues of theoretical foundations, often come together in the form of the social values and value standpoints that, whether social researchers always readily confess them or not, are an essential feature of social research design and execution. 'Ethics', 'theory' and 'values' form a mighty triumvirate underpinning research methodology, and researchers who have a positive and confident awareness of them *really are* more likely to produce 'good social research'.

# Dedication and Acknowledgements

This book is dedicated to the memory of Dr Paul Ransome, much-loved father, husband and son who died on 15th October 2011. He loved to write and was very proud of this book.

He had much more to give and is missed by his family, friends and students. *The Sociology of Gardening* will now never be written and this dedication would have been more erudite if Paul had written it himself.

This book would not have been published however without the help of Nick Stevenson. Thank you, Nick, for taking over and making sure the book was finished as Paul would have wanted. Also thank you to Anna Reeve at Palgrave Macmillan for her help and patience in bringing this book to press.

Harriet Ransome, 2012

The publisher would like to thank the following for their permission to reproduce material: the World Medical Association for the use of the Declaration of Helsinki, 2008; the British Sociological Association for the use of the BSA Statement of Ethical Practice, 2010 (the British Sociological Association is both a Registered Charity (no. 1080235) and a Company Limited by Guarantee (no. 3890729)); the UN for the use of the Universal Declaration of Human Rights: UN General Assembly, 1948; and Sage Publications Ltd for the use of the *Critical Social Policy* Editorial Statement.

# Introduction

The purpose of this short introduction is to:

▓ highlight the main themes that run throughout the book
▓ define some key terms
▓ summarize the focus of individual chapters

## Theoretical parameters of the book

The aim of the book is to help readers move their research projects and intellectual interests forward. Some parts of the content will reinforce understanding of methods and approaches that readers have already adopted, and some will help develop a wider perspective by reflecting on other approaches that are available in social research. While social research perpetually runs up against difficult practical issues, it is equally important to recognize and overcome intellectual barriers.

Throughout the book issues are explored, as far as possible, from the point of view of the social researcher. This is done in order to press the point that ultimately social researchers are answerable to their own good conscience when carrying out social research. Doing research within the rules defined by various codes of professional and ethical practice (discussed in Chapter 2) is a necessary but not sufficient condition for social research to be considered truly ethical and moral.

A guiding principle of the discussion throughout the book is to reassert the importance of the link between the practical and the theoretical aspects of social research. Understanding the theoretical characteristics and implications of social research is a profoundly practical matter. By its nature social research is a reflexive undertaking and so social researchers are necessarily expressing views about the nature of knowledge (*epistemology*) and the substance of social matter (*ontology*). These are practical questions that form part of the foundation of social research. Awareness of the role played by ethics and values in social research is a fundamental part of research practice.

A second guiding principle of this book is to adopt a positive attitude towards what might appear to be the more abstract and esoteric concerns of social research. Rather than issues of ethics and values being peripheral, they add an interesting and important element to the overall processes of research design. Issues of ethics and values are, as we have already suggested, inherent features of social research and, as such, it is naive to proceed as if they can be treated in a superficial way or excluded from consideration altogether. Social researchers are increasingly required, for example, to seek clearance for their research proposals from their departments and institutions. They often have to negotiate access to data and respondents from key players in the research. They are obliged to seek permissions of various kinds from respondents in the form of consent forms. Each of these negotiations is essential in establishing the integrity of the research process, an integrity that is suffused with ethical and moral content.

## Theoretical consciousness

First, the main justification for responding positively to the challenge posed by issues of ethics and values in social research, and for adopting what we will call (with apologies to VI Lenin) a positive *theoretical consciousness*, is that it helps avoid developing an unnecessarily narrow approach in research design. In the same way that good social researchers have awareness of methods in data gathering and analysis other than those that they are already deploying in their own research, so also should they remain inquisitive about alternative theoretical possibilities. Having clear ideas, for example, about what kind of knowledge the researcher hopes to produce or about where that knowledge stands in relation to competing ideas about the nature of knowledge (discussed in Chapter 2) is part and parcel of the research process. It also helps articulate the age-old difficulty of whether the purpose of social research is to contribute to purely theoretical understanding of the phenomenon under consideration, or whether it is grounded research in the sense of making practical interventions such as developing new policy. It is often difficult to say where 'theory' ends and 'practice' begins. A first clear practical benefit, then, of theoretical consciousness is that it raises awareness of how other social researchers are doing their research and *why* they are doing it.

Theoretical consciousness is practical in a second sense, which is that such an attitude can assist in the development of innovative ways of combining elements from more than one research tradition. The different ways in which social researchers have resolved sometimes complex issues of ethics and values can add variety to the research design, first by showing that there is more than one way of defining these issues at the outset, and second by illustrating different ways of tackling them in practice (Hammersley 2000).

The third sense in which theoretical consciousness is practical is that it turns the spotlight onto the ethics and values of the *researcher* and the *research community*. If we take literally Max Weber's influential definition of social knowledge as something that is inherently and categorically the possession and expression of individual minds (see Chapter 3), then it is not unreasonable to argue that the real subject of social research is the social researcher rather than the research subject. We should, in other words, be wary of the myth that social researchers possess a uniquely independent or objective position from which to observe the activities of other social agents. The issue of research-led practice, for example, has attracted increasing attention in a number of fields of applied social knowledge and the questions raised cannot be adequately addressed without also addressing the motives and interests of those sponsored to carry out the research. Despite determined efforts continually to improve the factual content of research findings, social research remains saturated with opinion. The greater the number of stakeholders involved in evaluation research, for instance, a form of research that has become increasingly popular, the larger will be the number of opinionated voices seeking to be heard. Evaluation research is a technique that is specifically designed to do justice to the range of subject positions involved in complex social situations.

Two further benefits of theoretical consciousness can be noted here. One is its recognition that the terms of reference of the research, and the practical tools at hand for carrying it out, are products of *social construction*. There are no pure methods in social research, in the sense that each technique is essentially an intervention in the social phenomenon under consideration. Unlike the biological and medical sciences, in which the experimental apparatus is essentially separable from the matter being investigated, in social research this can never be so. The tools and techniques of social research are continually modified and recombined in order to achieve new analysis interventions. The devices used in social research are very much a *product* of the research process itself, although this is not always explicitly acknowledged. Through practice it has been found, for example, that different kinds of interviewing produce different kinds of data (e.g. Seale 1998, 1999; Silverman 2007; Hammersley and Gomm 2008).

This peculiar type of research outcome is readily incorporated into subsequent research design. Some pieces of social research are explicitly carried out in order to develop new techniques of investigation rather than to advance theory or recommend new policy. Awareness of the socially constructed nature of the whole process of social research again urges us towards a proper consideration of the theory–practice interface.

Since social researchers do not have at their disposal a measuring stick or other form of calibrated apparatus for analysing social action, the base methodology for all social research must be *comparative*. The logic of this reality obliges us to accept that there are no 'fixed fast-frozen social relations', no pure forms of social action against which all other forms of social action can be measured. A population is defined and a suitable research sample is drawn in order to examine in what ways this particular group of social actors acts or does not act *compared with* another selected sample or that population. Instances of conformity or non-conformity are further investigated in order to try to identify specific factors that have caused such forms of social action. The identification of causal factors that account for social non-conformity, usually through comparison of samples of that population, is the modus operandi of social research.

Finally, social research is *over-determined* both by pre-existing theoretical suppositions and by expressed policy objectives. While such over-determination is relatively explicit in the case of policy-oriented social research (discussed in detail in Chapter 7), a more subtle but nonetheless equally important process is taking place at the level of theoretical perspectives that are being relied on. Theoretical consciousness makes us sensitive to what we might call the 'gravitational fields' of social research: fields that pull the research intellect in one direction rather than another. The current hegemony in the United Kingdom of qualitative-evaluative social research, for example, which prioritizes small-scale intimate-ethnographic techniques, tends to enhance the perceived credibility of findings arrived at through this method compared with findings produced by large-scale, non-interactive social surveys, which used to dominate the paradigm.

Having sketched the broad theoretical and motivational parameters of this textbook, and acknowledging that it too is an act of social construction, we can briefly define some key terminology.

## Key definitions used in the book

So what do we mean by 'ethics' and 'values' and, more particularly, *whose* ethics and *whose* values are we interested in as social researchers?

### Ethics

Ethics are rules of conduct that people adopt when they act in social contexts. What distinguishes ethical behaviour from ordinary kinds of rule-following behaviour is that ethical behaviour is underpinned by systems of universal moral values that are characteristic of a particular social group, society or culture. To say that somebody is acting in an ethical way presupposes not just that they are controlling their social behaviour so that it falls within 'the rules', but that the rules in question derive from an underlying set of moral values. Reassuringly, one of these underlying moral values might be the belief that 'following the rules' is itself a moral way of acting.

Ethics are 'regulatory' in the sociological sense that Émile Durkheim (e.g. 1968 [1897]) develops the term, in that they establish a framework within which action or, in the context of the discussion in this book, research activity is deemed to be acceptable and outside which it is not. Frameworks of ethics compel researchers to behave in particular ways because they are backed up by sanctions: if the researcher fails to comply, and is found out, they will be 'punished' in some way. We can identify two basic categories of sanctions. The first are institutional-legal sanctions, which are operated by formal organiza-tions and professional associations (discussed in Chapter 2). Non-compliance with their ethical frameworks may result in censorship or exclusion from the organization or institution. If membership is a precondition for being able to find employment as a social researcher, then this kind of sanction, and the regulation to which it gives rise, can be quite restrictive. A familiar instance of professional exclusion is the medical profession, where bodies such as the British Medical Association or the American Medical Association have the authority to strike members off the list of those who are legally able to practise within the territories over which they have jurisdiction.

The second form of sanction resides within the moral conscience of the social researcher and takes the form of feelings of guilt or unease. Social researchers impose this kind of sanction on themselves. As Durkheim explains it:

> A regulative force must play the same role for moral needs which the organ-ism plays for physical needs. This means that the force can only be moral. The awakening of conscience interrupted the state of equilibrium of the ani-mal's dormant existence; only conscience, therefore, can furnish the means to re-establish it. (Durkheim 1968 [1897]: 248)

Frameworks of ethics and associated codes of conduct are especially powerful in the world of social research precisely because legal-institutional sanctions are backed up by powerful emotional-moral sanctions. Legal-institutional sanctions are often legitimated by underlying emotional-moral convictions. Although they share a number of characteristics with other kinds of legal-institutional regulation (a system of formal rules, a notion of membership or agreement to comply, a mechanism for investigating non-compliance) ethical frameworks are of a different order because of this underlying moral sanction. Breaking the traffic regulations by driving above the official speed limit, for example, might result in a sanction in the form of a fine or withdrawal of a licence to use the public highway, but is it much less likely to be experienced as morally wrong by the offender. Other kinds of motoring offences, however, span the divide between legal transgression and moral culpability. Government anti-drink-driving campaigns stress the moral stigma of causing injury to others rather than the practical inconvenience of losing a driving licence.

However, ethical 'commands' do not simply act as moral sanctions. There is also the sense that human beings gain a strong sense of purpose and meaning by simply being seen to 'do the right thing'. In the Aristotelian tradition ethics are not simply regulatory statements, but we need to consider the possibility that living the ethical life is also leading the virtuous life (Macintyre 1985). That is, the researcher's wish to behave ethically is motivated by the fact that it is simply the right thing to do. Sometimes this is expressed through the saying that virtue is its own reward. What, then, is good for the researcher is also good for the research community, the people being researched and the wider society more generally. This is less a matter of rules, but more an attempt to debate with others what good ethical research should be and then to carry this out in practice. While this is a different way of thinking from the Durkheimian tradition, we should be reminded that they are both sources of ethical behaviour and conduct and it is not necessary to make a choice between the two.

There is also a strongly *communal* dimension to codes of ethics, in that they shape the behaviour of whole communities of researchers or practitioners. In this sense they are *socially paradigmatic* and *hegemonic*. One of the unspoken rules of social regulation is that actors are willing to comply so long as other 'members' are willing to do the same. Potentially, and irrespective of the moral rightness or formal effectiveness of the regulatory framework, a regulatory code becomes utterly ineffectual if people no longer agree to abide by it. The effectiveness of a code of research ethics – in other words, its ability to shape the behaviour of social researchers in any way – is intimately connected with its popularity within the particular research community in which it operates.

The close association in social research between the legal and moral forms of sanction raises the interesting question of how researchers become subjectively aware of the rules of acceptable conduct: when do researchers learn to feel guilty or troubled by particular kinds of (non-compliant) research practice? Part of the answer is that researchers begin to be able to recognize particular research practices as 'bad' or unacceptable during the course of their professional initiation. Incorporation into the professional body means learning the rules of ethical conduct. Reading books like this one is part of that professionalization process. A further part of the answer, however, is that social researchers are already familiar with the principles of acceptable behaviour by virtue of their personal *socialization* into the social and cultural community that they are investigating. Finally, we might also consider the argument that ethical practice is also a practical form of everyday experience. In other words, through discussions with themselves and others, researchers will gain a great deal of information about what constitutes ethical behaviour in any given setting. It is of course not always the case that the 'right thing to do' is clearly signposted. There are inevitably a number of grey areas, debates and controversies when it comes to ethical practice that often require extended forms of discussion and consideration.

This takes us back to Durkheim and to the once popular functionalist perspective developed by Talcott Parsons (1951) and RK Merton (1949) that the *solidarity* of the social group is dependent to a large degree on the assimilation within the group of certain core values and beliefs. To say that social researchers are 'members of the social and cultural community they are investigating' means that they are already familiar with the prevailing belief system of that community and that they are prepared voluntarily to have their behaviour controlled by it. Social researchers can easily tell the difference between what is held in that society to be 'right' and what is held to be 'wrong'. Sociology contrasts with social anthropology precisely because social anthropologists are usually (although not always) *not part of* the social order they are investigating.

The sense of difference or otherness that the researcher experiences when moving outside the social and cultural groups with which they are familiar (as social anthropologists often do) arises from their unfamiliarity with the underlying value system of that community. Feeling comfortable moving between social and cultural groups might require the social researcher to be prepared to alter their own 'moral compass'. Most challenging for researchers who have been socialized within the western perspective, and who have travelled abroad to carry out their research, will be those cultures in which the basic principle of rule-following is itself not found. However, similar difficulties can be experienced within host societies as well. For example, many modern societies are divided along the lines of class, race, gender and age and, although there are undoubtedly overlapping ethical beliefs, we should not assume that this is always the case.

## Social values

Looking in more detail at the *social values* that underpin codes of ethics in social research, we can note that social values have the interesting property both of *expressing* underlying beliefs and of providing the *motivation* to act in a particular way. In Max Weber's theory of social action, for example (Weber 1949; Brubaker 1984), the motivation to act often stems directly from the desire (or in a religious or spiritual context the need) to express a particular set of values through action: to render those values real rather than leaving them in a state of abstraction. Social values have the potential to shape action both in terms of *restraining* some social actions, for example by inhibiting actions that are harmful to other social actors, and by *enabling* actions that are deemed to be socially worthwhile, for example actions that protect others from harm.

The peculiar way in which the social researcher is integrated into the research process (unlike the laboratory researcher who is not) raises the important question of what happens to the values of the researcher as research takes place. Again referring to Max Weber, we know that a distinction can be made between social research in which social values are the object of that research (research looking at the social values that people hold) and the various value positions that, although they are not the specific focus of the work, are nonetheless implicated in it. All social action is saturated with social values and so, like it or not, these are bound to have some impact on the events that occur. Within the general value context of the research we can also identify the social values held by the social researcher. Developing the influential notion of *value neutrality*, Weber recommends that the objectivity of social research cannot be protected unless the researcher makes a special effort to prevent their own value position from impinging on the research. And the first step towards achieving *this* is for the researcher to be aware of what their own value position *is*. Awareness of value position is a key aspect of theoretical consciousness:

> Nor need I discuss further whether the distinction between empirical statements and value-judgements is "difficult" to make. It is. All of us [...] encounter the subject time and again [...] The examination of one's conscience would perhaps show that the fulfilment of our postulate [i.e. maintaining value neutrality] is especially difficult, just because we reluctantly refuse to enter the very alluring area of values without a titillating 'personal touch'. (Weber 1949 [published in *Logos* in 1917]: 9)

Having sketched out some basic definitions, we can now summarize briefly the content of the chapters that follow.

## Outline of chapters

Chapter 1 continues the discussion we have just been having and discusses the *universal moral values* that underpin codes of professional and ethical practice used by social researchers. These values, which provide the fundamental basis for, and articulation of, the idea of moral behaviour, are transposed into *social values* as a practical means of distinguishing behaviour that is ethical from behaviour that is unethical. The core social values identified in this chapter are the preservation of the collective good, the preservation of individual life and liberty and the quest for knowledge. Given the inherently social context of human action, and its equally inevitable social consequences, the values that govern people's action, including that of social researchers, must be social values.

Chapter 2 looks in detail at examples of codes of professional and ethical practice that are currently applied in doing social research. Key elements from the Nuremberg Code 1947 and the Declaration of Helsinki 1964/2008 are discussed, followed by consideration of examples of codes from academic and professional bodies, such as different social science associations' statements of ethical practice and university 'Guidelines on good research practice'. The focus is on how the various codes help moderate the professional relationships between researchers and respondents, between researchers and other members of the research team, between researchers and those who provide sponsorship and funding, and between researchers and the professional associations and institutions with which they are associated. Issues of the justification for carrying out the research, the competence of the researcher, *informed consent* and technical considerations of ethical research design (including issues of privacy and data protection) are discussed in this chapter.

Beginning with a discussion of the underlying intellectual and philosophical principles of what constitutes social-scientific knowledge (*epistemology*), Chapter 3 discusses comparatively the advantages and disadvantages of the most influential methodological paradigms, including *positivism, empiricism, interpretivism* and *constructivism*. The discussion offers guidance on how different research traditions provide social researchers with valuable conceptual tools for resolving the practical problems of ethical research design.

Chapter 4 looks in detail at the value content of social research. The vehicle here will be a discussion of one of the most recent approaches in social research, *evaluation research*. Established questions about the ability of the social researcher to remain value neutral, and about doing research into the values that other people hold, provide a platform for a discussion of research that seeks actively to evaluate the success of policy and programme interventions. Balancing the different value positions of key *stakeholders*, and acknowledging that social researchers are themselves key stakeholders in the research process, is one of the most difficult tasks facing social researchers.

Chapter 5 moves the focus towards social research that adopts a critical orientation towards its subject matter. The chapter discusses how traditional principles of social research such as value neutrality, open-mindedness and political neutrality are displaced by an informed expectation that things could and ought to be different. A first example is *critical realism*, which offers a way of investigating social phenomena without assuming that they, and our understanding of them, are inherently beyond our control. This requires the development of a contingent notion of *causality*, in which understanding is defined as a context-driven process, rather than as a formulaic observation of cause and effect. The chapter also looks briefly at Marxist-standpoint and feminist-standpoint social research, in which the researcher abandons objectivity in favour of becoming an advocate for a particular political and ideological position.

Chapter 6 considers a further set of innovative and increasingly influential approaches to social research comprising various forms of *practitioner research*, including *action research* and *self-reflexive practice*. By closing the distance between the researcher and the research subject or research respondent, participatory modes of social research shift the data-gathering process away from a potentially intrusive, sterile and anonymous experience towards a mutually beneficial conversation for all participants. The linear model of investigation is, so it is argued, displaced by a circular one in which the researcher/subject distinction is dissolved away. The implications of this new perspective for traditional views of ontology and epistemology in social research are explored here. The chapter also reflects on the ethical implications of these procedures.

The final substantive chapter discusses the important topic of the relationship between social research and the policy-making process. It focuses on the role of social policy research and social policy analysis in the field of social and welfare policy, and reflects on the role that social researchers play in the political and ideological discourse about social and welfare policy. The basic argument presented here is that although social policy research and analysis struggle to meet the strict standards of objectivity demanded by positivist definitions of scientific evidence, they do have the virtue of contributing positively to the general ethical and moral discourse *about* social and welfare policy.

The brief concluding chapter revisits issues raised in the opening chapter and reflects on how successfully social researchers are able to accommodate underlying issues of ethics and values in their research activity. The impact of public expectations about social research is also discussed.

# Social Values and Social Research: The Collective Good, Life and Liberty and Reason

1

The ways in which professional codes of ethics regulate the social relationships of social research are discussed in the following chapter. We set the context for this discussion now by looking at the *universal moral values* as well as the *social values* to which they give rise, and which, ultimately, regulate these various kinds of relationships.

## Universal values: Life, liberty and the pursuit of happiness

We noted in the introduction that the base method of social research is *comparative*, in that the findings of social research can only be made sense of in the context of other social research that has been carried out. There are no universal objective standards or infallible criteria for measuring social phenomena, hence the powerfully *interpretive* character of social research methodology. This raises the question of whether assessments of the *ethical and moral* dimensions of social research are similarly comparative: is social research deemed to be ethical and moral only in comparison with other social research that has been carried out?

These dilemmas were notoriously demonstrated in the furore surrounding Stanley Milgram's research into obedience to authority (Milgram 1963, 1973). Forty subjects had volunteered to take part in what they had been told was an experiment on memory. Having assigned these volunteers to groups of 'teachers' and 'learners', Milgram deceived the respondents who were taking on the role of teacher into thinking that they were administering painful electric shocks to the other respondents who were playing the role of learners. Each time a learner gave an incorrect answer to one of a series of questions, the strength of the electric shock was increased. The maximum shock of 450 volts was clearly a very serious if not fatal level of punishment. The teachers could not see the learners, but they could hear complaints and screams that ostensibly came from the learners they were punishing for giving incorrect answers. The teachers were required to continue with the procedure despite their clear reluctance to do so, hence this was a study of the teachers' obedience and not of the learners' memory. At the end of the experiment, the teachers were debriefed and told that they had in fact not administered any electric shocks.

The results of the research were deeply troubling, as 65 per cent of 'teachers' were prepared, on the authority of the instructor, to inflict electric shocks up to the maximum 450 volts. They continued with the experiment even after (at 350 volts) the 'learner' had fallen silent, which implied unconsciousness or even death. Even more serious for members of the research community was the outcry at Milgram's method, which depended on deliberate misdirection and deception. As a direct result of the controversy surrounding Milgram's research design, social researchers have become much more circumspect in devising procedures involving the deception of research subjects (Baumrind 1964; Miller 1986).

Although judgements about the ethical and moral status of social research always include elements of comparison and subjective interpretation, it is clear that the comparative approach is rather precarious given the serious consequences if the research turns out not to be ethical and moral. In the context of control experiments in social psychology, for example, the Milgram experiments have set a baseline for judging the ethicality of such procedures. Apart from the potential harm to research subjects and research respondents, the credibility of the findings and ultimately of the researcher and funding body will be undermined if the research is ethically dubious. Milgram was heavily criticized for his research design on all these grounds. There has also been an important shift over the past 20 years in the kind of social phenomena in which social researchers are interested, away from general features of social life such as orientations to work and social class, and towards the more personal aspects of people's lives such as intimate relationships, mental incapacity, age and disability. The more sensitive the realm of investigation, and the more vulnerable the research respondents, the more important it becomes to have robust guidelines for ethical and moral research conduct (Pitts and Smith 2007). The Mental Capacity Act of 2005, for example, which defines mental capacity in terms of the ability to act and make decisions, includes in its Code of Practice (2005) a chapter on how researchers must comply with the Act.

Concern over these issues has resulted in the development of criteria for judgement and of practical guidelines in the form of codes of ethics (discussed in detail in Chapter 2) designed to improve the moral and ethical integrity of social research. Comparison continues, this time not against the variegated array of other research but against a set of specified criteria that are deemed to be universally applicable in the conduct of social research. Codes of ethics attempt to provide a single point of comparison to which social researchers can refer as they design their research. To the extent that the social research community is prepared to follow these criteria, they become universal through practice; indeed, a research community can be defined as a group having in common a specified professional code of ethical conduct. Over time the credibility of the code and that of those who abide by it become mutually reinforcing. Codes of professional ethical practice are thus *hegemonic*, in the sense that they demonstrate coherence of behaviour and intent. However, this does not mean that they do not need to be interpreted and deliberated in respect of the different contexts to which they are applied.

The effectiveness of an ethical code obviously depends on the perceived legitimacy of its contents. If the contents of a putative code are insufficiently persuasive, then it is unlikely to attract many followers. The major factor affecting code appeal is its basis in *universal moral values*: are the contents of the code irrefutable in the sense that no sensible human being, let alone a humble social researcher, could deny their virtue? Again, a powerful process of mutual reinforcement is in play, since the greater the number of people adhering to the code, the more certain it appears that the contents of the code do in fact have universal appeal. The credibility of the social researcher who wishes to stand outside a code of ethics based on universal principles is undermined to the extent that others are prepared to abide by it. Before very long, abiding by the code becomes a precondition for the credibility of the researcher and of the research they are proposing to carry out. However, it may be important that these codes are challenged occasionally so that their legitimacy is put to the text. This may result in the code being revised or, depending on the reaction of the researcher and the wider community, reaffirmed. This edges us towards the question:

---

What are the universal moral values that form the basis for a code of professional ethics for social researchers?

---

One possibility is to seek guidance from religious codes of behaviour and belief. Religious codes make very strong appeals to universality, since spiritual virtue is deemed to be attainable by all persons. Indeed, many now point to the extent to which religious ethical beliefs actually overlap with one another. The difficulty here, however, is the implication that these beliefs originate from a divine or at least supra-human source of knowledge that, although it has been partly revealed to humankind, ultimately remains 'beyond all human understanding'. The necessary condition for basing a code of universal ethics on religious precepts is the exercise of religious faith. However, in practice many of a community's shared ethical beliefs and practices are religious in origin. This pointed Macintyre (1985) to argue that the Enlightenment project was ultimately doomed to failure. This was because reason can only offer rationalizations rather than moral commitment, which remains closely tied to religious worldviews. The project to find a rational basis for moral and ethical beliefs is, then, unlikely to bear much fruit. If there is no wider human purpose (like that described by the religious traditions) then morality seems to collapse along with it.

Furthermore, we also note the extent to which universal ethical statements can equally take on a religious character. Much of the writing concerning human rights lifts the status of the documents themselves from the profane to the sacred. Again, this argument potentially questions the extent to which universal forms of morality are based on reason alone. Nevertheless, this view can be pushed too far: although much of the moral thought associated with the Enlightenment simply revised pre-existing religious arguments, what was given added importance was the idea that morality needed to be rationally discussed and debated.

A different possibility for social researchers wanting to base their code of ethics around universal moral values is to invoke *humanist* intellectual principles. This perspective originates in the *Enlightenment* conception of the uniqueness of the human subject and the exercise of *Reason*. Human-beingness, so it is claimed, possesses a transcendental quality that enables human consciousness to rise above the particular material conditions in which it finds itself. The human capacity for creative imagination enables *Homo sapiens* to envisage alternatives to the current situation and to take practical steps to bring them about. These steps invariably involve active cooperation with others, thus the inherently social and cooperative constitution of human social action.

This humanist perspective strongly implies the existence of a universal human nature: a set of drives and characteristics that all social actors possess irrespective of the particular time and place they occupy. This conception of a universal human nature sits very comfortably with the idea of universal human moral values and associated responsibilities. Any transgression of universal human values is deemed to be a crime against the whole of humanity. The strength of the legal and psychological sanctions that are applied to social actors infringing universal moral values (for example, war criminals and terrorists) stem from the fact that, morally, these values are held to apply equally to all persons without exception.

A third possibility, and one that again relies on universal assumptions, is to base a code of research ethics for social researchers on political declarations of human rights and values. The Declaration of Independence made by the General Congress of the then 13 united states of America in 1776, for example, offers the following pithy definition of political rights and values:

> We hold these truths to be self-evident, that all men are created equal, that they are endowed by their Creator with certain unalienable Rights, that among these are Life, Liberty and the pursuit of Happiness. (Declaration of Independence, 1776)

These core rights and values are also evident in the Universal Declaration of Human Rights set out by the General Assembly of the United Nations in 1948:

> All human beings are born free and equal in dignity and rights. They are endowed with reason and conscience and should act towards one another in a spirit of brotherhood [...] Everyone has the right to life liberty and security

of person. (Universal Declaration of Human Rights, General Assembly of the United Nations 1948, Article 1 and Article 3)

These political value ideals are again repeated in the European Convention for the Protection of Human Rights and Fundamental Freedoms issued by the Council of Europe in 1950 (last amended in 2010): 'Everyone's right to life shall be protected by law [...] Everyone has the right to liberty and security of person' (Article 2 and Article 5). The European Convention also asserts that 'Everyone has the right to freedom of thought, conscience and religion [...]' and 'Everyone has the right to freedom of expression' (Article 9 and Article 10). Freedom of expression includes 'freedom to hold opinions and to receive and impart information and ideas without interference by public authority and regardless of frontiers'. These latter rights are especially important since they reinforce the legitimacy of freedom of enquiry embedded in the pursuit of Reason and, notwithstanding the rights *of others* not have *their* rights infringed, offer some researchers some protection from being prevented by the state from pursuing their quest for new knowledge.

## Social values

In terms of their fundamental moral foundations, the codes of professional ethics governing the conduct of social research are an attempt to combine powerful assumptions about universal rights and freedoms with a pragmatic orientation towards the pursuit of knowledge. To this end, universal moral values are translated into *social values*. A key feature of social values is that they attempt a synthesis between the concept of individual lived experience (that which is personal and unique to the individual) and the concept of universal experience (that which is part of the common or shared experience). Although social actors are preoccupied with meeting their own individual *existential* and *ontological* needs, the same essential needs are experienced by all social actors. What makes social values 'universal' and 'moral' is not that they stem from a single point of origin, but the profound *mutuality of experience* that characterizes human social life. Referring to the kinds of values in which social researchers are interested as *social values* (rather than simply as 'values') reminds us that they originate from, and ultimately take their legitimacy from, actual lived experience. Universal morality is implied in social values because of this quality of universal experience. Applying their capacity for empathy, social actors can place themselves in the position of 'the other' and thus make judgements about their own actions in light of this knowledge. There might be a strong coincidence between this sense of altruistic responsibility and a specifically religious or spiritual set of values, but one is not required to explain the existence of the other.

Philosophically speaking, the capacity and willingness to take core moral principles into account when deciding how to act are what make somebody a moral person. The practice of thinking about the consequences of what one is about to do in light of the core moral values can be described as *moral practice*. The notion of criminal responsibility in the United Kingdom, for example, is often cast in moral terms. It is presupposed that persons below a certain age, or having particular mental impairments (including temporary ones), are unable to understand the difference between what is morally right and morally wrong, and so cannot be held 'morally' responsible for their actions. Above this age, and assuming no mental impairment can be proved, the culpability of the accused is often expressed specifically in terms of moral reprobation.

Emphasizing the pragmatic, experiential and empathic aspects of social values brings into the foreground the crucial importance of the *social contexts* in which action takes place, and the *social consequences* (i.e. the impact on other social actors) of that action. Although it is not impossible for social actors to develop values that are unique to them as individuals (the difference between one social actor and another often relates to differences in their values), what makes values socially meaningful is the impact they have on activity at the level of the social group. Social values are thus inherently *communal* and *collective*. Individuals regulate their actions according to the values they hold, but the benefits of such regulation are social rather than psychological (it is a moot point whether individual meaningfulness is truly separable from social meaningfulness). The social effectiveness of values stems from the way in which they cause social actors to cohere in their actions to a greater extent than would be the case if there were no values in play. The solidarity of social groups presupposes sufficient overlap between individuals in terms of the values they recognize and adhere to. Social values are thus sociali*zing* and collectivi*zing* in their effects. They constitute a medium of communication between social actors, enabling them to produce accounts and exchange views about how they are acting and why.

## The strong society thesis

Developing what we might call a 'strong society thesis' in social theory, Émile Durkheim and Talcott Parsons suggest that the collectivizing and socializing effects of social values help explain how social order can be maintained in modern society despite the strong urge for individual expression and freedom of action. As Parsons puts it in his seminal analysis of *The Social System*:

> The problem of order, and thus of the nature of stable systems of social interaction, that is, of social structure, thus focuses on the integration of the motivation of actors with the normative cultural standards which integrate the system, in our context, interpersonally [...] The basic condition on which an interaction system can be stabilized is for the interests of actors to be bound to conformity with a shared system of value-orientation standards. (Parsons 1951: 36–7)

For theorists using a functionalist or collectivist perspective (and concentrating for the moment on the mechanism by which social values operate rather than on the content of any particular value system), it is the development within society of the capacity for transmitting social values both across the population at a particular time and between one generation and the next (socialization) that produces the essential conditions for the emergence of social order (Joseph 2003). Society could usefully be defined as a collectivizing force that emerges at the point at which the reliable transmission of social values has become possible. The European Convention on Human Rights refers, for example, to the importance for 'the governments of the European countries' of 'a common heritage of political traditions, ideals, freedom and the rule of law, to take the first steps for the collective enforcement of certain of the rights stated in the Universal Declaration' (Preamble). Similar appeals to a common cultural and political heritage, although in this case in a voice of disappointment, are made in the American Declaration of Independence, which refers to 'Native justice and magnanimity' and 'Ties of common kindred' (Declaration of Independence, 1776).

One could go a stage further than this and argue that, in recognition of the crucial collectivizing and socializing effects of social values, one of the most important social values of modern society is the idea that 'the social' itself is worth preserving ('social values' being defined specifically as the inherent value of preserving 'society'). The maintenance of social order becomes one of the most important social values in modern society. Indeed, the notion of the collective good, and of its importance for the development of individuality, is noted in the Universal Declaration of Human Rights: 'Everyone has duties to the community *in which alone* the free and full development of his personality is possible' (Universal Declaration of Human Rights, General Assembly of the United Nations 1948, Article 29, emphasis added).

To the extent that the preservation of society is seen as a prerequisite for social order, paradoxical situations arise in which the value of maintaining society becomes more highly valued than the preservation of individual lives. In war, for example, soldiers are required to kill and be killed in order to preserve the interests of the collectivity that has sent them into battle, *even if* this means losing their own lives in the attempt. Whether or not one believes that the preservation of the collectivity takes priority over the lives of all its members, social order provides a value context or value platform in which these and other kinds of values can be expressed. We can also note in passing that even the most categorical assertions of individual rights in the various declarations and conventions to which we have been referring can be overruled by the state if it can be shown that this is *in the interest of preserving social order*. The European Convention on Human Rights (Article 10), for example, states that 'since it carries with it duties and responsibilities' the exercise of freedom of expression:

[may] be subject to such formalities, conditions, restrictions, or penalties as are prescribed by law and are necessary in a democratic society, in the

interests of national security, territorial integrity or public safety, for the prevention of disorder and crime, for the protection of health or morals.

## The strong individual thesis

An alternative conception of the role of social values in shaping social order is put forward by Max Weber. Developing what we can call a 'strong individual thesis', Weber's general theory of social action is *individualist* rather than collectivist. Philosophically speaking, Weber believes that since knowledge can only be experienced through human consciousness, and since the only consciousness the individual can experience is their own, the only orientation social actors can adopt to the world around them is an individual orientation. The collective aspect of some social events is a secondary effect of persons acting individually. It makes no sense to Weber to treat collectivities as if they were actually existing phenomena with the ability to act in and of themselves. Where, one might ask, does the consciousness of the collectivity reside if not in the mind of the individual?

Having said this, and while rejecting one of the core assumptions of the strong society thesis that the preservation of society or 'the needs of society' always or necessarily take priority over 'the needs of the individual', the way in which social values shape individual social action still produces important integrative effects. In his influential essay *The Protestant Ethic and the Spirit of Capitalism* (1976 [1904–05]), for example, Weber attempts to account for the emergence of modern capitalism as arising from a historical coincidence between the religious values of ascetic Protestantism (hard work, thrift, industriousness, abstemiousness) and a 'rationalistic economic ethic' (Weber 1983: 128; exact calculation of costs, highly rational approach to investment and decision making). The widespread influence of the Protestant work ethic in the West from the late seventeenth century onwards is attributable to the fact that it combines a powerful set of religious values (focusing on taking individual responsibility for spiritual destiny) with an innovative business ethic (ensuring the prosperity of the business *as evidence of* spiritual and civic virtue). In pursuing spiritual salvation and monetary prosperity as individuals, social actors in modern society are, at the same time, producing social coherence, since they are participating in essentially the same undertaking as everyone else. Collective participation in the value system of capitalist enterprise, just like collective participation in the capitalist division of labour, is a prerequisite for being able to reach individual commercial goals. The use of money, calculation of risk and exercise of trust, for example, all of which are somewhat abstract concepts relying entirely on social agreement and compliance, become essential for the conduct of commercial transactions across time and place.

For Max Weber, then, social values not only provide a means of synchronizing social action, they also provide key objectives *for* social action. Social values, in other words, have emerged not just in order to help social actors achieve particular ends, sometimes the pursuit of a particular social value 'is itself an end, or an end in itself' (Brubaker 1984: 42). This conception of the integrative effects of social values draws on a further important distinction that Weber makes between the *formal rationality* of acting in a particular way and the *substantive rationality* of so acting. Some actions are deemed desirable because they are effective (rational) in the formal and practical sense of bringing about particular desired ends. Officials follow the bureaucratic rules of a government department, for example, because they are seen as the most efficient way of conducting the business of that organization (efficiency that is continually challenged). Awareness of *the aims of* the organization, however, such as delivering a progressive taxation or benefits system, invokes a different kind of rationality, since these aims reflect substantive decisions about what the organization is trying to achieve (the role of the organization in society). Decisions about the best way of achieving particular ends are irrelevant if the substantive objectives they are designed to achieve are no longer seen as necessary or desirable. The technical question 'What is the best way of achieving ethnic cleansing?' becomes a non-question if one believes that ethnic cleansing is a practice that can never be morally justified.

Having looked briefly at the constitution of social values and the mechanisms by which they originate and operate, we can consider the core contents of the universal-moral value system underpinning social research. Once again, we should recognize that as a social construction this core will continue to change over time. Elements are added and refined as new approaches in social research are developed.

## The contents of the universal-moral social value system

So what are the core social values that guide social action in general and actions of social researchers in particular? (See Table 1.1 for a summary.) Core values are drawn from the strong society thesis, from the strong individual thesis and, as a manifestation of the attempt to reconcile these two sets of values, the pragmatic quest for knowledge based on lived experience.

From the social side is the central notion of the *preservation of the common good*: that social order has to be maintained as a precondition for almost all other forms of social action. Associated with this is recognition among members of the social group of the *importance of social values in maintaining social order*. It is difficult to imagine a form of social orderliness that does not have a recognizable set of social values. Social actors sometimes struggle to say specifically what the social values are by which they live, but almost all acknowledge that such things do exist and have a powerful influence over the action choices that individuals make. Actions that disrupt the ordinary state of social orderliness and the processes of social ordering (including fundamental processes such as the socialization of children into society) are regarded as unwelcome. This principle might be carried to the point of *valuing the social collective* as a

**Table 1.1**   Core social values that underpin social research: Life, liberty and the pursuit of Reason

| Social side | Individual side | Lived experience |
| --- | --- | --- |
| **Preserving of the collective good** | **Preservation of life and liberty** | **Free expression of Reason** |
| Maintenance of social order | Promoting a strong concept of individuality | Empathy, sympathy, identification with 'the other' |
| Propagation of social values to maintain social order | Independence and integrity of the individual | Expressing balance and critical distance |
| Preserving the means of communicating social values | Freedom of expression and belief | Protecting the dynamic and interactive quality of human social action |
| Recognizing and acting in accordance with a sense of collective responsibility | Freedom from threats, intimidation and harm | Freedom of curiosity and enquiry and the social value of knowledge |
| Defending the collectivity in the interests of all its members | The right to be heard | Freedom to question orthodoxy |

key objective of social action. Given their important role in social order, *propagating social values* across the population and from one generation to the next is also a social value. Inevitably this also means *preserving the social means* by which values can be expressed and discussed. The preservation of what the social theorist Jürgen Habermas (1984) has called 'communicative action' is essential to this process:

> If we assume that the human species maintains itself through the socially coordinated activities of its members and that this coordination has to be established through communication – and reaching agreement – then the reproduction of the species also requires satisfying the conditions of a rationality that is inherent in communicative action [...] The utopian perspective of reconciliation and freedom is ingrained in the conditions for the communicative sociation of individuals: it is built into the linguistic mechanism of the reproduction of the species. (Habermas 1984 [1981]: 397–8)

Awareness of social order, either as a deliberate goal of action or as a necessary condition for social action to take place (including action that expresses individuality), reinforces acceptance of the strongly collective constitution of human social life. Awareness of being a member of a wider social group (family, tribe, community, society, species) invests in the individual consciousness a *sense of responsibility towards the collectivity*. Actions that harm or jeopardize the well-being of the collectivity are thus deemed unacceptable. *Preserving cultural activity* that is part of the collective identity of the group (language, dance, foodstuffs, dress), for example, expresses a concern for phenomena that are social-cultural rather than individual. Maintaining social order, and *preserving the practices and artefacts* that give social order its particular substance and identity, is a key social value and a marker of civilization.

From the individual side, and beyond the preservation of the physical and mental well-being of life and liberty itself, there is a deeply held conviction in promoting and preserving a *strong concept of individuality*. The claims of social actors to express their own individuality, and to act as individuals (rather than as hostages to the collective will), are a powerful driving force in the social value system. Principles of *freedom of expression and belief, freedom from intimidation, oppression and harm* and *freedom of action* all rehearse the core virtue of the fundamental independence, integrity and liberty of the individual. Also important, particularly in the context of democratic social systems, is the right of the individual for their *opinion to be heard*.

Where, though, does the balance lie between the freedom to act individually and the interests of *other* social actors also wanting to express *their* individuality? This is the point at which social values change from being statements of principle into practical guides for action; the point at which individual social actors become citizens.

Philosophically speaking, an indication of the real strength of the sense of individuality that pertains in society is the extent to which individuals are able to step outside their individual position and evaluate their actions *in terms of the system of social values* that surrounds them. Preparedness to act in accordance with the core principles of the value system is a measure of individuality. The presence of the value system, in other words, removes the potential for incompatibility between the expression of strong individuality and the preservation of a strong collectivity by specifying and regulating the terms on which the two come together. Individuality does not mean isolation; it means social participation.

As noted previously, social actors are able to make judgements about how other social actors are acting by referring to the value system. All individual action is, in this sense, judged against the social values that pertain in that society and situation. Social values provide the moral parameters within which individual action takes place and according to which it is or is not deemed acceptable. The alternative would be to compare the actions of one individual with the actions of another or all other individuals. Clearly this is impossible and so the value system provides a unifying central authority against which individual actions can be compared. When a sufficient number of individuals wants to change the basis on which comparisons are made, or to modify or clarify whether such and such an action is acceptable, further discussion will take place about where the revised guidelines should be drawn. For example, it used to be regarded as acceptable for parents and teachers to administer corporal punishment to children as a way of maintaining discipline. Today, however, the general moral principle of not deliberately causing harm to others has been strengthened to make it clear that children are no longer an exception to this general rule. This debate arguably has further to go and may eventually include non-human life like plants and animals.

Thirdly, core social values originate from the *lived experience* of the human condition and the quest for knowledge that is incumbent on this. *Empathy, sympathy* and *identification* with 'the other' are essential characteristics of human social activity; qualities that are regarded as worth protecting. It is these core features of human experience that enable social actors to see the world (albeit imperfectly) from a point of view other than their own. This capacity for reflexivity establishes a sense of *social perspective* or *critical distance*, enabling social actors to imagine how they would feel if they were in the position of the other and to modify their behaviour accordingly. The consciousness of the individual provides a unique vantage point from which to view the world, but one that is nonetheless tempered by experience, including the experience of empathizing with others. Protecting the *dynamic and interactive quality of human social action* is a core social value. The physical need and intellectual desire to reconcile individual freedom with the collective good give rise to the pragmatic orientation referred to above. This in turn generates the need for knowledge. The category of lived experience is thus intimately connected with intellectual and scientific enquiry: a mode of systematic investigation that expresses and embraces principles such as *freedom of curiosity and enquiry*, belief in *the social value of knowledge* and *freedom to questio*n the orthodox view. A shorthand way of expressing these virtues is simply to refer to the *exercise of Reason.*

In summary, we have argued in this opening chapter that the codes of professional ethics that social researchers use to regulate, authenticate and legitimate their investigations have their roots in universal moral values. These values, which provide the fundamental basis for, and articulation of, the idea of moral behaviour, are transposed into social values as a practical means of distinguishing behaviour that is ethical from behaviour that is unethical. Social values are a forthright attempt to reconcile the need to preserve the collective good with the demands of individuality. Ultimately, there can be no abstract or philosophical reconciliation of these twin forces and so human intellectual effort is diverted instead towards understanding the nature and quality of lived experience. If quality of life and the prospects of individuality are unevenly distributed among a population, interest is bound to develop in the likely *social causes* of this situation (it is highly improbable that relative social disadvantage can be accounted for in terms of identical weakness of individuality among members of the disadvantaged). Given the inherently social context of human action, and its equally inevitable social consequences, the values that govern people's action must be social values.

This brief exploration of social values is helpful for our discussion of the various relationships in which social researchers become involved, since social research is itself a form of collectivized social action. Like the solidarity of groups in society in general, the solidarity and integrity of the research community and its individual members, and the coherence of social research as an intellectual undertaking, depend on sufficient sharing among members of that group of sets of social research values. We can now turn our attention in this direction.

# Social Research and Professional Codes of Ethics

*2*

This chapter considers leading examples of professional codes of ethics used by social researchers. We will look carefully at four such professional codes that illustrate general principles and the particular requirements of specific organizations. The four codes are:

- Nuremburg Code 1947
- Declaration of Helsinki 1964/2008
- British Sociological Association Statement of Ethical Practice 2002
- a university code of ethics

Professional codes presuppose the existence of underlying universal moral values, and of social values, which provide them with an aura of indisputable legitimacy. It is possible to argue against the content of a particular code, or even to challenge the relevance of professional codes more generally, but such attempts are likely to fail because they go against the weight of professional and public opinion. The force of collective will and of collective conscience embedded in social values makes their denial antihuman and undemocratic. Challenging a code potentially serves to reinforce the legitimacy of the fundamental moral principles on which it is based and which it seeks to express. In its own way, and at varying levels of specificity, each of the professional codes we are looking at in this chapter is grounded in a fundamental belief in the preservation of the collective good (social), the preservation of individual life and liberty (individual) and the free expression of Reason (lived experience: see Table 1.1 for a summary).

We noted in the introduction that social research is a profoundly social and *collective* form of activity. This being the case, we can usefully reflect on the ethical and moral considerations inherent in social research in terms of four kinds of relationships in which social researchers become involved. These are relationships between:

> ▓ researchers and research subjects and respondents
> ▓ members of the research team and research community
> ▓ individual researchers and their professional bodies
> ▓ researchers and other stakeholders, including research sponsors and funders and institutions

These relationships are mediated to varying degrees by professional codes of ethics, in the sense that the codes provide a common point of reference to which all participants can refer in planning, participating and funding the research project. The presence of the professional code sets the ethical tone for the research process. Awareness of a code and its impact is uneven, however, since not all participants in the research process will be equally aware of it.

## The complexity of research relationships

The complexity of social research stems in part from the cross-cutting nature of the four kinds of social relationships listed above. Awareness of codes of practice is part of the context informing research relationships. Research relationships also vary according to other contextual circumstances, such as:

> ▓ differences in the power or *authority* of participants (social)
> ▓ degree of *intimacy* or familiarity between participants (individual)
> ▓ previous research *experience* of participants or stakeholders (lived experience)
> ▓ taking *responsibility*

### Authority

Although good ethical practice places an obligation on social researchers to try to make research relationships as equal as possible, it would be naive to disregard the power differentials that exist within research relationships. Respondents might have superior knowledge of the substantive research issue (which is why they have been included in the sample), but they are likely to occupy a subordinate position to the researcher in the conduct of the research. Senior or experienced researchers occupy a more authoritative position in relation to their less experienced or junior colleagues. This issue might affect the planning and conduct of the research, but also the distribution of authorial credit accruing from subsequent publication of the findings. Researchers might also be required to accept the authority of those funding their research if, for example, conditions or limitations are attached to the funding.

## Intimacy

The relationships between researcher and respondent, and between one respondent and another (for example in a focus group), are also likely to influence the conduct of the research. Selecting a sample of respondents from a population with which the researcher is familiar is bound to increase the researcher's sense of identification with respondents and with the attitudes and opinions they might express. Conducting research using a sample from an unfamiliar population might increase some aspects of objectivity (the researcher takes a more dispassionate view), but yet undermine their interpretation of 'what is really going on' (the 'insiders' view' is discussed in Chapters 6 and 7). Familiarity between members of the research team might also become an issue if it increases the number of tacit assumptions being made about the conduct of the research, how to interpret the data and how to report the findings. Similar risks to the integrity of the research could arise if the research team has a particularly familiar relationship with other stakeholders, especially those providing the funding. Competition for government research council funding in British universities, for example, has become so intense that it increases the risk of systematic favouritism towards particular research topics and research teams (Tapper and Salter 2004). However, there are a number of global issues at stake here involving the ability of research institutions to protect their autonomy from the market, state and other social pressures that seek overly to influence the content, practice and outcomes of the research. These are mostly contextual problems that need to be thought about on a case-by-case basis.

## Experience

In this context, experience refers to the fact that researchers and research funders and, with the exception of those whose mental capability prevents them from making sense of such experience, a majority of respondents enter the research situation with at least some previous understanding of what research is. Social research is often characterized as a false situation in the sense that it is not usual to answer questions according to such formalized procedures, although respondents and participants will find some aspects of it reasonably familiar. As is the case with authority and intimacy, however, this sense of familiarity will vary from one participant to another. Some respondents and some stakeholders will be more competent in dealing with the research situation than will others.

## Taking responsibility

A key role of professional codes is to help researchers make the best possible choices in planning and carrying out the research. One way of approaching these difficult issues is to think about *responsibility*. Professional codes of ethics are all about taking responsibility: working out where responsibility lies and who has the authority to challenge whether proper responsibility has been taken. Increasingly, social researchers are expected and required not only to take responsibility in a personal sense, but to be seen to be doing so. An awareness not only that professional codes of ethics exist but of their precise content has become one of the main responsibilities of the social researcher. Reading books such as this one raises awareness of the ethical dimensions of social research.

The idea of taking responsibility moves us beyond seeing professional codes of ethics as simply mediating the various relationships involved to their actively *regulating* such relationships by making explicit the parameters within which the research takes place. The notion of regulation establishes that overall and ultimate responsibility for the research rests with the researcher. Second, it establishes the principle that, if the researcher fails to acknowledge responsibility and/or does not design the research so that it complies either with the spirit of the code or with its practical intent, then the researcher will be held to account for these shortcomings. For professional codes to be effective, in other words, researchers have to be convinced that their work will be scrutinized with reference to the terms of the code and that they will face sanctions for non-compliance. Ultimately, however, and as noted in the Introduction, social researchers are answerable to their own good conscience when carrying out social research. Doing research within the rules defined by various codes of professional practice is a necessary but not sufficient condition for social research to be considered truly ethical and moral. Because of the complexity of the various interconnecting relationships in which the researcher becomes involved during the course of their research, the only cogent fixed point from which the researcher can assess the integrity of the research is *their own* perception of it.

Bearing in mind the complexity of the research relationships, and that each researcher is likely to be involved in more than one of these relationships at the same time, we can sketch out the basic function of the professional codes in each of the four main relationships listed above.

## Researchers, research subjects and respondents

Unless research respondents have previous knowledge of social research (a sample of respondents might be drawn, for example, from the academic population or a population of professionals having their own code of ethics), all they know about the professional code is what the researcher tells them. Their awareness of the code is implicit rather than explicit. Clearly, it would not be reasonable for the researcher to absolve themselves from responsibility for the outcomes of research on the grounds that respondents were aware of the terms of the relevant professional code when in fact they only have a very superficial knowledge of it. As we will be discussing in detail shortly, the central issue at stake in the relationship between researcher and respondent is the issue of *informed consent*. Although informed consent focuses mainly on the requirement that respondents and research subjects knowingly and voluntarily take part in the research, and that they have a working understanding of the purposes of the research and the involvement of other stakeholders, being properly informed can be taken to include some broad awareness of the general rules governing social research.

Reference to a code of ethical practice might form part of the information provided to respondents at the outset and, in this respect, forms a tacit part of the researcher–respondent relationship. To the extent that the relationship between researcher and respondent is, at least in the first instance, likely to be a relationship of strangers, reference to the existence of a professional code helps establish a sense of trust between them. Recalling our brief reference in the previous chapter to Stanley Milgram's (1963) obedience experiment, many respondents rationalized their willingness to continue administering electric shocks to their co-participants precisely on the grounds that they believed that the people in charge of the experiment were ethically and morally responsible for what was taking place.

### Relationships with members of the research team and research community

We will reserve our main discussion of relationships with the wider research community and the professional bodies until later in the chapter, but it is important to note here that relationships between members of a research team are also moderated by codes of professional and ethical conduct. Researchers' responsibility for making themselves properly aware of the existence of the various professional and institutional codes applicable to their proposed research also means making sure that colleagues are similarly aware. In addition to the impact that the codes might have on between-researcher relationships at the level of their personal conduct towards each other, there is the profoundly practical consideration that acknowledgement of the appropriate professional codes is a necessary first step in developing research proposals, which must gain approval by an ethics committee before the research can proceed. The moral undergirding provided by the codes has an important practical bearing on whether the research can proceed.

Differences in levels of experience between members of research teams might require that a senior colleague takes the lead in *interpreting* the terms of a professional code and in deciding *the extent to which* it applies in the particular research context. This is not to suggest that professional codes are insufficiently explicit in the guidance they provide, but that questions of degree might need to be resolved. Greater familiarity with the possible negative consequences for respondents of being involved in research, familiarity gained through previous research involvement, can provide a useful guide when applying in practice the principles of professional codes.

## Relationships with other stakeholders

While adherence to a professional code is not a condition of participation for other key stakeholders such as sponsors and funders in quite the same way that it is for researchers (although charitable organizations and educational foundations will have their own codes of professional conduct limiting the kinds of research they are able to fund), sponsors and funders might reasonably assume that the person or team carrying out the research has carefully considered its ethical dimensions and is aware of the relevant codes. It is not unreasonable for funders and sponsors to assume further that permission to carry out the research is based in part on the researcher having satisfied the professional codes of the institution through which the research is taking place. Although researchers are then not so immediately confronted by the ethical basis of what might sometimes be a rather remote relationship with, for example, a government research council or large public charity, the code provides an important part of the background conditions of their relationship. The code underwrites reasonable assumptions of trust between researcher, funder or sponsor. A little more abstractly, and certainly in the case of research in the field of social and welfare policy (discussed in more detail in Chapter 7), researcher and sponsor are likely to occupy the same moral position in terms of wanting to improve the collective well-being of people in society. The underlying social value of supporting the collective good not only informs *how* the research is to be carried out, but also provides an important justification for *why* it is necessary.

The same sense of shared moral purpose also underpins a further important stakeholder relationship, that between researchers and the academic and research institutions where they carry out their research. Although this relationship is often framed by a contractual relationship between employee and employer, and in addition to the ordinary presumption of duty of care towards fellow employees, students and faculty, research activity is subject to further professional scrutiny. As we will see shortly when we discuss an example of an institutional code, the institution will require researchers involved with animal or human subjects to show that the research conforms to the professional code applying to that kind of research.

Having sketched some of the general background factors and contexts of social research and the kinds of relationships involved, we can look in detail at the chosen professional codes to see what practical help they provide in preserving the ethics and values in social research. The content of the professional codes centres around three basic questions:

- is the research *necessary* in the sense that the ends justify the means; are there valuable outcomes that can be obtained?
- is the researcher *competent* to carry out the research?
- assuming that the first two general conditions can be met, have research subjects and respondents given their *informed consent* to taking part in the research?

The key relationship in social research is that between researcher and research subject or respondent, and the ethical foundation of *that* relationship is that respondents are aware of what they are agreeing to become involved in. We begin with the Nuremburg Code of 1947 and the Declaration of Helsinki.

## Professional codes of ethical practice: Nuremburg Code of 1947 and Declaration of Helsinki 1964/2008

The Nuremburg Code of 1947 and the Declaration of Helsinki, which was first adopted by the General Assembly of the World Medical Association (WMA) in 1964 and most recently revised in 2008, are both professional codes dealing with the ethical conduct of medical research. Their relevance for social researchers is that they specify very clearly what limits there are to research involving human subjects and how human subjects should be treated. Although, in most instances, social research constitutes a far less critical or immediate threat to research subjects and respondents than might be the case with medical experimentation or treatment, many of the same ethical principles apply. Guidelines developed to specify what is and what is not ethically acceptable in the field of medical research on human subjects apply to the treatment of human subjects and respondents in any kind of research, including social research.

The need for such codes arose as a result of concern in the medical profession and in society more generally that human subjects had been used, without their willing consent, for medical experiments in Nazi Germany and possibly elsewhere during the 1930s and 1940s (for discussion see Arendt 1963; Kren and Rappoport 1994; Cesarani 2004).

### Justification for the research

*General benefits of the research*
Consideration of the aims, purposes and justification of research involving human subjects obliges the researcher to be certain that the research really is *necessary* since, clearly, if no significant advantage is to be gained then research respondents have been put at risk unnecessarily (which can never be justified). There are different kinds of anticipated outcomes and different interpretations of the possible benefits of social research. At the least specific level, social research can be justified intellectually on the grounds that findings from the research will contribute to the general human quest for knowledge. This argument is well supported by the powerful underlying social value discussed previously, which is to preserve the right of individuals to exercise reason in developing new knowledge and understanding. One of the ways in which the state of human knowledge moves forward is by conducting social research. If researchers are challenged over why they are doing a particular piece of research, and assuming it is causing no harm to others, they could

Table 2.1   The Nuremburg Code 1947, 10 key points (abridged by the author)

| | |
|---|---|
| 1 | The voluntary consent of the human subject is absolutely essential |
| 2 | The experiment should [...] yield fruitful results for the good of society |
| 3 | [Prior scientific knowledge is sufficient to ensure that] the anticipated results will justify the performance of the experiment |
| 4 | The experiment should [...] avoid all unnecessary physical and mental suffering and injury |
| 5 | No experiment should be conducted where there is an a priori reason to believe that death or disabling injury will occur |
| 6 | The degree of risk to be taken should never exceed that determined by the humanitarian importance of the problem to be solved by the experiment |
| 7 | Proper preparations should be made [...] to protect the experimental subject against even remote possibilities of injury, disability, or death |
| 8 | The highest degree of skill and care should be required |
| 9 | [T]he human subject should be at liberty to bring the experiment to an end if he/she has reached the physical or mental state where continuation of the experiment seems to him to be impossible |
| 10 | [T]he scientist in charge must be prepared to terminate the experiment [...] [if he/she believes] that a continuation of the experiment is likely to result in injury, disability, or death to the experimental subject |

simply respond 'Why not?' on the grounds that the quest for knowledge is justification in itself. Here research practice is justified through criteria such as curiosity or simply the desire for greater levels of human understanding. It is probably hard to think of research that does not at least minimally conform to these questions in one way or another.

A second general kind of justification beyond the intellectual concerns the likely *social benefits* of the proposed research. Items 2 and 6 in the Nuremburg Code, for example (summarized in Table 2.1), specify that 'the experiment should [...] yield fruitful results for the good of society' and that 'the degree of risk to be taken should never exceed that determined by the humanitarian importance of the problem to be solved by the experiment'. Item 18 in the Declaration of Helsinki specifies:

> Every medical research study involving human subjects must be preceded by careful assessment of predictable risks and burdens to the individuals and communities involved in the research in comparison with foreseeable benefits to them and to other individuals or communities affected by the condition under investigation.

There has to be a clear balancing of risks: 'Medical research involving human subjects may only be conducted if the importance of the objective outweighs the inherent risks and burdens to the research subject' (Declaration of Helsinki 2008, Item 21).

Beneath these general assertions of the justification for social research on intellectual grounds, and on the grounds that it will support the collective good (both of which are amply supported by the underlying social values already discussed), will be more specific or localized expectations arising from circumstances in a particular national society or individual case.

### Specific benefits of the research

In medical research the direct benefits to particular individuals might be fairly clear if an experimental treatment saves their life. The saving of an individual life also has wider social benefit, however, since others could be treated in the same way. The situation is a little more opaque in social research as the kind of interventions that arise from it are likely to be more dissipated. Applied social research, for example, is justifiable on the grounds that research findings help governments, charitable and other formal organizations develop effective social policy. While there might be specific beneficiaries whom the researcher could identify, the stronger justification is that the research will be of benefit to social actors in general. Evaluation research (discussed in detail in Chapter 4) is justifiable on similar grounds, since it aims to test the *effectiveness* of policy for improving the situation for particular social actors. Effectiveness is assessed at least partly by considering the number of identifiable beneficiaries and the extent to which they have benefited from a policy intervention.

Although we are especially interested in the ethical justifications for social research, other kinds of justification are in play that might include perceived political advantage, improving the status or reputation of the funding organization, or simply whether the research represents value for money. Ethical justification obviously has to come first, but researchers might reinforce their arguments by referring to these other kinds of justification. Making a successful funding application requires ethical clearance from the institution where the work is to be carried out, but it also needs to be persuasive on political and practical grounds. In this sense the burden of justification for social researchers might be higher than it is for medical researchers: the latter 'only' need to show that the proposed intervention saves life, whereas social researchers might need to demonstrate that the research is justifiable on social, economic and political grounds as well. At all times, however, social researchers need to be wary of allowing these external forms of justification to undermine the ethical integrity of the research.

### Competence of the researcher

The second key theme in codes of ethical conduct focuses on the *competence* of the researcher to carry out the research. Although the qualifications of medical doctors to carry out surgical procedures and other kinds of intervention are relatively obvious, the same general issue of competence applies to social researchers and to any research assistants who might be hired to carry out interviewing and other tasks bringing them into direct contact with respondents.

The competence and qualifications of the researcher to be carrying out the research are highlighted in both the Nuremburg Code and the Declaration of Helsinki. For the medical practitioner, professional responsibility is combined with moral responsibility, which is often referred to as the Hippocratic oath. Items 3 and 11 of the Declaration of Helsinki, for example, state:

> 3. It is the duty of the physician to promote and safeguard the health of patients, including those who are involved in medical research. The physician's knowledge and conscience are dedicated to the fulfilment of this duty.

> 11. It is the duty of physicians who participate in medical research to protect the life, health, dignity, integrity, right to self-determination, privacy, and confidentiality of personal information of research subjects.

In similar vein, items 4 and 7 of the Nuremburg Code state that 'all unnecessary physical and mental suffering and injury' should be avoided and that 'proper preparations should be made [...] to protect the experimental subject against even remote possibilities of injury, disability, or death.'

This explicit commitment of the researcher to the well-being of the research subject is further reinforced by the requirement that the researcher will exercise the highest levels of *knowledge and skills* in carrying out the research. Item 8 of the Nuremburg Code, for example, states that 'the highest degree of skill and care should be required'. Item 12 of the Declaration of Helsinki expresses this as follows:

> Medical research involving human subjects must conform to generally accepted scientific principles, be based on a thorough knowledge of the scientific literature, other relevant sources of information, and adequate laboratory and, as appropriate, animal experimentation. The welfare of animals used for research must be respected.

Research has to be carried out using the best available knowledge in the field and it is a further responsibility of the researcher to make themselves aware of this. If harm were done to a respondent, the researcher cannot retrospectively claim ignorance of information from previous research that might have prevented such harm occurring. (The competence of the researcher to carry out the research also includes the choices they make over technical matters in research design and methodology. These are discussed below.)

### Informed consent

The third key theme of professional codes is whether respondents have given their *informed consent* in agreeing to take part in the research. Informed consent is very much the linchpin of the relationship between researcher and research respondent and the point in the research process at which ethical considerations are brought decisively into the foreground. Coercion is not acceptable because it infringes the principle of liberty. It is also a failure of research design, since data obtained against the respondent's wishes is likely to be deeply flawed. Research findings based on data obtained through coercion or deliberate misdirection are likely to be discredited (for example, Miller's 1986 account of the Milgram obedience experiments).

The principle of informed consent is deeply embedded in professional codes of practice. The first item of the Nuremburg Code states this very directly: 'The voluntary consent of the human subject is absolutely essential.' The Declaration of Helsinki is equally clear:

> Participation by competent individuals as subjects in medical research must be voluntary. Although it may be appropriate to consult family members or community leaders, no competent individual may be enrolled in a research study unless he or she freely agrees. (Item 22)

Informed consent also implies the right to discontinue taking part, to withdraw consent, even once the research is underway: 'the human subject should be at liberty to bring the experiment to an end if he has reached the physical or mental state where continuation of the experiment seems to him to be impossible' (Nuremburg Code Item 9). The Declaration of Helsinki states:

> Physicians may not participate in a research study involving human subjects unless they are confident that the risks involved have been adequately assessed and can be satisfactorily managed. Physicians must immediately stop a study when the risks are found to outweigh the potential benefits or when there is conclusive proof of positive and beneficial results. (Item 20)

Although the circumstances of discontinuing research might appear less acute in social research than in medical research, situations can arise in which respondents begin to experience anxiety and distress. During a focus-group encounter, for example, respondents might begin to exhibit signs of stress or upset if the conversation becomes heated or confrontational. Respondents might overestimate their willingness to participate and/or find themselves in a situation that they had not expected. A life-history session, for example, might elicit strong emotional reactions if previously repressed memories come back to the surface. The social researcher must remain sensitive to these possibilities and always be prepared to end the session early if necessary (Roberts 2002). However, there is clearly an ethical line to be drawn between what we might term tolerable discomfort and situations in which participants might be said to have been harmed. Where this line is drawn in practice needs to be a matter of ongoing debate for the researcher and within wider research communities.

If one utters the words 'informed consent' quickly enough, this stipulation seems not to present too much of a difficulty. For social researchers, however, and again placing them in a more ambiguous position than is usually the case for medical researchers, questions arise as to what being 'informed' means and what constitutes properly given 'consent'.

Taking the notion of 'simple' consent first, this is especially important if the proposed research involves the participation or other involvement of children or young people, or subjects with mental or psychological impairment. The critical issue, then, is whether a potential respondent or research subject is *competent* to make a decision about their participation in the research. Competence is defined in the 2005 Mental Capacity Act Code of Practice (2007) as a capacity to act, in the following way:

> Whenever the term 'a person who lacks capacity' is used, it means a person who lacks capacity to make a particular decision or take a particular action for themselves at the time the decision or action needs to be taken. (Introduction)

Although Section 2(1) of the 2005 Act focuses in particular on incapacity 'because of an impairment of, or disturbance in the functioning of, the mind or brain', the general definition it uses of the capacity to make timely decisions provides a useful guide for social researchers in making their own decisions about the competence of research respondents to make informed decisions about participation.

Part of the underlying reason *why* it matters whether a person has the capacity to express informed consent is because of the possible negative impact that participation might have on people who are deemed to be vulnerable. This is becoming an increasingly common ethical consideration given the trend towards social research into intimate and personal aspects of people's lives (Pitts and Smith 2007). Researchers need to take seriously the possibility that participation in the research might cause mental or psychological discomfort, or in some other way result in a further deterioration of respondents' conditions of living. *The* Mental Capacity Act Code of Practice just referred to, for example, includes a lengthy and detailed chapter on the responsibilities of researchers who wish to carry out research with people whose mental capacity is clearly impaired, such as those with Down's syndrome, Alzheimer's disease or dementia. Defining 'intrusive research' as that which, 'if a person taking part *had capacity*, the researcher would need to get their consent to involve them', the Code states categorically:

> Intrusive research which does not meet the requirements of the [2005 Mental Capacity] Act cannot be carried out legally in relation to people who lack capacity. (Section 11.5, emphasis added)

Where research subjects or respondents are unable to give consent (usually on grounds of age or mental capacity), then the researcher must obtain consent on behalf of such respondents from an intermediary who can act as their legally authorized representative. This might be a parent or guardian, a legal custodian or person in authority in an institution. If in all good conscience, however, the researcher feels that despite obtaining appropriate legal consent, and despite the minimal possibility of causing harm to a vulnerable respondent, the research still constitutes a moral infringement of the rights of the respondent, then an alternative form of research design will have to be devised. The inability or unwillingness to involve vulnerable respondents can in itself be considered a 'research finding' in the sense that it demonstrates one of the most important constraining factors in conducting social research, which is the moral dilemma of affecting the lives of others.

However, we need to proceed carefully here. While most codes wish to offer special protection to the status of children, others also wish to recognize them as moral agents in their own right. This means that it is overly paternalistic simply to gain the consent of a parent, teacher or guardian: researchers are urged to gain the consent of the child as well. Ethical codes of practice under some headings explicitly state that researchers are required to gain consent 'from the child as well as the adult' (Social Policy Association 2009: 4). Here again, researchers are urged to consult the specific code of ethics that governs their professional practice and to proceed on a case-by-case basis.

### Subjects and respondents

The question of respondents' ability to give their consent can be considered in relation to the important distinction between research respondents and research subjects. Subjects might not be aware that they are the subject of research, whereas respondents will be. The issue when dealing with research subjects is whether or to what extent it is justifiable to deprive research subjects of any opportunity to give their consent. Simple observation, for example, does not ask for consent to be given at all, but it might constitute a breach of the individual's right to privacy (see below).

Slightly different is the case of observing subjects in public. Data gathered in this way could be justified on the grounds that the ordinary expectation of citizens that their actions are not being systematically observed is mistaken. It is a matter of simple fact that in the modern surveillance society very many public places are equipped with cameras whose purpose is to observe and monitor behaviour. It would be impossible for social actors to make a journey of any length through any urban district in the United Kingdom today *without* their actions being recorded in this way. The political justification for this is that the modest infringement on individual liberty imposed by 'mass' or 'undirected surveillance' (as distinct from 'targeted surveillance') is balanced by the need of the state to prevent disruption to social order. State observation of citizens, so it is claimed, reduces crime and increases security both of which are deemed to be valuable social benefits (House of Lords Report 2009, Item 24).

A famous illustration of the ethical difficulties of observation research is Laud Humphries' study of casual homosexual sex in public lavatories, published as *Tearoom Trade* in 1970. Humphries carried out covert observation in men's public lavatories (the tearooms) to study encounters between homo-sexual men meeting for sex. Although he did not lie directly to the people he encountered about his real purpose, he did take advantage of the fact that the men assumed he was there for the same reason they were. Without their knowledge, he also made detailed notes of their activities. In a later stage of his research, Humphries used the car number plates of men he had observed in the tearooms to find their names and addresses and, under the pretext of conducting social research for different purposes entirely, interviewed a sample of the men in their own homes. There is no evidence that Humphries' research harmed the men in any way, but, given that homosexual activity was illegal at that time in the United States, it would have been extremely serious if the men's names had become public.

Similar methodological dilemmas arise in participant observation, since the researcher has to decide whether they are at ease with the albeit moderate form of misdirection or plain deception they are using in order to get the data they claim they need. Consideration should be given to what level of deception is strictly necessary to gather the required data and/or whether it is possible to get the data by some other means. The ethical and practical difficulties of partic-ipant observation are likely to increase further, and might become impossible to keep up, if the observation takes place over a number of weeks or months, since the fiction is likely to become increasingly difficult to maintain. A classic example of the ethical dilemmas posed by participant observation techniques is William Foote Whyte's study *Street Corner Society* (1993 [1943]. Although Whyte explained in some detail what his research was about to his key infor-mant 'Doc', and although Doc became 'in a very real sense a collaborator in the research', other members of the Italian gang community in the North End of Boston knew very little about the study other than that 'I was writing a book about Cornerville' (Whyte 1993: 300–01).

For researchers intending to incorporate simple observation and participant observation into their research design, an ethical judgement has to be made between the benefits of the research and the potential harm it could do. If it is unlikely that any harm will come to those being observed, the consequences of infringing their rights to anonymity and privacy can be balanced against the potential benefit to society of the knowledge that might be developed. The onus is very much on the researcher to make the case that the benefits outweigh, and in fact can be used as grounds for justifying, moderate infringements of the right to privacy. Reflecting some years later about his Cornerville study, Whyte writes: 'What impact did the book have on the North End? I have no evidence of any major influence or even that it was widely read in the dis-trict' (Whyte 1993: 342). However, he goes on to explain that Doc, whose real identity has subsequently been revealed, 'did everything he could to discour-age local reading of the book for the possible embarrassment it might cause a number of individuals, including himself [...] The last letter I received from him was a request that I henceforth not tell anyone who "Doc" was' (Whyte 1993: 347).

These potential difficulties can be reduced when respondents are approached directly and openly (rather than covertly). In answering questions through surveys, questionnaires, interviews or focus groups, for example, respondents will be aware of what they are doing and so the risk of deception is considerably reduced. The situation is a little different when respondents are to be contacted via particular institutions such as their place of employment or residence. In such cases the initial conversation with representatives or *gatekeepers* of the organization will usually include an account of the various kinds of protection that are built into the research design. It is probable that individual respondents will also be contacted individually and so assurances and information provided to the organization act as a kind of preliminary to the granting of full consent. In some observational studies, however, or in studies where it is necessary for respondents not to be aware of their participation for reasons of research design, although consent has been given by organizational gatekeepers respondents might not be contacted directly for permission. This raises a number of important issues to do with the liberty of the individual, including their right to privacy. If respondents are part of a captive population, for example in a prison or psychiatric institution, the right to privacy still needs to be properly considered. One justification for research where informed consent cannot be obtained in the usual way is that the research will be of benefit to the general good and thus, albeit indirectly, to those who have taken part, even if they were not, or could not be, consenting to it (Pitts and Smith 2007).

Turning from 'simple' consent to informed consent, a key issue for social researchers is whether respondents are sufficiently well informed to give their consent. With what kind and quality of information are respondents being provided? Information can be given orally, for example a brief statement that is read out as part of the preamble to asking questions in a questionnaire or interview. Where there is no direct interaction, a brief written statement is provided so that respondents have an opportunity to read for themselves what the research is all about. In the case of self-completion questionnaires, for example, it is standard practice to include such a statement at the top of the questionnaire. Statements should be clear and open, explain who the researcher and/or research organization is, and say what the research results will be used for and how they will be disseminated. Respondents might not be required to agree with the intended outcomes of the research, or even to understand fully their widest implications as a condition of participating, but in order to treat their consent as *informed* consent respondents need to be *sufficiently* aware of the context and purposes of the research.

However, there are circumstances in which we may need to abandon the usual procedures of informed consent. In these cases we might say that there are 'waivers' of informed consent (American Sociological Association 1997: 14). There are many circumstances in which this might apply. One such example could be research into a group of 'illegal' migrants or a group who do not have formal citizenship status or who are subject to human rights violations of various kinds. Here the presentation of an informed consent form may give the impression that the research is connected to state practices of surveillance and control. It may be necessary to fit the process of informed consent to the research context in ways that are sensitive to the needs of the research and the participants. Such cases should be monitored by wider research bodies and the university requiring that researchers gain ethical clearance before the work is allowed to proceed. Again, it may not be possible to decide in advance whether such research is ethical, but very careful forms of deliberation and consideration will be required.

## Privacy, anonymity and confidentiality

The foregoing discussion has referred a number of times to privacy. To the extent that social researchers obtain personal information from people, observe and interview them, and generally intrude on their lives, the issue of privacy is something that needs to be taken seriously. The Universal Declaration of Human Rights (1948), for example, states:

> No one shall be subjected to arbitrary interference with his privacy, family, home or correspondence, nor to attacks upon his honour and reputation. Everyone has the right to the protection of the law against such interference or attacks. (Article 12)

This right is repeated in the European Convention for the Protection of Human Rights and Fundamental Freedoms: 'Everyone has the right to respect for his private and family life, his home and his correspondence' (Article 8(1)).

However, despite clear endorsement for the right to privacy, the European Convention seems to take this right back by saying that 'public authority' (i.e. the state) can *disregard* the right to privacy 'in the interests of national security, public safety or the economic well-being of the country, for the prevention of disorder or crime, for the protection of health and morals, or for the protection of the rights and freedoms of others' (Article 8(2)). One might suggest that, at a push, not much goes on in the 'private' home that could *not* be treated by the state as grounds for the official invasion of privacy. It is unlikely, however, that a humble social researcher would be able to justify disregard for privacy, home, honour and reputation on the grounds of 'national security'.

Further protection is offered to the individual by the laws on confidentiality and the protection of personal data. The Data Protection Act of 1998, for example, stipulates that personal data must be:

- obtained fairly and lawfully (i.e. with permission from the 'data subject')
- adequate, relevant and not excessive in respect of the purpose for which it has been gathered
- stored securely
- accurate and kept up to date

■  kept only for as long as is necessary for the stated purpose
■  not transferred from one country to another without permission from the 'data subject'

Although it is unlikely that a respondent will subsequently exercise their right under the Act to request a copy of the data being held, or to make a legal challenge over the way the data is being stored, used and so on, best practice dictates that social researchers should treat personal data very respectfully. Assurances will usually be given as a condition of respondents being prepared to take part in the study, for instance a clear undertaking that any information they provide (including personal data of the kind specified in the Data Protection Act) will be recorded and anonymized in such a way that the data cannot be traced back to them.

Anonymity is relatively easy to achieve with quantitative data obtained, for example, from a social survey, since the analysis will usually be limited to the cross-tabulation of responses in various categories in search of interesting co-relations between responses. Assurances about anonymity and confidentiality are more complex in the case of qualitative data gathered, for example, through an interview, since social researchers will need to refer in detail to what respondents said. In each case the basic technique is to record personal information separately from the main body of data and to use a system of codes to link respondents with the data they have provided. Only the principal researcher should have access simultaneously to both parts of the information and thus respondents can be assured that, even though there is a record of their taking part, nobody can attribute any particular response to them. The special case of 'patient confidentiality', as applied in the context of medical examination and record keeping (and as specified in the Health and Social Care Act 2006) is unlikely to apply in the case of data collected by social researchers.

Issues of anonymity and confidentiality become more complex in the case of data that is gathered during a participatory event such as a focus group or evaluation-research discussion. Although the researcher will take trouble to ensure that the final presentation of findings and results will protect individual identities (perhaps from other stakeholders in positions of authority), it is clear that participants will know who else was there and indeed what they said. These issues are discussed in more detail in Chapters 4 and 6.

In summary, respect for the integrity of research respondents not only includes protecting their physical and mental well-being (as stipulated in the codes of medical ethics) but also their political rights as citizens, particularly their right to privacy (as stipulated in the European Convention, the Universal Declaration of Human Rights and the Data Protection Act). Unless respondents specifically agree otherwise, a condition of participation is that respondents remain anonymous and their personal details are treated as confidential. Even if personal information has to be recorded, it is essential that, including in relatively small-scale or intimate studies, individual respondents should not be identifiable from the published findings. While respondents might recognize themselves, others should not be able to recognize them. This basic expectation of privacy, anonymity and confidentiality reflects the underlying social value of preserving the integrity and liberty of the individual, as discussed in Chapter 1. It is expected that researchers should 'take reasonable precautions to protect the confidentiality rights of research participants' (American Sociological Association 1997: 11).

## Technical considerations and research design

For respondents to be properly informed they also need to have some awareness of the research situation they are letting themselves in for. This introduces consideration of the ethics of the *technical or practical aspects* of the research design, including the competence of the research team. An important difference between surveys and interviewing, for example, is the relative exposure of respondents to the researcher and research instruments. Questionnaires administered remotely via post and email protect respondents from direct contact with the research team, but with a corresponding lowering of response rate. Surveying by telephone or email, and some forms of face-to-face interview, retain quite a high degree of anonymity, in the sense that the questioning process is not especially intimate, but questions arise over the quality of the resultant data. Respondents have been shown to answer more honestly in fact-to-face interviews.

Ethical considerations also vary between different kinds of interviewing. In individual interviews respondents are protected by the relative intimacy and privacy of the interview situation. In a focus group session, in contrast, respondents are under pressure to perform (and possibly to conform) under the scrutiny of fellow participants. Respondents are likely to vary considerably in terms of how well they cope with this situation, a variation that might have an impact on the data that emerges from the session (Seale 1999; Hammersley and Gomm 2008). It has also already been noted that differences in the power or relative status of respondents affect the conduct of social research. If senior and junior colleagues from the same organization are participating together in a focus group or evaluation session, for example, consideration needs to be given to the dynamics of the group and to the possible impact of the research on their subsequent working relationships (evaluation research is discussed in Chapter 4).

A number of contemporary methods encourage the *active participation* of subjects or respondents in the research process. This being the case, consideration also needs to be given to agreeing how and to what extent respondents will have opportunities to change or withdraw the data they provide or comment on emergent findings. If the method claims full participation of all stakeholders, then the process by which this is to be achieved needs to be agreed at the outset. In some instances research sponsors or funders might increasingly expect to be more actively and directly involved in the design of the research process.

Providing respondents with adequate information includes information about what use will be made of the data they provide and, further along in the research process, how and in what form the *results* of the research will be published. A state of deception could arise if, even having provided a précis of the research and having obtained a signature on a consent form, the findings were subsequently used for a purpose that was not specified at the outset. In participatory forms of research design, such as action research and evaluation research, the purposes of the research might also change over time, raising difficult questions of whether fresh consents will be required. These techniques also raise the bar with respect to informed consent, as it might be impossible to say clearly at the outset what the likely uses, consequences and outcomes of the research are likely to be. Indeed, researchers who characterize participatory evaluation as a learning experience might actively reject the notion that final outcomes can be anticipated in detail at all. Consideration also needs to be given to whether consent will have to be reviewed and/or renewed during the course of the research if, for example, new gatekeepers or respondents become involved, or if the research uses a longitudinal methodology.

Supporting the principle that 'Publically-funded research data should be openly available to the maximum extent possible' (ESRC 2010: Item 4), the UK Economic and Social Research Council obliges grant holders to agree to place their data in a national data archive administered by the ESRC's Economic and Social Data Service; the ESRC will 'withhold final payment of an award if the data have not been offered for archiving to the required standard within three months of the end of the award' (ESRC 2010: Item 10.5). Although the ESRC also declares its intention to adhere 'to the government data security requirements and recognises the need to meet the confidentiality commitments and maintain the security of data' (ESRC 2010: Item 5), making data available in this way does tend to undermine the original researchers' assurances about the purposes of the research and, bearing in mind our earlier reference to the protection of personal data, who might have access to it. The ESRC Research Data Policy instructs grant holders to make respondents aware of the likely future use of the data they provide *rather than* allowing grant holders not to archive their data:

> Where research data are considered confidential or contain sensitive personal data, award holders must seek to secure consent for data sharing or alternatively anonymise the data in order to make sharing possible. The ESRC regards a waiver of deposit as an exception and reserves the right tor refuse waivers where there is insufficient evidence to prevent the data sharing. (ESRC 2010: Item 32)

In addition to researchers being aware of the terms of the Freedom of Information Act 2000 and the Data Protection Act, further practical considerations include issues of safety and risk, copyright clearances if filming in any public

**Table 2.2**  Checklist of items when preparing a consent form

---

- Respect for the personal integrity of the respondent.
- Clear statement of the aims and purposes of the research.
- Clear statement of who is funding the research and for what purpose.
- Firm commitment to protecting the anonymity and privacy of respondents.
- Clear commitment to treat personal and sensitive information confidentially.
- Reassurance that secure procedures are in place for analysing the data once obtained.
- Clear explanation of who will have access to the data respondents provide.
- Brief explanation of where research findings will be published.
- Offer to provide respondents with further information about research if they ask for it.
- Reassurances about possible future uses of the data.
- Any issues relating to the Data Protection Act.
- Any issues relating to the Human Rights Act.
- Any issue relating to copyright of data and other materials used in the research.
- Precautions regarding the safety of respondents.

---

place, and any copyrights respondents might have over the material they provide, for example diary entries or photographs over which they have intellectual property rights.

Table 2.2 provides a checklist of items that should always be considered when informing respondents about the research and preparing the consent forms that might be required.

Ultimately, and aside from reminding us of the moral, ethical and philosophical dimensions of social research, the problem of gaining informed consent is a profoundly practical matter that, by focusing the mind of the researcher on the integrity of the data, contributes significantly to the practical development, design and conduct of the research.

## Professional codes: British Sociological Association Statement of Ethical Practice

Very much following the template for ethical medical research practice established in the Nuremburg Code and the Declaration of Helsinki, professional organizations in the social sciences, and institutions where social research (research involving human subjects) takes place, have also developed detailed codes of ethical and professional practice. The principles of the *justification* for carrying out the research, the *competence* of the researcher to do so and *informed consent* are diligently repeated in these codes. One UK university statement on ethical practice begins with the simple assertion: 'Research is premised on a fundamental moral commitment to advancing human welfare, knowledge and understanding.' The Statement of Ethical Practice of the British Sociological Association (BSA; 2002) is equally explicit:

> Sociological research is a valuable activity and contributes to the well-being of society. Members should strive to maintain the integrity of sociological enquiry as a discipline, the freedom to research and study, and to publish and promote the results of sociological research including making data available for the use of researchers in the future. (Item 5)

> Although sociologists, like other researchers are committed to the advancement of knowledge, that goal does not, of itself, provide entitlement to override the rights of others. (Item 11)

In addition, the American Sociological Association adds that sociologists should also seek to communicate their findings in a spirit and language that are both 'respectful' and 'understandable' to the participants involved in the research (ASA 1997: 15). This is clearly a difficult requirement to meet in practice given the inevitable use of theoretical terms and abstract concepts. However, research should make an effort to meet these requirements and avoid the practice of being deliberately obtuse.

Beyond the quest for knowledge and respect for the integrity and dignity of research subjects and respondents, however, codes produced by professional associations and institutions also seek to regularize the relationships between social researchers and the organizations and institutions at which they work. Between the codes of high ethical principles discussed in the previous section (Nuremburg and Helsinki) and the code of the professional association discussed in this section (BSA), there is a definite shift in emphasis away from codes that are principally preoccupied with ethical conduct and the morality of research on human subjects, towards codes that have been developed to guide and regulate, in a more pragmatic way, the *professional conduct* of social researchers. From the perspective of the professional body or institution, the spirit that lies behind good ethical practice carries over into the kinds of behaviour that researchers are required to exhibit across all of their professional activities.

As indicated in the quotation above, members of professional associations and researchers who claim solidarity with its ethical standpoint (for example, in declaring their ethical commitments when applying for funding and/or as a condition for receiving ethical approval from their institutions to carry out the research) are also under an obligation not only towards research subjects but also to protect the reputation of other sociologists and of sociology as an academic discipline. This point is reiterated a number of times in the BSA Statement:

> During their research members should avoid, where they can, actions which may have deleterious consequences *for sociologists who come after them*

or which might undermine the *reputation of sociology as a discipline.* (BSA 2002: Item 40, emphasis added)

In their relations with the media, members should have regard for the reputation of the discipline. (BSA 2002: Item 9)

There is no suggestion here that the interests and reputation of sociology should come above those of researchers, research respondents, sponsors and funders, but it is a moot point whether responsibility for protecting the reputation of an academic discipline is an ethical consideration of the same order as those we have been discussing so far in this chapter. In the BSA Statement, expectations of how professional relationships with fellow sociologists, and especially with BSA members, will be conducted are suffused with the same spirit of ethical integrity as that which is necessary in dealings with those outside the profession.

The difficulty of sustaining the ethical and moral force of professional relationships between researchers (one of the key sets of relationships that we identified at the start of this chapter) is also evident in respect of issues of *enforcement* and *regulation.* Although the BSA is in a position of authority relative to its members and other researchers wishing to be associated with its Statement, *responsibility for* ethical conduct remains with the individual researcher. There is no suggestion in the BSA Statement that the Association makes itself in any way responsible for the ethical conduct of its members and associates. Rather, and as the BSA Statement puts it in its introduction, its force is really only manifest through a rather general appeal to the collective solidarity or *hegemony* of the discipline:

> The strength of this statement and its binding force rest ultimately on active discussion, reflection, and continued use by sociologists. In addition, the statement will help to communicate the professional position of sociologists to others, especially those involved in or affected by the activities of sociologists. (BSA 2002: 1)

Perhaps reflecting awareness of its limited ability actually to enforce the rules among its own membership, the BSA Statement also adopts a somewhat cautionary tone in the way it offers its advice on ethical conduct. Having noted that 'the advancement of knowledge' does not 'provide entitlement to override the rights of others' (Item 11), the Statement does leave quite a margin for individual interpretation of what might otherwise be regarded as hard-and-fast rules of individual rights and informed consent:

> In some cases, where public interest dictates otherwise and particularly where power is being abused, obligations of trust and protection [to respondents] *may weigh less heavily.* Nevertheless, these obligations should not be discarded lightly. (Item 15, emphasis added)

> *As far as possible* participation in sociological research should be based on the freely given informed consent of those studied. (Item 16, emphasis added)

This obviously leaves the door open to different interpretations of what is or is not acceptable 'within the rules' as set out in the BSA Statement. These difficulties become especially acute in respect of covert research.

### Covert research

> Covert methods violate the principles of informed consent and may invade the privacy of those being studied. Covert researchers might need to take into account the emerging legal frameworks surrounding the right to privacy. Participant and non-participant observation in non-public spaces or experimental manipulation of research participants without their knowledge should be resorted to only where *it is impossible to use other methods to obtain essential data*. (BSA 2002: Item 32, emphasis added)

The BSA Statement goes on to suggest: 'In such cases it is important to safeguard the anonymity of research participants. Ideally, where informed consent *has not been obtained* prior to the research it should be obtained post-hoc' (BSA 2002: Item 33, emphasis added). The obvious practical difficulty here is that, having completed the fieldwork and possibly part of the analysis, the researcher might find that retrospective consent is not given and the data cannot be used in the direct way that might have been intended originally. In this instance data from covert observation might have to be used much more indirectly, perhaps forming part of the general background research material only. It is somewhat contradictory to ask for consent after the event.

In addition to this practical difficulty, however, is the more pressing one that, from a strictly ethical point of view, obtaining data without consent is unethical. At the very least, the extent to which consent given in retrospect is 'informed' consent is questionable. Whatever uses are subsequently made of data obtained by covert methods, the social researcher is obviously taking a major risk in deploying a method that violates the core principle of informed consent. The BSA Statement again tends to combine the basic ethical issue (informed consent is a precondition for participation) with a pragmatic concern with the feasibility of social research. According to the BSA Statement, the privacy of research subjects can be infringed in cases where '*it is impossible to use other methods to obtain essential data*' (Item 32, emphasis added). There is no guidance in the Statement as to what constitutes 'essential data' and so decisions about this are left to the discretion of the researcher.

Clearly then, and quite unlike the situation in the medical profession where failure to abide by the terms of the professional code may result in withdrawal of the right to practise at all, codes of ethical and professional practice used by social researchers are not backed up by such powerful sanctions.

In social research the process of maintaining ethical integrity, of making sure that researchers actually are practising what their associations and institutions preach, depends very largely on the discretion of the individual researcher and on the process of peer review (see below). As we have already emphasized, in the end it is up to the individual conscience of the social researcher to decide whether the research they are proposing is, or is not, ethical.

We have already noted that the underlying purpose of codes of professional and ethical conduct, such as the one provided by the BSA, is to help regulate professional relationships between social researchers and other stakeholders in the research process. A key area in which professional codes seek to offer guidance is over possible conflict of interest.

## Conflict of interest

Conflict of interest arises in a slightly different form in social research than in medical research, in the sense that differences in the interests of the various parties involved cannot be resolved simply by asking whether the patient will survive the procedure and benefit from subsequent treatment. If the proposed medical research cannot be shown to benefit patients then, whatever other financial or institutional interests are involved, the research cannot proceed (or if it does proceed in a clandestine or covert way it cannot be deemed to be ethically robust). Here, social researchers are reminded to 'disclose relevant sources of financial support' (ASA 1997: 7).

Issues of conflict of interest are not just between different stakeholders in the research process (the different kinds of research relationships discussed at the start of the chapter), but may also arise *between* aspects of the research design and the responsibility of the researcher towards their research respondents. As we have just been discussing, for example, covert techniques of data gathering clearly infringe the rights of the respondents to privacy and anonymity, and yet might be the only practical way of getting at the information required. The ambitions and determination of the researcher could push the limits of what is ethically acceptable in terms of technique and research methodology.

Issues of conflict of interest might also arise between researcher and respondent over the levels of confidentiality to which researchers are able to commit. Unlike medical research, for example, where special restrictions and assurances about 'patient confidentiality', the protection of personal data, apply (for example the Health and Social Care Act 2006), the relationship between social researcher and respondent does not carry the same kind of legal sanction. Potentially, and at the behest of the state acting to protect the public interest, the researcher could be required to disclose information they have obtained during the conduct of their research *and without the permission* of the respondents who gave it to them. In this instance, a clear conflict of interest arises not only between researcher and research respondents – who, in order to comply with the principle of informed consent, should be told that the information they provide is not legally protected – but also between the social researcher and the forces of the state.

A covert social researcher, for example, who observes criminal activity might be faced with the double dilemma of breaching the privacy and confidentiality of those they have observed *and* of being legally compelled to report that activity to the authorities (e.g. Smyth and Robinson 2001). Here we have to consider obvious aspects like breaking the law in carrying out the research or, more complex, of doing research into law-breaking behaviour. By not blowing the whistle, the social researcher is, technically, putting themselves in the position of being a witness after or even during the fact. These issues are illustrated in Dick Hobbs's participant-observation study of criminal activity in the East End of London *Doing the Business* (1988). By participating in the criminal activities he was observing, Hobbs certainly put himself at risk of discovery both by the police authorities (some of whom were also part of the study) and by his local informants (some of whom were family and friends): 'I was willing to skirt the boundaries of criminality on several occasions, and considered it crucial to be willingly involved in "normal" business transactions, legal or otherwise' (Hobbs 1988: 7).

More subtle conflicts of interest might arise in situations in which social researchers have the potential to have an impact on the lives of their respondents and, in cases where access to respondents has to be negotiated with a gatekeeper, on the relationships that those respondents have with their employers, wardens or colleagues. Again, the interests of the researcher in trying to gather key data for their research might come into conflict with respondents' interests not to have their existing relationships disrupted:

> Since the relationship between the research participant and the gatekeeper may continue long after the sociologist has left the research setting, care should be taken not to compromise existing relationships [i.e. with organizations and gatekeepers] within the research setting. (BSA 2002: Item 25)

Situations in which respondents have to be approached via organizations and gatekeepers who might have agendas of their own, which are different from those of respondents or the researcher, might also give rise to conflicts of interest. Social scientific ethics statements are keen to point out that social researchers need to remain robustly independent of sponsors and funders and not allow their findings to be interpreted and reported in ways that favour the interests of particular stakeholders: 'Research should be undertaken with a view to providing information or explanation rather than being constrained to reach particular conclusions or prescribe particular courses of action' (BSA 2002: Item 44).

Researchers *themselves* also have a clear vested interest in the research, since their ability to secure further funding will depend on the success of their current projects. If the researcher is aware, for example, that key funders are

developing new priorities, it might be tempting to produce findings that recommend further research in that particular direction, even if the findings do
not 'naturally' lead in this direction or could at least be interpreted in a different direction: '[BSA] members should also be careful not to promise or imply
acceptance of conditions which are contrary to their professional ethics or competing research commitments' (BSA 2002: Item 45). As we will be discussing in
detail in Chapter 5, which looks at critical and standpoint orientations in social
research, the personal motivation of the researcher often presupposes a commitment to a particular political or ideological point of view. Social research
that is framed in terms of a critical realist orientation, such as Marxism, feminism or environmentalism, for example, is already breaching some aspects of
the professional and ethical code that specifies objectivity and value neutrality.
Critical approaches might also contravene some of the basic assumptions about
positivist social *science*. Even if the research strategy and method are assidu-
ously empirical and objective, the analytical framework used to make sense of
it is certainly already skewed towards a preferred reading of the data. The pressure to identify the future priorities of funders and sponsors is especially acute
in the field of research into social and welfare policy, where awareness of the
political and ideological context might be a precondition for making successful
research applications (these important issues are discussed in Chapter 7).

In summary, the underlying ethical presumption when issues of conflict of
interest arise in social research is that, *even if* the research is not of direct
benefit to individual respondents or subjects actually involved in the research
project (and assuming that they are not being placed 'at risk'), it will have
indirect benefit to them and to society as a whole. As we also concluded in
our discussion of medical research ethics earlier in this chapter, professional
codes are intended to help the social researcher strike a morally defensible and
ethically robust balance between the rights of individual freedom and liberty,
and the preservation of the common good (see Table 1.1).

In reflecting on possible sources of conflict of interest, social researchers
might ask themselves again what the grounds are on which their research can
be *justified*:

- the public good
- the public right to know
- the sponsor's prerogative
- the aims and reputation of the funder
- the interests of the profession
- the professional self-interest of the social researcher

Where it seems likely that these different justifications might come into conflict with one another, the researcher should do their best to anticipate such a
situation and prepare to alleviate it in advance.

## Professional codes: A UK university's guidelines on good research practice

Finally in this chapter we look briefly at how matters of ethical and professional conduct are treated by institutions at which social researchers are often employed. Typically, in documents on ethical research practice provided by UK universities, the shift continues from a preoccupation with purely ethical matters towards a more pragmatic orientation that characterizes the codes of professional organizations and associations like the BSA. The emphasis is very much on *institutional procedures* for emphasizing that social researchers are aware of *their* responsibilities and for checking that robust procedures for obtaining ethical approval are being followed. Institutions take no responsibility themselves for enforcing adherence to appropriate ethical and professional standards (this remains firmly the responsibility of individual researchers), but institutions do want to be seen to have procedures for monitoring it. The 'Policy Statement for Ethical Research' offered by Swansea University (which happens to be my own), for example, emphasizes: 'It is the responsibility of all researchers to be aware of good research practice and codes of ethics that apply to their own areas of research' (Swansea University 2008: 2).

Underlining the limits of its own responsibility in respect of ethical probity, this university simply refers social researchers back to the codes issued by the appropriate professional bodies:

> The University endorses the ethical principles and guidelines published by the range of professional associations to which staff in the University belong and under which relevant ethical principles for the conduct of research are set out. (Swansea University 2008: 1)

> The University expects researchers to observe the standards of research practice set out in guidelines published by scientific and learned societies, and other relevant professional bodies. (Swansea University 2008: 5)

Turning away from responsibility towards procedure, under a section entitled 'University Research Committee: Responsibilities on issues of ethics', the Swansea University guidelines state that the research committee's responsibility is 'To monitor the management of good research practice and research within Schools and Departments. This will be done in accordance with the provisions set out in this procedure' (Swansea University 2008: 2).

The university thus devolves responsibility for 'monitoring the management' of good research practice to the research committee, as limited and determined by the procedures it has set out for so doing. This is very much an administrative approach to the issues of research ethics and good research practice, but says little *enforcing* the regulations: 'This Committee [university research committee] needs to be satisfied that through an audit process the appropriate quality of research is maintained across Campus' (Swansea University 2008: 3).

As long as the *audit process* is maintained, which includes making sure that ethical approvals are documented, no further action is required.

If breaches of ethical practice arise, the research committee is 'to refer instances of suspected research misconduct to the appropriate committees within the University' (Swansea University 2008: 3). In effect, the regulations provide a mechanism for passing decision-making powers from one committee to another. There is no indication of whether or how the 'appropriate committee' is qualified to comment on research ethics. Without suggesting that university research committees and their various ethics subcommittees are disinterested in research ethics, or are unsympathetic to the underlying social values that they reflect, it is nonetheless not untypical of institutional codes that they tend to be preoccupied with *procedure* rather than with *substance*. Adopting a fairly pragmatic attitude of ethical responsibility is dissipated to the extent that, once again, final responsibility rests with the researchers themselves. Institutions should be aware, however, that grant-awarding bodies like the Economic and Social Research Council in the United Kingdom do hold *the institutions that employ grant holders* responsible for ethical probity:

> The responsibility for ensuring that research is subject to appropriate ethics review, approval and monitoring lies with the research organisation seeking or holding an award with the ESRC and which employs the researchers performing it [...] Breaches of good ethics practices [...] could result in the immediate suspension of the individual project and other projects based at or under the co-ordination of the contracting institution, and a halt to the consideration of further applications from that institution. (ESRC 2011: 3–4)

### Peer review

By making individual researchers responsible for obtaining appropriate ethical approval, institutions such as UK universities are, like the professional associations discussed above, relying heavily on peer review. A practical solution to the problem of lack of ethical expertise across the institution (and an attractive way of protecting the institution from criticisms of its procedures) is to pass responsibility for ethical scrutiny to the community of peers. Lawyers, trustees and board members of professional associations and university committees are not competent to make 'final judgements' about ethical practice in social research, so this responsibility is passed to fellow social researchers.

Ethical conduct is exposed to peer review at several stages in the research process. Research proposals – including, increasingly, proposals at undergraduate level – are required to show awareness of ethical issues and to take these into account in research design. Applications for funded research are scrutinized both by prospective sponsors and by funding organizations, including government or state research councils. The latter will send proposals out for external review to experts who are sufficiently experienced to identify areas of ethical concern. Although, as we have just been discussing, institutions where the research is to take place do not take it on themselves to be experts in ethics, they do expect researchers to provide documentary evidence that they have referred their research *to somebody who is*. Once permission has been granted and the research is underway, ethical considerations continue to receive close attention both from respondents and from fellow researchers, who might subsequently raise an objection to some aspect of what they are being asked to do. Peer review also controls the final publication of the research findings, since external reviewers are at liberty to raise ethical concerns retrospectively, not only about the conclusions reached but about the integrity of the data that has been obtained. One of the criticisms made, for example, of the data Stanley Milgram obtained from his obedience experiments was that the procedure *never was* an adequate measure of 'obedience' (Orne and Holland 1968; Milgram 1973).

The issue of publishing research findings draws attention to the ethical obligation placed especially on *academic* social researchers, which is to report their findings *truthfully*. It is regarded as a major crime in academic circles to falsify evidence, or to deliberately misinterpret or misrepresent one's findings, yet the line between the dramatic and original interpretation and the mundane and commonplace is not easy to resist. Interpretation, especially of qualitative data, is problematic in this respect, because of the interpretive nature of social research. Complex procedures for peer review within the community of academic researchers have been devised to try to deal with this problem. This does pose other questions, however, such as whether cartels of interest form around fashionable research areas, thus creating, even if benignly, an aura of respectability or authenticity for styles of research or data interpretation that at other times might be rejected as 'false'.

Although there is an element of self-reference, even of tautology, in the peer review process (researchers confidently declare conformity with published codes of ethical and professional practice, but are at the same time being judged by them and being asked to enforce them), the network of peer review in social research still provides respondents (and institutions where the research is based) with reasonably robust protection against ethical misconduct. Social researchers who are found to have acted unethically might subsequently find it difficult to attract research funding, to gain access and to have their work published.

## Conclusion

Taking a step back from the three kinds of professional codes that we have been considering in this chapter, there is a clear transition within the codes from protecting the individual research subject or respondent, to protecting the researcher, to protecting the reputations of the professional association and, finally, to protecting the institutions at which social research takes place. Although the latter kinds of codes do foster awareness of ethical standards and want to support them in principle, they combine this with a pragmatic intention to protect the reputation of the association, discipline or institution. Arguably, institutional codes of good research practice are as concerned with retroactive legalistic defence of the organization as they are with the proactive protection and integrity of the research subject.

The use of codes of ethics by professional bodies and organizations also raises an important point about the degree to which, or the intensity with which, the social researcher is expected to apply the code in their own work. Professional codes are usually expressed in an authoritative idiom, implying that nothing short of total compliance will do. In most practical research situations in which social researchers find themselves, however, matters of absolute life and death, or real permanent harm to respondents, are unlikely to arise. The choices the researcher makes need to follow the spirit of the code, and where possible its practice, but without making the situation more dramatic than it already is. To take an example from the world of animal rights, members of animal protection agencies like the RSPCA are there to enforce minimum standards of animal care and welfare. The RSPCA might be asked to monitor the living conditions of laboratory and farm animals. Animal rights activists, in contrast, advocate a much higher level of animal welfare in which virtually any kind of captive situation is rejected as cruel and exploitative. While accepting the superiority of the moral case offered by the full animal rights agenda, most people most of the time would settle for the less ambitious and more moderate position represented by the RSPCA. In social research using human subjects there can be no absolute guarantee that research respondents and subjects will not suffer any negative consequences of any kind from their participation, yet social research is still carried out. The risks to individual respondents are deemed to be low enough, and the possible gains for society as a whole sufficiently worthwhile, for the research to proceed. One could go so far as to argue that the real beneficiary, in this balancing of the rights of the individual to life and liberty and to improving the common good, is the search for knowledge: the triumph of reason over ignorance.

However robust the codes of professional and ethical practice are, social researchers continually need to consider *their own position* as social researchers, located as they are somewhere between personal moral values, public social values and the expectations imposed on them as they carry out their various professional roles and duties. Ultimately, it is the personal conscience of the social researcher that moderates ethical research activity. The ethical pull to do 'the right thing' is indeed its own reward.

# The Intellectual and Philosophical Underpinnings of Social Research

3

The purpose of this chapter is to look briefly at the underlying theoretical and philosophical perspectives that are commonly used by social researchers in formulating their research questions and in analysing their data. We begin by comparing two alternative views of what knowledge is (epistemology). These are the *rationalist* view, which presuppose that all knowledge must be a product of conscious reflection, and the *empiricist* view, which argues that all knowledge must originate in physical sensation (sense data). We then consider how these approaches have been deployed in various combinations, in developing *positivist*, *functionalist* and *interpretivist* accounts of social phenomena. Although the more abstract and esoteric aspects of social research philosophy might initially seem to be disconnected from practical research issues, it will be argued here that they remain fundamental to the whole undertaking. Knowledge of these underlying principles provides an intellectual resource on a par with other kinds of material and financial resources without which the research process would hardly be possible. It will also be emphasized that social research does not always fit neatly into one methodological type or another. Social researchers should be willing to find innovative ways of combining elements from more than one perspective.

In developing the kind of theoretical consciousness described in the Introduction, we are particularly interested in the impact that the theoretical and philosophical dimensions of social research have on the development of what we will call the question-forming or question-asking process that lies at the heart of social research. Each stage in social research can be treated as a series of moments marked by developing a particular set of questions. The four basic question-forming stages are listed in Table 3.1.

We will develop this theme throughout the chapter, but the basic point to grasp is that there is a logical continuity linking these four basic stages together: the questions are interconnected in important ways. The questions put to respondents at Stage 3, for example, are not random but are carefully selected in order to provide specific pieces of information. This information is required to provide data that has the potential for developing an answer to the research question at Stage 2. The research question is subsequently linked to

**Table 3.1**  The question-forming process in social research

| | |
|---|---|
| 1 | Selecting the initial *topic* for investigation, the first moment when stakeholders and researcher express curiosity about a particular social phenomenon or aspect of social life |
| 2 | Formulation of the *research question* itself, which refines general interest in the topic into a more specific and formal question about it |
| 3 | Developing the research *instruments* through which questions will be put to respondents in surveys, questionnaires, interviews, focus groups and other question-and-answer sessions |
| 4 | Interrogating the *data* in light of phases 1, 2 and 3 |

the kinds of question the researcher asks *of the data* during the analysis phase at Stage 4 in the hope of illuminating the initial questions at the first stage.

We begin with a brief summary of the debate over what constitutes knowledge (the debate over epistemology).

## Intellectual knowledge: Rationalism versus empiricism

The essence of debates over the nature of knowledge is simply whether the exercise of intellectual reasoning in making sense of physical sensations and experiences (and later of recording them for the purpose of communicating them to other people) is *the only way* of becoming conscious of the exterior material world. If there were no physical sensation, no sense data, the conscious human intellect would have nothing to work on; yet without the *capacity* for intellectual reflection (a capacity that is keenly, perhaps uniquely developed in *Homo sapiens*) there would be no means available for making (intellectual) sense of (physical) sense experience. The earliest physical sensations of the human infant, for example, are undeniably real (their effects can easily be witnessed by others), but the infant has yet to apply the labels 'hungry', 'cold' or 'wet' to the experiences they are having. Infants living in convivial circumstances soon 'learn' the concept of cause and effect, since their distress provokes a definite response in the carer. The sensation of hunger makes the infant cry and crying brings relief from hunger. It would be stretching a point, however, to say that young infant 'know' what they are feeling. This fundamental dilemma lies at the heart of all philosophical debates between social scientists who advocate a rationalist approach, emphasizing the essentially processed and intellectual nature of knowledge, and those who advocate an empiricist approach, giving priority to the raw data of experience.

An essential property of rational intellectual knowledge is that by virtue of its being processed in the mind and recorded in some way, intellectual knowledge becomes available (albeit as mediated knowledge) to others. What social researchers are typically referring to when they speak of 'knowledge' is a distinctive subcategory of intellectual sensations or effects on the conscious mind that are codified in the form of oral or written statements. Compared with emotional knowledge (physical sensations of the brain), intellectual knowledge (constructions of the mind) is codified and refined. Because it takes on a communicable form, intellectual knowledge becomes part of the common or shared consciousness of the social group. Social groups can in fact be defined as such by virtue of the shared intellectual knowledge they hold; shared intellectual knowledge is a basic characteristic of social groups. Part of the shared intellectual knowledge of the community of social researchers, for example, is knowledge of the ethics and values of social research. Social researchers cohere as a group because they are prepared to regulate their professional behaviour in accordance with intellectual knowledge recorded in the form of codes of professional and ethical conduct, such as those described in the previous chapter. If there were no shared intellectual knowledge of ethics, and if there were no formal codes for expressing that, then it would make little sense to talk of the 'research community' at all.

The rationalist perspective is underpinned by the basic claim that intellectual knowledge is a product of processing information in the conscious mind. It is perfectly reasonable to refer to a category of emotional knowledge that is distinguishable from intellectual knowledge, but the understanding or meaning produced by the processes of the human intellect actively intervene between raw experience and consciousness of it. Although social phenomena clearly exist independently of the thoughts we have about them, it is the *process of thinking* that makes them available to consciousness in an orderly, rather than disconnected and chaotic way. Thinking introduces discipline and organisation into a process that would otherwise be utterly anarchic and, in this sense at least, unknowable. Rational knowledge is not the only way of experiencing or knowing the exterior world, since many social practices are based on faith and emotion rather than reason, but it is the only way of knowing the world *rationally.*

Although without data the mind has nothing to work on, this does not preclude the possibility that the necessary input can be provided internally by thoughts rather than its having to come from some exterior form of stimulation. Some thoughts give rise to powerful emotional responses and sensations, suggesting that the usual process of physical sensation followed by thought is reversed; it is thought that stimulates a physical sensation. The sensations that draw people towards aesthetic activities in literature, art and music, for example, would seem to enter the person largely through their conscious mind (it is an intellectual input), but are experienced emotionally and thus physically. The process is somewhat circular, however, as the individual has to have had sufficient previous experience to establish a reservoir of emotional experiential knowledge with which to respond to the emotionally provocative thoughts they are having.

Looking for a moment at the facilities available for producing intellectual reasoning, advocates of the rationalist position are persuaded by the suggestion that it is not until the conscious human mind applies linguistic labels to the sensations being experienced by the organism (what the mind *thinks* about it as distinct from what the brain *feels* from it) that those sensations really do become truly digestible in the intellectual sense. The factuality of matter is only confirmed intellectually at the point at which, literally, it is put into words. This approach received considerable support from the study of structural linguistics and semiotics (the science of signs), which, following the work particularly of Ferdinand de Saussure (1916 [1915]), Ludwig Wittgenstein (1961) and Roland Barthes (1973 [1957]), demonstrated that intellectual knowledge of actually existing and exterior phenomena is entirely mediated by the system of word-signs that we use to describe and discuss such phenomena.

Also supportive of the rationalist position is the *structuralist* proposition that the internal logic of language (the rules of grammar and syntax that make linguistic utterances coherent and meaningful) must have a very important influence over the structures of intellectual reasoning. Language might not determine the capacity for intellectual reasoning in a physiological sense, but is difficult to know of what such a process might consist if it were not for the existence of a linguistic structure *with* which to think. The philosopher René Descartes, for example, brought great clarity to the rationalist position by saying 'I think therefore I am' (the capacity for reflective thought proves the existence of the individual), but without the facility of language he could neither have formulated this conclusion meaningfully nor communicated it to the rest of us.

We need not discuss this separately here, but the epistemological debate over how knowledge should be defined (physical sensation versus rational construction) and what the substance of knowledge is (electro-chemical repercussions of physical sensation in the brain versus an emergent property of human consciousness) intersects with the *ontological* debate over what the essence of matter itself is. The basic division here is between *idealists* who assert that the essence of matter is essentially 'thoughts' or 'ideas', and *materialists* who claim that matter consists primarily of tangible material. Although the associations are neither fixed nor immutable (ideas can be regarded as constituting a special kind of 'physical' matter: ideas cause physical change when they are translated into action), idealists also tend to be rationalists and materialists also tend to be empiricists.

Social researchers generally adopt a pragmatic attitude towards these basic philosophical dilemmas. One practical solution is to accept that 'knowledge' embraces both experience (which may or may not be put into words) and intellectual understanding (which usually is). 'Knowledge' becomes materialized (available, accessible) only when it becomes communicable to others. If something is purely experiential then, despite the significance or meaning it might have for the particular individual (the impact it has on their physical senses), there is no way of conveying it to others and thus it must remain purely a possession of that individual. It becomes part of the 'knowledge' of the individual but is unavailable to anyone else. To the extent that the social researcher does attempt to describe and analyse the subjective experience of other social actors (describing one's own subjective experiences is an entirely different matter and raises a different set of issues), they also have to accept that this knowledge is always mediated by a process of supposition and interpretation.

Social researchers are also *realists*, in the sense of accepting that phenomena have an existence independent of the mind of the observer. Although the repercussions in the brain caused by physical sensations are subsequently processed through the conscious mind, exterior reality is credited with an actual independent existence that is not conditional on the intellectual reasoning of the human mind. The only alternative is to argue that nothing can be shown definitely to exist, since everything must be a figment of an observer's imagination. Clearly, the researcher must believe in the independent existence of the object of their analysis (whether this be other social actors, institutions, social practices or cultural phenomena of various kinds) or there would be no point in trying to investigate it. If nothing else, we need to account for the objective existence *of the observer*. The phenomena of subjective experience, and phenomena like ideas and beliefs, are more problematic in terms of knowing of what they consist, but they can still be categorized as social phenomena. For social researchers, the philosophical debate is thus set aside in favour of dealing with the *methodological* question of how robust and reliable intellectual knowledge *can be arrived at*.

## Positivism

Accepting as it must the realist assertion of the independent existence of stuff and associated with this the empiricist presumption of the need to observe and study it as objectively as possible, scientific intellectual knowledge is treated as *positive* knowledge, in the sense that it comprises statements about actually existing phenomena that are *reliable* in that they offer faithful or accurate representations and *stable* in the sense that the same statement was true yesterday and will still be true tomorrow. Social-scientific knowledge thus makes propositions about social phenomena in the belief that they can be shown to be 'true'. Spontaneous statements based on emotion and feelings, in contrast, are not truly positive in the scientific sense, since they do not fulfil the positivistic criteria of reliability and stability. In disciplines that claim the special status of 'science' (as distinct from academic disciplines in the arts and humanities, which generally do not), the refined positive definition of intellectual knowledge is closely aligned with the idea of *fact*, understood as knowledge statements that absolutely and incontrovertibly describe something as it truly is. The pursuit of positive scientific intellectual knowledge is largely coterminous with the pursuit of facts.

In cultures in which scientific knowledge occupies a dominant position (relative to other discourses on knowledge such as metaphysics and aesthetics), the criterion of truth is itself increasingly defined in terms of empirical scientific knowledge. Facts are legitimated as true and the truthfulness of facts is validated to the extent that they have been arrived at by means of the scientific process of dispassionate intellectual reasoning. Positive scientific knowledge is established as *the* criterion of factuality and truth in such cultures (the dominance of scientific rationality).

Faith and superstition express a kind of metaphysical knowledge that is characteristically different from the positivist scientistic definition of intellectual knowledge, since faith and superstition do not rely for their legitimacy on the existence of independent evidential facts. They are statements of feeling and emotional attachment rather than of rational thought and objective assessment. Furthermore, and introducing an issue to be discussed in more detail below, we could argue that faith and superstition undermine the *capacity of the observer* to remain separate and independent from the object of their study, since the observer's intellectual machinery is already predisposed to one particular sense of reality.

Scientific knowledge is also positive knowledge in the sense that it is often concerned with uncovering the underlying laws, or basic principles, of social action. This belies an important core assumption of rationalist thinking, which is not only that facts can be indicative of, or imply the existence of, a larger overall system of knowledge (intellectual knowledge is cumulative at a higher or more aggregated level of analysis, the 'tree of knowledge'), but that individual facts can often only be understood *in relation to* the larger whole of which they (allegedly) form a constituent part. From a scientific perspective in general, and particularly so for rationalists, individual facts are relatively meaningless: it is the connectedness of one fact with another that makes them truly interesting. Positive social-scientific intellectual knowledge is very much concerned with understanding the nature of the connections *between* the individual facts. Even though each individual piece is necessary to complete the final picture, having only a few pieces of a jigsaw puzzle hardly makes for an interesting afternoon's entertainment.

## Positive social science

The first definition of knowledge used by social scientists that emerged during the nineteenth and early twentieth centuries originated from the same positivist, realist, scientistic definition of intellectual knowledge used in the natural sciences. Each of the founding figures of sociology such as Auguste Comte (1974 [1830]), Herbert Spencer (1969 [1873]) and Émile Durkheim (1964 [1895]) promoted the possibility of a distinct science of social phenomena that would make a valuable contribution to the general scientific quest for intellectual knowledge. All were fully committed to the Enlightenment idea that the quest for knowledge and understanding is one of the basic social values of human activity (discussed in Chapter 1). In his book *The Rules of Sociological Method* (1964 [1895]), for example, Émile Durkheim argues that a distinct social science is possible precisely because there is a category of facts that are only found at the level of society; they are not biological facts nor psychological facts but social facts:

> Here, then, is a category of facts with very distinctive characteristics: it consists of ways of acting, thinking, and feeling, external to the individual, and endowed with a power of coercion, by reason of which they control him [...] They constitute, thus, a new variety of phenomena; and it is to them exclusively that the term 'social' ought to be applied. And this term fits them quite well, for it is clear that, since their source is not in the individual, their substratum can be no other than society. (Durkheim 1964 [1895]: 3–4)

A famous illustration from Durkheim's own social research is his study of the suicide rate in France at the turn of the twentieth century (1968 [1897]). Suicide is a profoundly personal matter, but *the rate at which suicides occur* in a given population and *how rates vary* between populations are social facts. Durkheim claimed that he had statistical evidence to show that rates of suicide were generally higher among Protestants than among Catholics and hypothesized that this was an effect of the more intense levels of integrative activity characteristic of Catholicism, in contrast with the more individualist constitutions of Judaism and Protestantism. Lack of social integration gives rise to egoistic suicide, whereas an excess of integration, which thus hampers the individual's desire to be an individual in the full sense of the term, causes altruistic suicide. The third main type of suicide described by Durkheim is anomic suicide, which arises under circumstances in which society fails to regulate what are otherwise the unrestrained appetites and desires of individuals: 'No living being can be happy or even exist unless his needs are sufficiently proportioned to his means' (Durkheim 1968 [1897]: 246).

## Functionalism: Rationalist theory as knowledge

Although all of the key theoretical concepts and constructs that underpin academic accounts of social reality owe their existence to the theoretical frameworks from which they emerge, this is especially so of accounts relying on the rationalist definition of knowledge. The rationalist perspective invests heavily in the theoretical framework through which intellectual knowledge is generated and expressed. It is the theoretical framework that gives rationalist knowledge integrity and coherence. A clear example in social research is the *functionalist* approach, associated particularly with the American social theorists Talcott Parsons (1951) and R.K. Merton (1949), which has developed the concepts of 'function', system' and 'structure' in its attempt to build a comprehensive account of how all social phenomena are fitted together.

The concept of function is simply that all objects and actions become meaningful in terms of the function they perform. Functionality, the capacity to fulfil a particular function, provides the basis for explanation. Utility and purpose coincide with function. Functions, and thus the objects and actions that enable them to be performed, can be understood hierarchically in terms of the simpler functions on which they are based, and of the more complex functions to which they contribute. Functionality further implies very high levels of integration and co-dependence between one function and another; hence the strong association in functionalist theory with the concepts of system and structure.

A system, for example the cooling system in a motor vehicle, comprises a number of individual components (radiator, pipes, pumps, thermostat, valves, coolant), each of which performs a particular function. Each component can be identified and its function described. This structure becomes a *system* when the engine is switched on and the structure enters a state of motion. Function is thus a highly inclusive concept, because the purpose of each individual function contributes towards the functioning of the entire system. The overall function of the motor vehicle – that is, to move people and cargo around – *is implied in* the functioning of each component of the system, including the cooling system and its various subsystems. Correspondingly, the satisfactory functioning of the overall system *depends on* the correct functioning of its individual parts, including those elements whose primary function is to maintain the system itself. Even in the case of very simple systems, 'systems maintenance' is a prerequisite for the system to be able to perform any of the other purposes that it was brought into being to serve (mechanical and social systems) or that led to its evolution in the first place (biological systems).

The concept-heavy rationalist approach illustrated by functionalist theory inevitably has a number of important consequences for the kind of 'knowledge' that rationalist and functionalist social theorists try to develop. Typically, the theory takes the form of generalized and often quite sweeping propositions about the nature of social phenomena and the 'general laws' that govern them. It is called 'general theory' because it attempts to develop a theory covering social phenomena of whatever kind. Functionalist theory is thus a theory not just of this or that social phenomenon taken in isolation, but of the social world *as a whole*. This is a top-down approach, in which the theory is developed in advance of any detailed examination of 'real' data. As the name suggests, functionalism posits 'functionality' as an indispensable characteristic of social action and social systems. Functionalists impose an all-embracing general theory of functionality, as it were from above, and thereafter develop various subsidiary arguments to substantiate it. It is not surprising that functionalists are predisposed to select for investigation social phenomena that appear to have a capacity for functionality.

It is also a characteristic of the positivist approach that the language used to outline general theory tends to be quite technical and sometimes rather obscure. There are three reasons for this. First, because the theory is constructed at a very general level, it has to make use of concepts that are also quite abstract. Abstract concepts tend to require abstract language to describe them, especially so when one concept is required to explain another abstract concept (for example co-dependent functionality to describe system integration). Second, high levels of precision are required in describing the relations between one abstract concept and another because, even more than is the case when describing physical objects empirically, the theory has no real substance beyond the words and concepts used to describe it. I can demonstrate the physical phenomenon that physicists have labelled 'gravity' by letting an object fall to the floor, but the *theory* of gravity only exists abstractly as word sounds in the air or marks on a page.

Third, relations between different parts of the theory, and indeed the way in which the theory develops, involve a process of *logical abstraction*, in the sense that the likely properties of actually existing social phenomena are *deduced* from the theory. The observation that stable social systems are more successful than unstable ones *bears out* the theoretical proposition that 'stability' and 'success' are positively linked. The theory might also point towards some useful places to look in order to find out why this tends to be a general rule in human social organisation (for example the kind of family structure or type of governance), but this need not be its main purpose.

### Criticisms

One of the major criticisms raised against rationalist approaches, and especially against functionalist accounts of social phenomena whose hypotheses are deduced from a grand theoretical design, is that they tend to impose on the data the properties of functionality or systemness whether they really exist or not. Clearly, it is a basic part of the scientific process to ponder various alternative explanations of how things are (or appear to be) and how individual facts are fitted together, but it might be difficult to prevent the theoretical construct from bullying the data, especially if there is *no other way* of proving whether the theory has explanatory power. If, for example, a functionalist social researcher is determined to see relations between two organizations in terms of how they function together, they might not be sufficiently aware of other forms of relatedness simply because they are not really looking for them. A strong theoretical framework can provide a sense of robustness and coherence, but it can also create intellectual prejudice against alternative interpretations of the data. Although rationalism is highly intellectual, one might say that it lacks imagination.

This illustrates a further dilemma facing social researchers adopting a theory-heavy rationalist approach, which is whether they are primarily interested in proving an existing theory to be 'true' or whether they are simply identifying social facts as discrete entities in and of themselves. Is the primary purpose of the social sciences to look for factual data in order to support an already existing theoretical account of reality (a version that might run the risk of becoming an intellectual substitute for exterior reality) or does the theory come after the facts (the basic empiricist position)? Since the *theory* only exists abstractly, the only way of establishing whether the claims it makes are valid is by developing hypotheses specifically for that purpose (that is, looking for examples of systems-maintaining activity in society as a way of proving that such activities are necessary). Questions that are *not developed* in order to test the theory might never be asked, and it might be difficult to see the relevance to functionalist accounts of results from other empirical investigations designed to answer other kinds of (non-functionalist) questions. An unproductive tautology can develop in which research questions are only asked if they explicitly help prove the validity of the theory, and the validity of the theory can only be established if appropriate research questions can be formed to test it. Answers provided by subsequent investigation are judged purely *in terms of* whether they do or do not achieve this specified outcome.

The alternative, it would appear, is to develop empirical investigations that are free from theoretical intimidation altogether. Perhaps having only a single piece of the jigsaw puzzle really is enough so long as it provides sufficient complexity to hold the attention of the observer.

## Interpretivism

We can usefully pursue some of the difficulties of the rationalist, theory-heavy method of analysis used by functionalist social researchers by comparing it with an approach that places greater emphasis on the empirical or grounded conception of intellectual knowledge. *Interpretivism* still aims to produce positive, robust, reliable scientific knowledge of actually existing social phenomena, but in a way that starts out from the observation of individual cases rather than looking for empirical examples to prove the validity of a grand social theory. The key differences are summarized in Table 3.2.

In contrast to the rationalist, 'top-down' approach, interpretivists argue that knowledge is not really about theory but about making clear descriptions of concrete situations. Interpretivists thus hold to a more empiricist rather than rationalist definition of knowledge, which gives rise to a different kind of social-scientific investigation. For empiricists, the proper subject matter of social inquiry is real-life encounters between actually existing individuals having real physical presence. The notion of intellectual knowledge favoured by empiricist thinkers develops from the 'bottom up' by looking first at particular examples of a social phenomenon, and only later attempting to infer a more general theory of what might be going on. Theory is *induced* from the evidence

**Table 3.2**  Key characteristics of interpretivist approaches in social research

Operates at a micro rather than macro level of investigation and analysis
Emphasizes actually existing situations rather than theoretical speculation
Is inductive rather than deductive in approach
Seeks to understand situations and experiences from the point of view of
    those who are experiencing them (*methodological individualism*)
Seeks to interpret the meaning of the situation (*verstehen*)

rather than evidence being *deduced* from the theory (hypothetic deduction). If done properly this method will, so it is claimed, produce a genuinely 'accurate' representation of the real world 'out there'. The whole point of the strictly empiricist inductive method, the virtue of the empirical knowledge it produces, is to try to eliminate entirely the distortions produced by the observer's creative imagination. The mind of the observer is required to observe, not to imagine.

The emphasis in rationalist theory on constructing elaborate abstract frameworks of explanation is thus displaced by an attempt to see social phenomena in and of themselves. Essentially this means shifting the scale of the analysis away from grandiose, macro-level hypotheses characterized by inclusivity, towards much more intimate, micro-level observations where difference and variability are accepted as inevitable (even if inconvenient) features of social happenings. In view of the financial and other costs involved, the level of detail necessary for making a thorough analysis of real events inevitably imposes tough practical limits on the number of observations that can be made. As the level of detail increases, the number of cases that can be examined is reduced. Large-scale ethnographic social research is seemingly a contradiction in terms.

Setting out as it does from empirical observation of actual events (and notwithstanding the particularly elusive nature of some of the phenomena in which social researchers are interested), interpretivist social research tends not to presuppose that social phenomena can be adequately explained through the application of a relatively small number of general concepts. The fact that much variation is found when observing different instances of what is ostensibly the same event not only proves the empirical fact of variation between social phenomena, but implies strongly that real life cannot be fitted easily into a single analytical framework. This is not to say that robust conclusions can never be reached, but that the *scale* of the phenomena under consideration and the *specificity* of the conclusions drawn must be at a much more detailed level of analysis. This is why the conceptual tools used by interpretivist social researchers, and the language in which they express their conclusions, are usually referred to as grounded rather than abstract. The relative closeness of the research to the actual events under investigation (the ground) means that, rather than having to refine one abstract concept by inventing another abstract concept, interpretivism uses language that is sometimes simpler and more accessible compared with the jargon-ridden prose of rationalist-functionalist accounts of social phenomena.

Confronting head on the elusive and problematic nature of many social phenomena, the interpretivist approach has a very different sense of the qualitative nature of the phenomena being investigated and thus of the kind of explanation being attempted. From a rationalist-functionalist perspective, it is the concept of functionality that drives the analysis. From an interpretivist point of view, although social actions can sometimes be described in terms of the functions they appear to serve, human social action is characterized as possessing a much more depthful quality of purposefulness, which includes the expression of values and is imbued with meaning.

## Methodological individualism

Emphasizing the way in which social action is infused with values and with meaning, one of the most influential contributions to interpretivist methodology comes from the German theorist Max Weber. Weber (e.g. 1949 [1903–17]) wrote on a wide range of topics, but in the realm of methodology two concepts have been especially influential: the idea of *methodological individualism* and the technique of *verstehen* or interpretation. Weber believes that since knowledge can only be experienced through individual human consciousness, and since the only consciousness the individual can experience directly is their own, social actors must adopt an individual orientation to the world around them; individual social actors can empathize with the actions of other social actors and can imagine how they are feeling and speculate why they are acting, but concretely speaking the only data they have to go on are those generated by their own experiences and thoughts.

Unlike *collectivist* social theorists such as Émile Durkheim and Karl Marx, who believe that collective phenomena such as societies and social classes acquire an independence that is greater than the sum of the individuals and events of which they are composed, Weber adopts the *individualist* position that the collective aspect of social phenomena is merely a secondary effect of persons acting individually. Terms like 'society' and 'class' are just that, words for describing certain kinds of phenomena. It makes no sense to Weber to treat collectivities as if they were actually existing phenomena having the ability of acting in and of themselves. Where, one might ask, does the consciousness of the collectivity reside if not in the mind of the individual? The basic point of departure, then, for Weberian social research is to try to see social phenomena from the only point of view that makes any sense; that is, from the point of view of the individual social actor.

Weber was also very interested in the kind of knowledge human beings have and how another individual, in this case the social researcher, might go about recording and understanding that knowledge. One difficulty he foresaw was that although some aspects of individual experience and understanding could be observed and described using the empirical methods of the natural sciences, much of human experience cannot be studied in this way. Adopting ideas developed by fellow German social philosopher Wilhelm Windleband (1901 [1898]), Weber agreed that whereas natural scientists were concerned with material objects and with describing the general laws governing their origins and interactions, social and cultural scientists were concerned with the ethical realm of human action and culture. Although knowledge of natural phenomena could be achieved directly through observation and experimentation, knowledge of human motivation, of norms and patterns of conduct and of social and cultural values necessarily had to be based on a more abstract process of theoretical reasoning. You can only *infer* that somebody is in love; you can't actually *see* 'love'.

The association of social phenomena with values was also considered by the German philosopher Heinrich Rickert (1986 [1896]), who argued that the natural sciences are 'sciences of fact' and so questions of value were necessarily excluded from the analysis. The social sciences, in contrast, are 'sciences of value', because they are specifically concerned with understanding why social actors choose to act in the ways they do. While it is appropriate to disregard questions of value when studying the physical or chemical properties of things, it is certainly not appropriate to do so when studying human social action and its consequences. It is relatively easy to show through laboratory experimentation what the properties of carbon are, where it comes from and what will happen if you combine it with some other material. What you never need to do is explain how carbon atoms *feel* about any of these things.

### Interpretive understating or *verstehen*

Distinguishing between two kinds of phenomena and two kinds of knowledge in this way has important implications for the methodology of social research. It is reasonable to study natural phenomena with a view to identifying the general laws applying to them, and by using established empirical methods of observation and experiment, because this was the appropriate way to study phenomena that had no capacity for acting on their own initiative. It is not reasonable, however, to search for general laws of motion of social and cultural phenomena, nor to use deductive empirical techniques alone, because social and cultural phenomena do have some capacity for independent action. They are just not the same as natural phenomena and their interactions are not regulated in the same ways.

While some of the physical and exterior aspects of social phenomena can be observed, measured and described in the manner of a scientific experiment, only the inductive method can explain and account for the inherently subjective and 'unobservable' factors and judgements underlying social action. Social researchers are therefore concerned with 'understanding' and 'interpreting' the actions of social actors and of trying to grasp what those actions mean to them. This method of interpretation or *verstehen*, as Weber calls it, is a defining characteristic of social research and one that is flexible enough not only to see things from the point of view of the individual social actor (to see things as they are most likely to appear to the individual), but also to try to understand the *meanings* that social action conveys to those individuals:

> [Interpretive understanding] accomplishes something which is never attainable in the natural sciences, namely the subjective understanding of the action of the component individuals [...] The additional achievement of explanation by interpretive understanding, as distinguished from external

observation [in the natural sciences], is of course attained only at a price – the more hypothetical and fragmentary character of results. Nevertheless, subjective understanding is the specific characteristic of sociological knowledge. (Weber 1978 [1921]: 15)

The interpretive method also partly overcomes one of the limitations of theory-heavy rationalist approaches that, as noted above, are not very good at explaining individual differences and/or instances where an observation is not consistent with the theory. Interpretivism still positively attempts to find regularities and patterns in order to analyse social phenomena in terms of causes and effects, but it tends to presume the likelihood of variation and difference from the outset rather than attempting to theorize a way around it.

### Criticisms of positive intellectual knowledge

A key objection raised against the positivist intellectual view of knowledge, whether in its rationalist, empiricist or interpretivist format, is that in spite of its attempts at objective purity, important questions remain about the status of one set of scientific observations compared with another set and, for that matter, any other set of observations whether or not they claim to be 'scientific'. Rationalist theory has grandiose ambitions in raising interesting concepts for testing in the 'real' world, the empiricist perspective is robust in terms of the techniques it uses to gather information and reach conclusions objectively, and the interpretivist approach is sensitive to values and meanings, but most social actors seem to operate quite successfully in a wide variety of social contexts and seemingly without participating in these kinds of complex procedure. The arrogance of scientific knowledge stems from its assumption that it occupies a privileged position in respect of all other accounts of social reality.

We have noted already that the perceived legitimacy of the scientific definition of fact and truth is perpetually confronted by the idea that, since it is just one socially constructed definition among others, it is always possible to question the apparent infallibility of scientific knowledge. The philosopher of science Karl Popper (1968 [1934]) has argued, for example, that the validity of scientific knowledge ultimately depends on attempts by other researchers to try to falsify those propositions. Rather than proceeding, as one might have thought, by a process in which confirmation is provided of current propositions, those propositions are held in a state of perpetual uncertainty by a research community set on showing them to be false. For Popper, therefore, scientific propositions and knowledge claims have to be expressed in ways that encourage others to challenge them. It is relatively easy to make weak scientific statements phrased in such a way as to make them easy to conform but difficult to challenge. For Popper, the robustness of a scientific claim depends on *refutability* rather than on *verification*. For example, the hypothesis 'the sun will shine' is undoubtedly 'true' and a billion empirical observations can be made to verify it. The hypothesis is, however, uninteresting, since there is no way of refuting it. The impossibility of reaching the 'final truth', however skilful the techniques of investigation might be, also seriously undermines claims about being able reliably to predict future outcomes. Future events, in the social universe as well as in the natural universe, are fundamentally unpredictable. More recently, the British social theorist Anthony Giddens has argued that the increasing reflexivity of knowledge in modern society further undermines the notion of scientific certainty:

> Modernity is constituted in and through reflexively applied knowledge, but the equation of knowledge with certitude has turned out to be misconceived. We are abroad in a world which is thoroughly constituted through reflexively applied knowledge, but where at the same time we can never be sure that any given element of that knowledge will not be revised. (Giddens 1990: 39)

Thomas Kuhn (1970) added to this debate by suggesting that the dominance of a particular worldview in science (as in any other domain of knowledge) depends in large part on the fact that that particular frame of reference, and the scientists who adhere to it, have come to occupy a dominant position within the intellectual community and cultural hierarchy. Kuhn introduced the idea of the 'scientific paradigm' to describe a process in which a particular scientific view or paradigm of explanation becomes widely accepted (for example Newton's Law of Motion), until such time as an alternative view emerges to challenge it. If the alternative view is able to establish itself, then it will achieve dominance (for example Albert Einstein's theory of relativity) until the next new idea comes along (something from the domain of subatomic particle physics, perhaps?). Even accepting that the reason the alternative view becomes dominant is often because it is simply better science or is based on better scientific technique, Kuhn argues that such claims do not in themselves prove that the knowledge produced is any more factual or final than that produced by previous paradigms of scientific knowledge that have since become discredited.

The context in which such knowledge claims are made, including historical circumstances and the cultural capital and political influence of participants, all have an impact on the kind of scientific knowledge that is being produced. The logic of permanent scientific revolution perpetually undermines the validity claims of scientists, who must accept that their own ideas are bound to be overturned some time in the future. Despite the persuasiveness of the positivist claim that empirical science can produce final factual absolute knowledge, the real truth is that such an ideal is not only questionable, but runs counter to the positivist urge to keep on looking for alternatives. Positivism feeds off the simple idea that what is already known should be challenged and that there is always something else that can be discovered. It is profoundly illogical to believe that scientific knowledge can ever be regarded as 'final'.

> So how does all of this interesting philosophical stuff help us with the practical business of developing research projects?

As noted at the start of this chapter, the research process is anchored to a series of question-forming and question-answering moments. The underlying philosophical debates we have been discussing have a direct bearing on the practical difficulties facing social researchers, precisely by drawing attention to the importance of this process. In their different ways each of the following issues poses a challenge to the *reliability* and *validity* of the research findings: would the same findings be reached if the study were repeated and do the findings adequately reflect the reality they claim they are investigating?

## Asking the right kind of questions and questions that are worth asking

### Definitions

A first key aspect of the question-forming and question-asking process is to remain aware of the multidimensional nature of the social reality about which the researcher is asking questions. The actual object under investigation (the referent) and the conceptual-linguistic terms used to refer to it are not the same thing. The words and concepts used to name and describe actually existing stuff might be more or less adequate to that task of naming, but judgements of adequacy in this context refer to relations between terms and their alternatives, not between the actual stuff and the name given to it. This relationship between the thing (signified) and the linguistic label given to it (signifier) is always arbitrary. A key difference, for example, between the sociological analyses of Marx and Weber is that Weber felt that although there are collectivities of individuals having particular characteristics in common that, for want of a better analytical term, could be called 'classes', this does not mean, as Marx had suggested, that classes are an integral part of the history-making process. Common and shared interests between groups of social actors give rise to collectivizing pressures of various kinds, but no single individual is infallibly or mechanically compelled always to behave in accordance with them. The force of the collective emanates from the fact of individual social actors already acting in similar ways; it is not an external influence that causes them so to act. Differences in the way the notion of 'class' is being used here obviously have a major impact on the kind of phenomenon Marx and Weber think they are investigating. Do the concepts being used adequately represent the actually existing phenomena under investigation? Is there a risk of slippage between the actually existing thing and the words used to name it?

Furthermore, if more than one concept is used in forming a research question, the researcher needs to be confident that the claimed relationship between these concepts is a reasonable one. For example, if a social researcher wishes to investigate the causes of 'poverty' among a particular 'social group' in the general population, a first critical issue will be how these key terms are defined. If poverty is defined as 'relative income poverty' and the social group as 'households with incomes above 50 per cent but below 75 per cent of average incomes', then, compared with those in the top 1 per cent of incomes, the conclusion would be that this social group is indeed living in relative income poverty. Intuitively, the concept of poverty usually implies serious disadvantage among households at the bottom end of the social hierarchy, but this is something that needs to be clearly incorporated in the way the research question is formed rather than being taken for granted. Additional clarification over the definition of key terms and conceptual assumptions would be required if the findings were to be compared with findings from other moments in time and/or from other samples of a national population.

### Range of phenomena

A second key consideration in the question-forming process is that the general category 'social phenomena' includes a range of objects, some of which exist in material form (such as social institutions and social practices), and some non-material or metaphysical phenomena such as values, ideas and beliefs, which do not. At Stage 1 of the question-forming process (see Table 3.1 above), the social researcher needs to specify the kind of phenomenon they are interested in and, if the phenomenon lies at the metaphysical end of the spectrum, what kind of proxy indicator they are proposing to use to investigate it. For example, if the research is an investigation into social attitudes towards poverty, some work will be required not only to indicate how information on attitudes can be elicited from respondents (the kinds of question formats that will be deployed at Stage 3), but whether expressed attitudes can be taken as a reliable indicator of what respondents (and by implication members of the wider population from which the sample is drawn) actually think about the issue of poverty. If there are doubts about the validity of attitude surveys (whether the data measure what they claim to measure), other additional procedures might be included in the research design, such as an examination of whether respondents behave in ways that indicate their attitudes towards poverty (e.g. giving money to charity, volunteering, explicitly supporting government policy aimed at alleviating poverty and its social causes).

### Kind of contribution

Third, social researchers need to be clear whether the research results are intended to contribute primarily to the theoretical understanding of the phenomenon under consideration, or whether the intention is to gather original data from which new kinds of questions might arise. If the research lies at the empirical rather than theoretical end of the scale, a related issue is whether the findings are intended to contribute only to academic debates (perhaps the further accumulation of empirical data on the issue of 'poverty'), or whether they are raising a fully grounded research question in the sense of making a direct practical contribution such as social and welfare policy interventions to *prevent* poverty. We know from the foregoing discussion that it is often difficult to say where 'theory' ends and 'practice' begins, but social researchers ought to be able to say where, approximately, among these various fields of research motivation and intention their research is located.

## Theoretical context

A fourth key consideration in the question-forming process is the conceptual and theoretical context in which the research question is located. To the extent that social research is always over-determined by pre-existing theoretical and philosophical suppositions, any useful interpretation of data at Stage 4 is necessarily already embedded in current knowledge of that phenomenon, knowledge that is not naive but is related in complex ways to earlier versions of the same research question. Although himself a leading functionalist thinker, which implies quite strong allegiance to the rationalist approach, R.K. Merton offers the suggestion that there are three levels of theory:

> Middle-range theories are intermediate to general theories of social systems which are too remote from particular classes of social behaviour, organization and change to account for what is observed and to those detailed orderly descriptions of particulars that are not generalized at all. (Merton 1949: 39)

Most abstract is general systems theory, where the ideas and concepts used are far removed from the empirical phenomena of the social world. Next is mid-range theory, which is sufficiently grounded to produce workable hypotheses for investigation. The most grounded form of theory takes the form of statements and conclusions of (claimed) empirical fact.

In a more recent formulation, Nicos Mouzelis (1995: 1) makes a similarly useful distinction between theory as 'conceptual framework, paradigm, metatheory or heuristic device' and theory as 'substantive theory', which is made up of actual detailed propositions about how the real world is. Social researchers have spent a good deal of time and energy reflecting on how the proving or disproving of substantive statements feeds back into either a confirmation or a revision of the conceptual framework that gave rise to the substantive proposition in the first place. Although there is continual discussion over how original ideas are taken up by subsequent researchers, the emergence of novel statements of fact that cannot be easily accommodated within either the mid-range or abstract frameworks currently available is certainly one of the ways in which new paradigms emerge. If a series of facts emerges that cannot be explained within the existing paradigms in social theory then, once the initial furore has died down, the solution is to develop a new paradigm that *can* accommodate them.

The relation between the three levels of theory reflects the intellectual process by which we come to know real reality. The work of theorists in the mid-range is to convert abstract theory into a form that can be tested against 'real' reality. General systems theory is not 'wrong' because it is abstract, nor is empirical knowledge wrong because it 'lacks' theory. They are two different phases or stages of the *same* overall process.

> The most pragmatic way of resolving the basic dilemma over whether the theory comes before or after the data, and thus over the relative status of theory building and data gathering, is to accept that empirical investigation and theorizing constitute two different moments in the *same* overall process of developing positive social-scientific knowledge of phenomena.

Also forming part of the theoretical context, it is important not to overlook the way in which the kind of knowledge produced by social research is over-determined by the kind of research question that has been asked. The specific research question sets the limits, in a remarkably precise way, of the knowledge subsequently produced in trying to answer it. This must be the case since, logically, researchers are bound to presume a close relationship between what they are asking and what they expect to find out. For example, if the research is developed to help a sponsor evaluate the implementation of managerial activity within its own organization, then, to the extent that the situation within that organization is unique, the knowledge produced will have only limited relevance to other cases. It is case-specific knowledge. Alternatively, if the research is formulated to explore the impact of a particular policy initiative on an identified population, then, to the extent that that sample population has characteristics in common with other possible samples of the same population, conclusions reached in the first case might be applicable in other cases as well.

### Political contexts

A fifth key issue relates to the political contexts in which the research is planned and carried out. Recalling our earlier comments about the social status of scientific intellectual knowledge, it is clear that no scientific research, and especially no *social-scientific* research, takes place in a social or political vacuum. We will be exploring this topic in more detail in Chapter 7, but here we encounter the issue of whose interests the research is intended to serve. We noted in the previous chapter, for example, that professional codes of ethical practice require social researchers to produce research outcomes that are honest and have intellectual integrity. One of the major challenges facing social researchers is to manage their relationships with sponsors and funders effectively, so that the interests of the different stakeholders involved do not impinge on the credibility, reliability and validity of the research findings.

In developing an initial interest in a topic (Stage 1) and in formulating this into a precise research question (Stage 2), social researchers need to acknowledge the various contextual pressures affecting the research. External pressure comes from the general attitude to social research and the prevailing research climate, the priorities of government, sponsors and funders and, especially for research funded by research councils, their own strategic directions and objectives. In the United Kingdom, for example, the Economic and Social Research Council (which spent a grant from central government of over £1.35 million in 2005–06) identified the following in its Strategic Plan in 2005–01 and 2009–14:

> Enhancing the performance of the UK economy, succeeding in the global economy; energy, the environment and climate change; education for life; understanding individual behaviour; population change; international security; and the complex interactions between religion, ethnicity and society. (ESRC 2005)

> Global economic performance, policy and management; health and wellbeing; understanding individual behaviour; new technology, innovation and skills; environment, energy and justice; social diversity and population dynamics. (ESRC 2009)

Broad continuity across the period 2005 to 2014 will be welcomed by researchers in those research domains, although it might tend to close off support for other equally important areas of social research. It is also interesting to note some subtle but still telling shifts in these priorities, for example the strong realignment of 'education for life' with 'technology, innovation and skills'; that is, employment (Ransome 2011). In the context of a tightening funding context, applicants to the ESRC will undoubtedly try to make their research proposals match as closely as possible the ESRC's stated strategic priorities.

Internal pressure comes from the expectations and ambitions of social researchers themselves, whose self-esteem and career prospects will certainly affect their research activity. Academic researchers working within the higher education sector are under continual and increasing pressure to do more funded research. The kinds of research questions asked by social researchers must remain independent of these pressures, but it is important to acknowledge that such pressures do exist and form part of the wider context in which social research questions are asked and answered.

### Intellectual modesty

Finally, and focusing this time on the personal interests and expectations of the social researcher, we should be very wary of the arrogance of scientific intellectual knowledge and the myth that social researchers possess a uniquely independent or objective position from which to observe the activities of other social agents. All social actors are *reflexive agents*, in the sense that they are able continually to alter their behaviour in response to the situations they are experiencing. Again quoting Giddens: 'The reflexivity of modern social life consists in the fact that social practices are constantly examined and reformed in light of incoming information about those very practices, thus constitutively altering their character' (Giddens 1990: 38). What is different about the reflexivity of social researchers is that they attempt to moderate their own responses while observing the responses of other social agents. It is naive to imagine that social researchers have perfect insight or that their capacities for observation and interpretation are infallible. What they can claim, however, is to be more aware of the factors affecting the question-forming and question-asking processes underpinning the investigation of social phenomena. Studying books like this one is hopefully part of the learning process of social research.

## Conclusion

If we stand back a little from the alternative definitions of knowledge and strategy outlined in this chapter, it is clear that none is entirely satisfactory. Against the rationalist conception it can be argued that unless one is prepared to accept the possibility that rational general theory might be a complete fantasy, some actual data are bound to be included in the analysis somewhere, *even if* these are based just on the personal experiences of the theorist (problems of verification and falsification). If the kind of social research in which one is most interested is based on abstract reasoning rather than examination of actual data, then that is fine as long as one does not claim later on to have said anything particularly concrete about real social phenomena. For this kind of theorist the primary object of social theory is not so much 'society' or actual social phenomena like families or bureaucracies, but the various ideas and propositions that are formulated *about* society. Against the objectivist/empiricist conception, one has to acknowledge that planning and carrying out a piece of research, let alone describing and analysing the data it produces, must involve some degree of theoretical-rational reasoning on the part of the researcher-theorist. The idea of theory-free or 'pure' data is just as silly as the idea of data-free or 'pure' theory:

> Science, we may say, is confronted with problems, at any moment of its development. It cannot start with observations, or with the 'collection of data', as some students of method believe. Before we can collect data, our interest in *data of a certain kind* must be aroused: the problem always comes first. The problem in its turn may be suggested by practical needs, or by scientific or pre-scientific beliefs which, for some reason or another, appear to be in need of revision. (Popper 1957: 121, emphasis in original)

Whether the methodological individualist social researcher tends towards the rationalist or towards the empiricist end of the scale (from the abstractions of theory to the groundedness of data) in framing their research questions and designing their research project, important issues remain about whether or not the social researcher (who like every other social actor can only see things from their own unique point of view) can still provide an 'independent', 'objective' and 'reliable' appraisal (interpretation) of what they have observed. The kind of intellectual knowledge produced by social research is unlikely to meet the strict demands of positivist scientific fact, but can offer a coherent assemblage of carefully formed interpretations. Grounded empiricist accounts of social phenomena offer a coincidence of interpretation rather than a body of indisputable scientific facts. In accepting the tendency towards difference and variation commonly observed among classes of social phenomena, inter-pretivist social researchers also have to moderate their expectations of being able to offer the kind of grand theoretical explanation favoured by hard-line rationalists.

Recalling the epistemological debate we started with between the rationalist and the empiricist definitions of knowledge, since it is not possible satisfacto-rily to deny the existence either of exterior or of interior reality, we are pushed towards the conclusion that, for the purposes of practical research, two dis-tinctive versions of reality co-exist simultaneously. One is the realm of actually existing stuff that is exterior to the individual's senses and consciousness, and the other is the intellectual replication of that actually existing exterior realm in the conscious mind of the observer (mediated by both sensation and con-sciousness). Intellect is the mechanism by which the imprint of the external world onto consciousness is rendered coherent and communicable.

One could say that, in respect of developing positive intellectual knowledge of the social world, the fundamental difference between rationalism, empiri-cism and interpretivism is a matter of *timing*. Depending on where the social researcher is positioned in the investigative loop, the phenomena under con-sideration will have either more or less actual substance, will be more or less experiential, more or less intellectually processed by the mind, more or less objective, and more or less reconstructed through interpretation.

Much of what we have been discussing in this chapter has implications for the position of the social researcher in the research process. Weber introduces the methodological concept of value neutrality, for example, to address the difficulty the social researcher faces in trying to analyse the value content of social action while preventing their own values from entering the research process. The claimed objectivity of the interpretations being offered can be seriously compromised if the values of the researcher contaminate the analysis. This issue is particularly significant in evaluation research, since questions of meaning, value and expectation are central to the research process. Evaluation research is the focus of the next chapter.

# The Values of the Researcher and Evaluation Research

4

Evaluation covers a range of professional practices, from relatively detached auditing as an outside observer at one end of the scale to full participation within the process at the other. *Participatory evaluation* inevitably poses particular challenges for social researchers because the researcher, acting as an evaluator, no longer occupies the position of a detached and objective observer of events, but becomes a full participant who is called on to make *judgements*. Evaluators who act as participants and facilitators may also be or become *stakeholders* in the evaluation and thus have vested interests that, like other stakeholders and participants, they carry with them into the evaluation process. While not all stakeholders will necessarily have a representative of their own present during the evaluation, it is part of the responsibility of the evaluator to bear these wider stakeholder interests in mind when making their judgements.

We need to acknowledge straight away, therefore, that the role of the social researcher and the role of the evaluator are not the same thing. Evaluators might take on the *appearance* of social researchers in doing their work, but the process of enquiry they use tends to diverge quite significantly from the positivist scientific approach discussed in the previous chapter. Conversely, whether constructed as an external audit used to assess organizational behaviour from the outside, or as an internal process of participatory self-evaluation, social researchers adopt some of the techniques and *characteristics* of evaluators in investigating the internal processes of organizations and programmes and how these affect outcomes. However, this does not make them fully fledged professional evaluators. To keep these important distinctions between evaluation and social research in mind, we will use the term *evaluation research* to refer specifically to social research that incorporates some of the techniques of evaluation in its methodology but does not claim to have become professional evaluation. We are interested in evaluation as a technique adopted for use by social researchers, rather than in evaluation as a distinct form of professional activity in its own right. As the following discussion will explain, the hybrid nature of evaluation research poses particular ethical and methodological challenges for social researchers who wish to use evaluation as a means of gathering their data.

Following a brief summary of the history and key characteristics of evaluation, this chapter offers a view as to why social researchers have been attracted to the techniques of evaluation. It then considers some of the epistemological and ethical difficulties that researchers might face when using these techniques. Evaluation has much to offer, but it differs in significant ways from conventional methods used by social researchers for gathering data, not least because it attempts to give equal voice to a number of participants, each of whom, in common with the evaluation researcher, has a stake in the outcomes of the research process.

## A brief history of evaluation

An evaluation is action oriented. It is conducted in order to determine the value or impact of a policy, programme, practice, intervention or service, with a view to making recommendations for change. (Clarke 1999: vi)

[E]valuation focuses on the aims of a program and investigates to what extent the intentions of the program providers are being realized. An evaluation report will comment on the effects of program provision on those involved in receiving or delivering it and usually indicate potential future directions. Evaluation thus implies a judgement of the worth or value of a program. (Hall and Hall 2004: 6–7)

Evaluations of past initiatives can help a policymaker avoid reinventing wheels [...] they allow policymakers instead to build on earlier interventions that *have* been effective, or are at least promising [...] The evaluator's role here is to bring the best available information to the decision maker on past experience with the problem to be addressed, and on strategies for addressing it. A second way decision makers use evaluation well is for timely monitoring of how established programs are doing, and for determining whether the assumptions underlying the policies or programmes appear to be correct, or are at least not *wrong*. Finally, decision makers use evaluation to establish results of their initiatives, both short-term and long-term, not only to decide whether or how they should be modified, but also to be in a position to defend their own records. (Chelimsky 1995: 11, cited in Pawson and Tilley 1997: 200–01, emphasis in original)

The outcomes of evaluation and the role of the evaluator have changed over time corresponding with developments in evaluation practice. Originally developed in the United States during the 1950s and 1960s by government departments that required relatively simple summative assessments of whether particular government-funded programmes and interventions were achieving the results they were meant to achieve, evaluation later evolved into an approach that attempted to look at the *process* of intervention, not just at its final outcomes. The logic here is simply that, particularly when considering government-funded programmes in education and social welfare, it is important to understand *why* some interventions work and others do not, *why* some programmes are successful and others less so, not merely whether they meet some relatively arbitrary measurements of success or failure. The development of new programmes is hardly possible unless this kind of qualitative understanding can be achieved. The earlier emphasis on objective summative assessment was thus replaced by a new approach to evaluation that offered formative assessments of the processes involved in the implementation of a new policy or programme.

Evaluation continued to change during the 1980s and 1990s when, especially in the context of non-commercial state-funded organizations providing educational and social care services to local communities, members of such organizations became direct participants in the increasingly informal evaluation process. The evaluation model more commonly found today is not expensive, large-scale, publicly funded and programme-wide investigation, but small scale, local, largely unfunded and based very much around the activities of a single researcher or very small group.

## Appraising evaluation

We can usefully appraise the technique of evaluation under three headings:

- role of evaluators
- nature of the evaluation process
- intended outcomes of evaluation

### Role of evaluators

The shift from summative to formative assessment described briefly above brought about significant changes both in the role of evaluators, and in perceptions of the nature and outcomes of the evaluation process. Evaluators no longer assumed the position of formal external inspectors appointed by the funding organization to record, check and report back on how their money was being used, but became instead expert contributors acting within the organization or local authority or with service providers to help improve programme delivery.

Although, as previously noted, not all stakeholders will be personally represented during the evaluation, the basic principle of participatory evaluation is that all stakeholders are given an opportunity to participate in the process, rather than allowing them to feel they are somehow peripheral to or excluded from it. Part of the skill of the evaluator is to ensure where possible that

**Table 4.1** Stakeholders in evaluation research

---

Sponsors*
Funders*
Managers of the organization being evaluated
Practitioners
Service users and clients
Partners in the sector
Related organizations
Evaluation researchers
Other members of the research group*
The institution where the evaluator works*

---

*indicates stakeholders who might not be direct participants
in the evaluation but who nonetheless have a stake in it.

all such stakeholder interests are adequately represented in the their eventual judgements and conclusions. To the extent that the business of service-type organizations is to provide people-centred services of one kind or another (rather than commodities like wheelbarrows or pencil sharpeners), the essence of the organization, its professionalism and expertise, are embedded within the activities of its staff members. In other words, enhancing the development of the organization, and improving its effectiveness in delivering the services for which it is responsible, actually means enhancing the capabilities of staff members. Participatory self-evaluation signals the full incorporation of all staff members into the evaluation process. Any residual distinction between 'us' (staff) and 'them' (evaluators) is removed: all colleagues are required to become quasi-professional self-evaluators.

Table 4.1 provides a list of likely stakeholders:

Looking at the continuing evolution of the evaluator role in participatory evaluation, Hall and Hall (following Weiss 1998: 99) suggest that three levels or stages of involvement can be identified (adapted from Hall and Hall 2004: 50):

---

■ *Stakeholder evaluation*, where evaluators remain in charge of the evaluation process but take care to include inputs from all stakeholders involved.

■ *Collaborative evaluation*, where evaluators become 'co-investigators with programme staff': stakeholders are included in the research process as 'equal' partners and all contributors 'take joint responsibility for the evaluation'.

■ *Empowerment evaluation*, which 'gives control of the evaluation to the practitioners, with advice and help from the evaluator. Ownership of the study aims to democratize the evaluation, empower the participants and ensure that the data are relevant to the stakeholders' concerns'.

---

These authors conclude:

> The role of the action researcher, as with the fully participative evaluator, is not to be an external expert but to act as a facilitator rather than a director, someone who offers expertise but cedes control to the practitioners and stakeholders for the research/evaluation process. (Hall and Hall 2004: 51)

### Nature of the evaluation process

Over time, the nature of the evaluation process has become increasingly intertwined with the development of the organization, and especially with developments necessary to improve programme implementation and programme delivery. In the commercial and business environment, for example, external audit is carried out by government- and agency-appointed officials to check that corporations are staying within the rules as required by law. Organizations also carry out quasi-objective internal audits of their own systems and procedures in order to ensure that, when the time comes for external scrutiny, compliance with external requirements is being maintained. Below this level of formal scrutiny, organizations have internal monitoring and feedback routines that both enable staff to know what is going on at a day-to-day level and increase their capacity to identify and fix problems (e.g. Kalling and Styhre 2003).

The original conception of evaluation as a professional activity that is separate and distinct from the organization being assessed has therefore been abandoned in favour of participatory evaluation that is fully embedded as a routine part of organizational behaviour. Members of organizations thus become quasi-professional self-evaluators of their own activities. Self-evaluation is characterized as a fluid process that might include moments of explicit reporting to colleagues, but generally operates in an open-ended manner and continues indefinitely.

### Intended outcomes of evaluation

Self-evaluation inevitably attempts to achieve very different outcomes from those associated with summative evaluation and with early forms of formative evaluation. These latter techniques are designed to measure activities and outcomes against fairly specific criteria of assessment, usually set out by the external agency that requires the evaluation to be done and the results recorded in a formal report. Throughout the 1990s and 2000s in the United Kingdom, for example, and associated especially with what has been labelled 'audit culture' and 'new public management' (Hood 1991; Pollitt 2003; Pollitt 2005), the effectiveness of primary and secondary education, and of health services, was assessed against targets set by the relevant government department. These metrics or quantitative data are then used to generate performance league tables, enabling, so it is claimed, parents, patients and taxpayers to see how well or badly local services are being provided. A school whose pupils do not achieve the requisite proportion of A to C exam grades, for example, or the hospital whose patients are not treated within the specified four-hour waiting time is deemed to be 'failing' compared with those that are meeting their targets.

The outcomes of developmental evaluation, in contrast, associated with formative rather than summative assessment, focus less on final outcomes and more on the *processes* of programme delivery. Since it is very difficult to develop satisfactory criteria for measuring and comparing the mechanisms and procedures taking place within particular organizations with what goes on in other organizations, assessment becomes much more a matter of *judgement* about whether one way of doing something is more likely to produce desired results than an alternative way. The evaluator is expected to offer an informed opinion about the current effectiveness of service provision in that organization. The formal evaluation report is replaced by action planning, which might include new procedures to facilitate the operation of feedback cycles and fluid self-evaluation. The emphasis is on shaping activities rather than on making final judgements about what works and what does not work. From the perspective of social research methods, formative evaluation is more like a case study than a social survey (summative assessment or audit), in the sense that it is context driven and context bound. It attempts to understand the dynamics and interactive character within a particular organization, rather than the dynamics of organizational behaviour in general.

In order for the informed judgements produced by formative-developmental styles of evaluation to be useful, processes must be in place that allow these judgements to influence the subsequent development of activities within the organization. Although there might be generic patterns of behaviour or 'ways of doing' that can be applied across organizations of the same type (for example, similarities in the exercise of discipline in the army, the navy and the air force, or similarities in financial compliance procedures between different government departments), patterns that an experienced evaluator might bear in mind when moving to their next job, the outcomes of the evaluation process are necessarily integral to the particular organization or situation from which it has emerged. The peculiarities of context, which tend to be disregarded when making summative assessments using quasi-experimental techniques, are now embraced as fundamental to understanding the dynamics of particular organizations and processes. Formative evaluation shifts the focus of analysis (and indeed the purpose of evaluation) firmly towards the process of implementation. It also moderates one of the perceived negative tendencies of summative evaluation, which is the tendency to define organizational failure in terms of individual failure. Formative evaluation, in contrast, emphasizes the idea of shared responsibility and, instead of blaming individuals, focuses instead on the 'failure' of organization and process. The ethos of formative-developmental evaluation is to be supportive of change rather than creating a negative atmosphere of blame and recrimination.

## From evaluation to evaluation research

We have already noted that professional evaluation has attracted the attention of social researchers, to such an extent that evaluation research has become established as a distinct method in the social sciences. Three aspects of professional evaluation techniques have been especially significant for social researchers:

- focus on context and process
- reflection and reflexivity
- the 'liberating potential' for researchers, respondents and stakeholders

### Focus on context and process

A first virtue of participatory styles of evaluation from the social researcher's point of view is recognition of the importance of context in the processes and activities that are taking place. Context is a profoundly sociological concept, since it shifts the analysis of cause and effect away from issues of individual personality and psychology and towards an appreciation of how social action is determined by the social circumstances in which it takes place. We will have more to say about the difficulties of the social constructivist approach to evaluation research shortly, but context overcomes the difficulties of relativism (that nothing certain can be known for sure because everything has to be compared with everything else) by asserting that 'action' is always determined in important respects by 'structure'. In the context of applied social research, structure refers to the pre-existing conditions, material and ideational, social and cultural, that shape social action and the choices that social actors make. Structure implies a sense of continuity and perhaps permanence.

In trying to devise new means of programme delivery and implementation, it is not enough simply to 'think differently' about the situation or to adopt the point of view of 'the other' (although both of these can be helpful); there is a requirement to understand how, in practical material terms, the situation needs changing. It is necessary to try to engage positively with the dynamics of the situation, to consider the situation as a process. Especially when using participatory evaluation techniques as a means of empowering participants, the kinds of power play surrounding stakeholder relationships also form an integral part of the context. As already noted, the techniques of evaluation research can be compared with the more familiar case-study approach in social research. Both attempt to draw into the analysis different types of information, and from a number of different points of view, in order to develop a depthful, holistic account of the situation. Descriptive and documentary materials, for example, as well as observation, are combined with information from individual interviews and from focus-group sessions with a range of stakeholders to try not only to develop an analysis of the surface features of the situation (whether the programme works or not), but also to uncover underlying forces and situational restraints (how this particular manner and style of programme implementation have developed in this particular context).

## Reflection and reflexivity

The second key moment of attraction for social researchers, and one that also emphasizes the positive side of the dynamic interaction between action and structure, is that stakeholder participation is a fine applied illustration of how, notwithstanding the restraining influence of the structural features of context, *reflexivity* is one of the key mechanisms enabling individuals to modify the conditions of their professional activity. Participatory evaluation gives social researchers an opportunity not only to gather quality information about the situation as it is (current policy implementation and effectiveness, current working relationships and procedures), but to witness how the *process of reflection* can generate social change. The general nervousness of many social researchers about the usefulness of input–output models of experimental design, a relatively static model of interaction on which first-wave summative evaluators tended to rely in producing their 'results', can be overcome in the participatory model because of the transformative impact on the organization of reflection and reflexivity. Operating in evaluation mode, the social researcher therefore has access to quality data that demonstrates the dynamic and transformative character of social interaction, and illustrates the way in which subsequent activity can be altered by virtue of reflection-based knowledge. The adoption by social researchers (for example Davies 2008) of the powerful social-theoretical concept of reflexivity, as described particularly by Anthony Giddens (1990), helps explain the transformative potential of evaluation:

> The reflexivity of modern social life consists in the fact that social practices are constantly examined and reformed in the light of incoming information about those very practices, thus constitutively altering their character [...] We are abroad in a world which is thoroughly constituted through reflexively applied knowledge, but where at the same time we can never be sure that any given element of that knowledge will not be revised. (Giddens 1990: 38–9)

### Liberating potential for researchers, respondents and stakeholders

The enabling potential of reflection at the level of the overall organization is repeated at the level of individual participants. Self-evaluation implies a process of the self-transformation of participants, which is an attractive concept for liberal-humanist social researchers, especially for those who are keen to see positive results emerging while the evaluation process is underway. Of particular importance here is the transformation of research respondents, and to some extent of the researcher (see below), into *equal partners* in the evaluation process. As Hall and Hall put it:

> [Participatory evaluation] is based on collaborative research between equals – researchers and organization members. The relationship is one of mutual benefit. The evaluation is conducted by negotiation, with respect being given to organizational goals and ethos and to the needs of the researchers and the researched. (Hall and Hall 2004: 9)

The conventional procedure in social research is to treat research respondents and research subjects as having a fairly limited and intellectually passive role in the research process. Those being observed, surveyed or interviewed are required to be involved only within the confines of what the researcher and the research design are prepared to allow. In evaluation, in contrast, which generally operates with a relatively open procedure, respondents are brought in from the periphery and occupy a central position in the process. Having become sensitive to the power differentials between researchers and research respondents, and to how this distorts the nature and quality of the data produced by standard interviewing techniques, evaluation offers an attractive alternative. Under the auspices of evaluation, the hierarchical and paternalistic notion that respondents provide information that clever researchers subsequently transform into valuable scientific knowledge is replaced by the idea that 'evaluation' is almost entirely about understanding the leaning process with which respondent-participants become involved. Holistic participant evaluation could reasonably be defined as an active learning process. The most intimate and committed forms of participatory evaluation constitute a mutual learning process premised on the core humanist-liberal notion that personal empowerment stems from this kind of self-awareness. Self-reflection, in other words, feeds into cycles of personal development and self-empowerment (Fetterman 2001). We can also note in passing that the idea of empowerment through social research is a concept that is also shared by standpoint social researchers (discussed in Chapter 5) and by researchers in the field of social and welfare policy (discussed in Chapter 7) who, by strongly advocating a particular ideological and political position, see social research as a legitimate means of trying to achieve real social change.

Always looking for ways of placing information gathered from evaluation in the wider theoretical context, social researchers have also been quick to identify the analytical similarities between participant evaluation, the process of learning by doing and the more radical libertarian principles of critical pedagogy described by activists such as Paulo Freire (1974) and Antonio Gramsci (1971; Ransome 1992). Like Giddens's theory of 'reflexively applied knowledge', the work of these theorists casts useful light on what goes on during evaluation and how its transformative potential on persons and structures can be realized. The transformation of research respondents and of research subjects into stakeholders, and indeed the concept of stakeholding itself, is attractive to social researchers both in adding a new dimension to the analysis and in attempting to democratize research relationships (critical social research is discussed in Chapter 5).

In summary, issues of context, reflection and individual development reflect and reiterate important properties of the universal social values of preserving individual life and liberty, promoting the collective good and the pursuit of knowledge outlined in Chapter 1. If applied social research can be described as a moral undertaking – or at least as an undertaking that expresses at the surface an underlying belief on the part of the researcher, in that social research makes a valuable and sometimes unique contribution to the social good – then sensitivity to context, the power of reflection and the empowerment of individuals can certainly be taken as strong indicators of moral commitment.

Having looked at some of the key characteristics of professional evaluation practice, and at the subsequent incorporation of some of its techniques into the distinct social research methodology called evaluation research, we now need to reflect on some of the epistemological and ethical difficulties that this process of incorporation raises for social researchers wishing to use evaluation techniques in their own data-gathering activity.

## Epistemological and ethical challenges faced by evaluation researchers

### Kinds of research, kinds of knowledge

The first major area of difficulty facing social researchers wishing to adopt evaluation techniques in designing and carrying out their research is the *kind of knowledge* produced by the evaluation procedure. First-stage evaluation assumes a positivist epistemology that a concrete reality exists that is independent of the mind of the observer, and that such a reality can be accurately described using scientific procedures. Given sufficient time and resources, it might also be possible to develop reliable knowledge of the 'general laws' or 'underlying principles' that govern the natural and social worlds. Operationally, audit-style summative evaluation (which often adopts simple experimental methods for gathering data) assumes a linear input–output model of causality, where evidence of outcomes following the introduction of a new policy or programme (for example, that crime rates have fallen or children have achieved higher grades at school) is taken as proof of the impact of those initiatives. Although more sophisticated, the same underlying assumption is made by second-wave evaluators adopting the formative-development style and by advocates of third-wave participatory evaluation, all of whom tend to assume a simple cause-and-effect model of *causation* that appears to produce a single valid set of conclusions and recommendations. The more inclusive the approach, the greater the certainty that the final outcome represents 'real' reality.

Reacting against what they saw as the impossibility of developing secure factual knowledge about programmes using summative and to some extent participatory evaluation techniques, Guba and Lincoln proposed instead a *social constructivist* approach. In *Fourth Generation Evaluation* (1989), these authors suggest that there are as many different versions of reality as there are participants and stakeholders. Each has a point of view that is just as 'valid', 'true' or 'real' as that held by any other. It is not plausible, therefore, for evaluators to reach final conclusions and judgements about the success or failure of a programme, because notions of 'success' and 'failure', and even of what might be worth measuring and describing, are contested.

In place of the notion of a single independent reality used by positivists, constructivists posit the notion of multiple realities, or of a reality that is formed pluralistically. Consistent with this logic, the interpretation or impression of the situation held by the evaluator/researcher also has to be seen as just another of the possible interpretations on offer. The evaluator/researcher still stands partly outside the evaluation situation, and has an outsider role that is distinguishable from that of other stakeholders, but the extent to which they can claim they occupy a privileged position in terms of the knowledge being produced is compromised.

Hall and Hall summarize the role of the constructivist evaluator as follows:

> It is the task of the evaluator to create a discourse with the many different stakeholders in a program, and to reflect back with them on the differing constructions held by participants within the program, in the hope of reducing the number of constructions to one agreed pattern. (Hall and Hall, 2004: 53)

While this collectivist, pluralist and participatory technique has the advantage of being relatively inclusive, democratic, enabling and possibly emancipatory for the stakeholders taking part (Fetterman 2001), the price the evaluator/researcher has to pay for abandoning the positive idea that knowledge is firmly anchored in a known reality that provides a fixed point for comparing different points of view is that the knowledge that emerges is highly *relativistic*. Each element can only be compared with other elements in the same field. A number of consequences flow from this.

First, the constructivist approach raises doubts over the *internal validity* of the data produced since, once the evaluation process is underway, it becomes very difficult to say clearly what exactly is being 'measured'. Changes obviously take place as a result of participatory evaluation (participatory evaluation could be defined as a process of organizational change), but with so many difficult-to-control variables in play (different stakeholders having different opinions and agendas, variation in the relationships between participants, pressure from sponsors and funders), it is difficult to distinguish cause from effect. The fluid conception of reality used by constructivists adds to the already pressing difficulty faced by social researchers, which is how to show that particular effects are unambiguously associated with particular causes. To the extent that the *evaluative method* becomes part of what is being evaluated, it is also difficult to know either whether the same methods will 'work' in a different research context and/or whether *other methods* might have produced a different reading of cause and effect.

There is the additional difficulty of internal validity here, which is that the data are likely to be quite uneven in nature, in the sense that evaluation seeks to bring together information from a number of different sources in the hope that the final account will represent a true or faithful account of the situation being analysed. Acting in the role of evaluator or facilitator, the social researcher is under pressure to try to blend or homogenize these varying sources in order to produce a coherent overall account. Unless the researcher has time to provide a detailed explanation of how each facet of the evaluation was combined and in what measure, so that other researchers can see exactly how the data from the evaluation phase of the research was manipulated, the reflexive method used in producing the 'final' account is likely to remain somewhat obscure. Unlike the analysis of numerical data, which involves relatively simple mathematical procedures and routines, the thought processes of the evaluator/researcher are thoroughly integral to the research process. A different investigator will almost certainly think differently, not only because they see things differently but also because they experience them differently as well. The reflexive involvement of the researcher/evaluator in the research process inevitably makes it very difficult for other researchers to retest the data and challenge the assertions being made about cause and effect.

Second, the highly contextualized nature of the evaluation procedure (its case-studyness) raises difficulties for *external validity*, as it is questionable whether the results of evaluation have meaning outside the context in which they are produced. If reality is recast as something that is perpetually elusive and inherently context dependent, this upsets the scientific presumption that 'conclusions' or 'results' that are reached in one case can be applied to other cases. This is not to say that evaluation in constructivist mode has no positive effects, since it has shown itself to be highly beneficial to stakeholders as they try to make sense of their own roles and activities (Chun Wei Choo 1998), but it does limit the extent to which insights produced by evaluation research can be used to shed light on other situations. The *practical experience* of facilitating an evaluation can be used again (possibly with the effect of producing 'better' data for the researcher, or that the researcher becomes 'better' at evaluation tasks), but the analysis remains trapped by context. The researcher has to moderate their underlying scientific-academic expectation that research-based knowledge is transferable between situations, and can be used to challenge existing theoretical propositions or propose new ones.

Third, and also an issue of the quality and reliability of the data, constructivism implies *interpretivism*, in the sense that the evaluation process, and indeed conceptions of what is being evaluated and to what purpose, has to embrace variations between stakeholders in terms of how they interpret the situation and even how they feel about it. Radical uncertainty about the idea of a fixed exterior reality that can be measured scientifically is complicated still further by the notion that part of what constitutes 'reality' is the meaning and significance that social actors attribute to it. Observation presents formidable difficulties, but interpretation raises the stakes even higher.

---

The more deeply the evaluator/researcher becomes integrated into the research process, the greater the extent to which they need to reflect on:

- their own role in the process
- the nature of the evaluation
- its intended purposes and outcomes

---

If, as we will be discussing shortly, the intention of the evaluation is entirely practical, which is to say that policy implementation and adjustment are the main drivers of the investigation, then academic concerns about lack of external validity and theoretical utility might be misplaced.

The constructivist approach is underpinned by what is sometimes called philosophical *hermeneutics*. Hermeneutics argues that there is no knowledge that is not interpreted knowledge. This philosophical position has a number of defenders within the social sciences. If all knowledge is interpreted knowledge, however, this radically opens the question of whether we can ever directly 'know' reality. If our knowledge is contextually bound by certain cultures, traditions and modes of understanding, to what extent could we ever say that we have stepped outside of these frameworks? The philosopher Richard Rorty (1989) argues that this basic recognition should induce an ironic disposition on the part of the researcher. That is the idea that the material presented in our research findings could always have been interpreted in another way. The ironist realizes that there is no 'final' or 'correct' interpretation, simply different vocabularies through which we might describe the world. For Rorty (1989: 74), the ironic researcher should be 'aware of the contingency and fragility of their final vocabularies, and thus of their selves'. The opposite of this philosophical position is a prevalent common-sense empiricism that can conceive of no other way of understanding the world. Alternatively, hermeneutics encourages the view that the world could always be redescribed in other ways. In Rorty's view it is only fundamentalists of different kinds who argue that there is merely one way to describe reality.

Many find such a view unsettling, whereas others see this argument as liberating. If there is no final language to describe reality, this makes the ways in which we understand the world a poetic achievement. It also questions the divide that is assumed within our culture between religion and science, literature and positivism or poetry and empiricism. Each offers a complex language revealing complex and always constructed and shifting realities. Such a view comes close to abandoning metaphysical questions altogether. Surely missing from these arguments, however, is the acceptance that some descriptions of the external world (even after having accepted that they are all constructed) are more plausible than others.

There has nevertheless been considerable debate about whether there can be a postmodern sociology along these lines. Zygmunt Bauman (1992) associates these concerns within a framework that talks of a broader intellectual crisis that relates to whether we can actually produce authoritative knowledge. Here, concerns about ethnocentric and Eurocentric bias within research rebound within sociology. If there are indeed no superior cultures but simply different ways of explaining the world, it is not altogether clear how to proceed in different social settings. However, while these are valid concerns that need to be faced within the research process, they inevitably raise the question of relativism.

### From constructivism to realism

The problems with the constructivist model proposed by Gubba and Lincoln are obvious, since constructivist evaluation easily collapses into *relativism*; that is, the idea that nothing really definite can ever be 'known' because there is an infinite range of variables that cannot be controlled. Knowledge becomes highly situational, context bound and relative. Knowledge is only 'real' in the sense of being a product of the collective imagination of those participating. In order to get around some of these epistemological difficulties, Pawson and Tilley (1997) have developed the idea of *realistic evaluation*. We will be discussing critical realism more directly in the following chapter, but the basic epistemology of the realist position is to reassert the existence of actually existing reality. Even accepting the existence of multiple viewpoints to any situation, viewpoints that contain rich varieties of meaning and emotional content, realists hold that social action takes place within social and cultural contexts that social actors are unable to control but that, nonetheless, produce identifiable patterns and regularities in their behaviour. In writing these words, for example, I am compelled to comply with the conventions of English grammar and syntax so that you can comprehend my intended meaning. Language thus regulates both my activities and yours, in ways that neither of us can control.

Without arguing that fundamental structures beyond individual control govern or determine every aspect of social action, the realist approach claims that when patterns and regularities are found, they can provide a kind of working hypothesis for theorizing the relations between forces, events, parties, persons, institutions and so on. Realist theory operates at the level of the *underlying mechanisms* that can be *inferred* as working 'behind the scenes' or 'beneath the surface' to cause various observable effects. The technique is highly pragmatic, in the sense that the emphasis is very much on 'what works' rather than on uncovering some universal truth about social relations. Working at the level of what R.K. Merton (1949: 39) described as 'middle-range theory', discussed in the previous chapter, the basis of Pawson and Tilley's realist approach to evaluation research is to consider the underlying mechanisms connecting 'outcomes' with 'mechanisms' in the specific 'contexts' in which they operate:

> [P]rograms work (have successful 'outcomes') only in so far as they intro-duce the appropriate ideas and opportunities ('mechanisms') to groups in the appropriate social and cultural conditions ('contexts'). (Pawson and Tilley 1997: 57)

> Realists do not conceive that programs 'work', rather it is the action of stakeholders that makes them work, and the causal potential of an initia-tive takes the form of providing reasons and resources to enable program participants to change. (Pawson and Tilley 1997: 215)

It is the reassertion into the analysis of the importance of context that enables Pawson and Tilley to move evaluation beyond what they see as a key deficiency of the constructivist approach, its tendency to disregard the structural, and pos-sibly the controlling, influence of situational factors, which cannot simply be 'imagined away' by participants. These authors think it essential to 'grasp those structural and institutional features of society which are in some respects inde-pendent of the individuals' reasoning and desires' (Pawson and Tilley 1997: 23). They describe their own realist approach as 'theory driven', in the sense that evaluation should, in their opinion, concentrate on finding out not just whether an intervention works, but how and why it works. It is valuable to know about the process of implementation not merely about final outcomes, as this generates valuable information about general processes that might also apply to other situations. It is transferable knowledge, not simply situational information.

Adopting the context-aware and process-dependent perspective described briefly above, Pawson and Tilley suggest that realistic evaluation is all about understanding how the causative impact of one set of underlying mechanisms, or one 'underlying generative force' (Pawson and Tilley 1997: 216), differs from the causative impact of another set of underlying generative forces. They assume that the difference between the situation before and that after a pro-gramme has been introduced (or between situations where there is a policy and where there is none) can be accounted for by differences between two distinct underlying generative mechanisms. We can *infer* that the programme has had an effect (and subsequently whether this effect is the one intended) because the situation at the surface after implementation is *different from* the situation before it has been introduced.

From a methodological point of view (that is, what procedure to follow in applying their technique of *analytic induction*), Pawson and Tilley are recom-mending that the established linear or 'successionist' model of cause and effect typically used in the positivist social sciences (factor A must and always does result in outcome B) should be abandoned. In its place, realist evaluators should apply a 'generative' model of causation, in which the possibility (sometimes probability) that particular outcomes will occur is seen as an *emergent property* of the various ingredients or factors in play (Pawson and Tilley 1997: 32, following Harré 1972). To the extent that it is reasonable not to regard surface outcomes as entirely random occurrences, and that any particular surface outcome is very unlikely to occur in the absence of the key situational and contextual factors, it is reasonable to infer the presence of an underlying causative mechanism of some kind.

The difficulty here, of course, is the continuing uncertainty of knowing whether different effects at the surface *are in fact attributable* to differences between one underlying causative mechanism and another underlying causative mechanism. Is it safe to infer the underlying mechanism of global warming to account for climate change in the late twentieth century, or is climate change something caused by some as yet unknown causative force? Since such generative mechanisms can never be observed directly (and thus have to be inferred from surface evidence), there is also the difficulty of knowing whether a programme or other intervention can safely be treated as operating as an underlying generative/causative mechanism *in that particular case*. Is it reasonable to assume that previous instances of climate change were also caused by the mechanism of global warming?

The ability of the inductive reasoner only to arrive at putative causes of surface events, and to accept that other causes (known or unknown) might also be playing an important part, invokes the use of a rather weak notion of 'causality'. Being unable to show unambiguously that a particular effect can be attributed to a particular underlying causal mechanism means that knowledge of cause and consequence can only proceed on the basis of general causes rather than of specific ones. While the inclination of the evaluation researcher is to *believe* that the effects they are observing are related in some fairly direct way with the programme they are assessing, a great deal of investigative effort is required to *demonstrate* that this is so. Notwithstanding its compatibility with the trend within evaluation research to understand process and context, inductive reasoning also tends to be a rather open-ended procedure, in the sense that any assertion about cause and effect has to be tempered with the possibility that even the current configuration of circumstances is likely to change in the future. The 'ideas and opportunities' and the 'social and cultural conditions' referred to by Pawson and Tilley (1997: 57) remain profoundly contingent and unstable, even if we have made some progress in understanding the kinds of outcomes they might produce. Pawson and Tilley are well aware of theses difficulties and, arriving back very much where we started, conclude in Rule 8 of their 'rules for the conduct of [realist] evaluation research':

Evaluators need to acknowledge that programs are implemented in a changing and permeable social world, and that program effectiveness may thus be subverted or enhanced through the unanticipated intrusion of new contexts and new causal powers. (Pawson and Tilley 1997: 214–18, emphasis removed)

The challenge facing social researchers remains that of knowing with certainty that particular effects can be attributed unambiguously to specific causes. And this necessity persists irrespective of whether 'causality' is conceived simply as cause and effect or as generative potential. The truism that all outcomes have multiple causes does not eliminate the desire to understand as much as possible about *particular* causes and *particular* effects.

### The role of the social researcher as evaluator

A second important area of difficulty for social researchers wishing to adopt the techniques of the evaluator is the complexity of the evaluator/researcher role and the moral and ethical issues surrounding it. The conventional position of the social researcher is to remain independent of the subjects or respondents who are being asked to provide information necessary for investigating the research question. The researcher's independence or separation from research subjects and research respondents clearly varies depending on the mode of data gathering being used. Completing face-to-face surveys, for example, requires less direct involvement than personal interviewing, interviewing is less interventionist than facilitating a focus-group discussion, and focus groups are less interventionist than eliciting personal life-history accounts. Evaluation tests the independence of the researcher still further since, assuming for the sake of this discussion that the researcher is acting as an evaluator rather than as an observer of an evaluation being conducted by somebody else, the evaluation researcher not only becomes integral to the conduct of the evaluation, but inevitably contributes to the information produced. The contribution of the researcher acting as evaluator cannot subsequently be removed from, or bracketed away from, the data that results.

Although social researchers strive to meet high standards of professional and ethical conduct in their dealings with research respondents and partners (discussed in Chapter 2), evaluation brings to the fore the important moral question of how effectively the researcher can keep their own interests and values separate from the interests of other stakeholders. The fact that the researcher has an agenda is not in itself an issue, since all stakeholders will have value positions and interests of their own. The attraction for any participant of being involved in an evaluation is that taking part might then bring some kind of advantage within the organization or situation and perhaps enable them to express a view that might otherwise go unheard. The attraction *for the researcher* will include a mixture of subjective curiosity or voyeurism about the organization at which the evaluation is taking place, a professional commitment to the research team of which they are part, and a material commitment to the sponsor and/or research funder. At a more personal level, the 'stake' the researcher has in the evaluation centres on the need to obtain reliable data in order to reach useful and interesting conclusions – conclusions that will meet the rigorous scrutiny of academic peer review. The participation of the researcher is driven ultimately by the desire to obtain publishable results that will enhance their academic career.

Accepting, then, that the researcher never does occupy the apparently value-free and interest-free position of the disinterested expert observer, but has a personal stake in the process that is at least equal to and might often be greater than that of other participants, the question becomes whether the researcher's personal stake in the evaluation is at odds with the stakes of other stakeholders. Is there a conflict of interests between the evaluation researcher and other stakeholders? To the extent that the researcher's interest is an academic-personal one, it might make very little difference to other stakeholders whether the research works out as planned or not for the researcher. However, the probability of success for the researcher is likely to depend on the support of some stakeholders more than others. Maintaining good relations with the management of the organization at which the evaluation is taking place, for example, or retaining the support of key respondents such as service users and clients, is key to retaining access to the data. There is, in other words, a tendency for the apparent neutrality of the researcher to be skewed more towards some of the participants in the evaluation than to others. Although all social research is vulnerable to the charge that results are likely to be influenced by funders, sponsors and senior research colleagues (who have vested career interests of their own), the likelihood of bias in evaluation research tends to be greater than in some other kinds of research design, because participants rarely enter the process on equal terms.

---

The mantra of participatory evaluation must be that 'all participants are equal', but from the researcher's point of view 'some participants are *more equal* than others'.

---

Turning from the basic ethical shell within which evaluation research takes place to the content of the data that emerges, we have already noted that the evaluation researcher is required to produce a homogenized summary, judgement or assessment incorporating quite a range of information. This raises the question of how well the evaluation researcher is able to prevent their own values from affecting this exercise of intellectual labour power. This issue is particularly significant in evaluation research since, as already noted in relation to the constructivist perspective, questions of value and meaning are open to negotiation.

We can turn again for guidance on this point to the German theorist Max Weber, who introduced the methodological concept of value neutrality to address the difficulty the social researcher faces in trying to analyse the value content of social action while preventing their own values from entering the research process:

> Nor need I discuss further whether the distinction between empirical statements and value-judgements is 'difficult' to make. It is. All of us [...] encounter the subject time and again [...] The examination of one's conscience would perhaps show that the fulfilment of our postulate [i.e. maintaining value neutrality] is especially difficult, just because we reluctantly refuse to enter the very alluring area of values without a titillating 'personal touch'. (Weber 1949 [published in *Logos* in 1917]: 9)

The claimed objectivity of the interpretations being offered by the researcher/evaluator can be seriously compromised if the researcher's values leak into the analysis. Personal values, and the undeclared or unrecognized values of other stakeholders, constitute difficult-to-control variables that can have a disruptive impact on the data and undermine internal validity. Table 4.2 lists the kinds of values that need to be taken into account by the evaluation researcher.

Although social researchers aspire to value neutrality more in hope than expectation, a first step is for the researcher to recognize and own the values they have already. These are likely to include the core social values of individual life and liberty, supporting the collective good and the quest for knowledge referred to previously. They are also likely to include elements of the professional-scientific work ethic of trying to produce objective analysis of reliable data in a trustworthy and open way. A second step is to anticipate the values that are likely to be in play within the evaluation process itself. These might include a preference for negotiating outcomes rather than imposing them, for listening to and empathizing with the point of view of other participants, and perhaps for the rightness of pursuing particular policy objectives. Inevitably, evaluation includes a complex mixture of personal values that stakeholders bring with them (their opening value positions), professional values that are expressed during the course of the discussion/negotiation (pragmatic value positions) and emergent value positions that provide the basis for final agreement (value outcomes).

As we will be discussing more fully in the following chapter in relation to critical approaches in social research, it is important not to underestimate the

**Table 4.2**    Values in evaluation research

| |
|---|
| Values of the researcher |
| Values of the various participating stakeholders |
| Values as the object of the analysis |
| Values as the kinds of outcome participants want to achieve |
| Values (ideologies) to which participants aspire |

influence of values driven by political and ideological views of various kinds. Some participants in the evaluation, for example, might believe that inadequacies in the internal organization of the organization, and/or in the way it services its clients, are caused by institutionalized gender or ethnic discrimination. Value positions underpinned by feminist beliefs, or by a desire to appreciate rather than deprecate 'difference', might have an important bearing on the outcome of the evaluation. Achieving a positive outcome from the evaluation might not depend on participants being recruited to a new value position, but *awareness of* others' value positions and beliefs constitutes an important moment of consciousness raising within the group; it is an important manifestation of the reflexive learning process of participatory evaluation.

A third step is for the evaluation researcher to be aware of their attitude towards the outcome of the evaluation. We have already noted that ultimately this is likely to be based on a desire to achieve good research outputs for personal career development, but an appreciation also needs to be developed of the hoped-for outcomes of other participants: outcomes that are themselves an expression of personal and professional values. Applying Habermas's (1984) theory of communicative rationality, for example, it is perfectly logical to assert that all those entering the evaluation process (as is the case in any other kind of conversation) do so *in the expectation* that a positive outcome or agreement is possible. It is profoundly non-rational to enter conversations unless one does believe this to be so:

> It belongs to the communicative intent of the speaker (a) that he performs a speech act that is *right* [appropriate] in respect of the given normative context, so that between him and the hearer an intersubjective relation will come about which is recognized as legitimate; (b) that he make a *true* statement [...] so that the hearer will accept and share the knowledge of the speaker; and (c) that he expresses *truthfully* his beliefs, intentions, feelings, desires, and the like, so the hearer will give credence to what is said. (Habermas 1984 [1981]: 307–08)

For Habermas, 'negotiation' is very much about resolving misunderstandings over what constitutes 'agreement', and 'agreement' is a basic operational principle of evaluation. Finally, in recognition of the fact that participatory evaluation constitutes a learning process, the evaluation researcher needs to prepare themselves for the possibility that they might experience important shifts in *their own* value position. Not only do participants all have stakes that they might lose, they also put at stake the preconceptions they already hold.

Awareness of the impact of values on the data-gathering process comes to a head at the moment when the evaluator/researcher delivers their 'final' judgement. In their conventional role as researcher, these results purport to be an analytically and theoretically informed set of conclusions derived from a dispassionate, independent and objective review of concrete data. While all social research drifts from hard data analysis towards interpretation in an attempt to emphasize the wider applicability or generalizability of the findings (to establish external validity), in evaluation research there is likely to be a much higher proportion of opinion right from the start. Assuming that the researcher is acting as facilitator for the evaluation (rather than being there as an observer), it is difficult to see how the evaluator/researcher can prevent their personal views and expectations, even if they believe these to be well informed, from having quite a powerful influence on shaping those conclusions. Hall and Hall (2004: 7) usefully point out that, while researchers attempt to apply rigorous techniques of systematic *investigation*, evaluators make *judgements*. One can add to this that whereas research produces *data*, evaluation produces *opinion*. The position of the researcher in evaluation research is inherently ambiguous, since a balance has to be struck between forthright judgement and strict objectivity.

### Practical outcomes versus theory

A third area of challenge posed by evaluation concerns the interface between theory and practice. As Hall and Hall put it:

> Evaluation can be seen as a specific type of research activity which is closely related to applied research. The emphasis is less on theoretical development than on practical implications. (Hall and Hall 2004: 6)

Pawson and Tilley are equally clear about the applied orientation of evaluation research:

> Evaluation is, after all, *applied* research. And although we have called throughout for injections of 'theory' into every aspect of evaluation design and analysis, the goal has never been to construct theory *per se*; rather it has been to develop the theories of practitioners, participants and policy makers. (Pawson and Tilley 1997: 214, emphasis in original)

Much depends, however, on what is implied by the use of the word 'theory'. In Pawson and Tilley's case, the theoretical element is provided by the basic investigative mechanism of analytical induction, in which the operation (existence) of the underlying forces that shape surface events is inferred from the existence of those surface effects. The key presumption is that, since social life is not utterly chaotic and irregular, something must have caused these regularities to occur. Working out what these causative mechanisms might be is a rational-intellectual form of activity. Speculating about the underlying causes of phenomena as they appear at the surface is a theoretical procedure, in the sense that knowledge of other causal/causative mechanisms found in other broadly similar situations is brought to bear to see whether the same kind of causative mechanism can be inferred to operate in the current situation as well. Pawson and Tilley (1997: 116), for example, introduce the idea of 'cumulation' to emphasize that the transferable element in realistic evaluation is not empirical knowledge (although descriptive comparisons between different situations can be made), but awareness of the underlying generative mechanisms in play. What cumulates is the intellectual understanding (knowledge) of causative mechanisms, rather than the empirical description of particular events.

'Theory' might also be defined as the various *policy positions* held by participating stakeholders. For sponsors, funders, managers and practitioners, 'theory' constitutes a preference for particular ways of doing and particular outcomes, perhaps informed by allegiance to a particular ideological position. General ideas about how policies in general are best implemented in organizations could be described as a kind of 'theory' that could be taken into account when other new policy introductions are being planned. Principles of successful implementation become theory. In this sense, 'theory' can be defined as the grounded knowledge of a situation based on previous personal experience. For practitioners, service users and clients, 'theory' can be defined in terms of 'practical outcomes', 'what works in practice'. The language might not be particularly abstract, but there is theory at the level of the transposition of information from one context to another.

Third, most social researchers approach their investigation using *academic theory*. In this definition, theory goes beyond the use of abstract concepts and vocabulary and tries to uncover the connections between social phenomena. The theoretical element here (the classic inductive method) is the abstraction/extraction/elaboration of general principles from particular observations. The intellectual (sometimes experimental) process of selecting and rejecting plausible accounts of how and why one effect, regularity or pattern can be explained draws on original data, but is also heavily dependent on explanations that *have already been put forward* by other social theorists. Existing scientific knowledge provides an essential resource on which social researchers can draw when trying to develop *new* connections of cause and effect, *new* kinds of explanation. Much of the preliminary work in developing a research question, for example, is taken up with surveying current theoretical explanations and models in order to produce a new research question (the classic deductive method). Social researchers might refer to themselves as 'experts' precisely because they have detailed knowledge of the academic literature in the field. Along with their equally expert knowledge of research methodology and, within this, knowledge of the techniques of gathering data (one of which is evaluation), it is this expert knowledge that constitutes the unique contribution of academics to the research/evaluation process.

Recalling what we have already said about the responsibilities of the evaluation researcher for producing balanced conclusions that are respectful of the various value positions participants hold, they need to be especially aware of the different ways of defining theory and how these are geared to the outcomes that different stakeholders expect to gain from the evaluation. As academic researchers, evaluation researchers also need to question whether they are defining theory as pure intellectual abstraction, as theoretical speculation, as the development of research questions or the search for practical solutions. Particularly in respect of the balance between academic-theoretical value and practical outcomes, there might be a significant divergence of opinion between stakeholders over what the evaluation is supposed to achieve.

One of the burdens carried by evaluation researchers (a situation that is strongly hinted at in Pawson and Tilley's reference to 'the theories of practitioners, participants and policy makers' quoted above) is that they have inherited from the practice of professional evaluation a firm emphasis on achieving practical outcomes for stakeholders and clients, rather than on expanding the general fund of social-scientific knowledge. In evaluation research, the generation of new knowledge is very much a peripheral outcome compared with the desire to achieve more immediate practical benefits. This contrasts quite sharply with the more gradual process in which carefully grounded scientific findings are reported and, after a period of professional and academic scrutiny and debate, are then incorporated into actual practice (in the form of what has been labelled 'research-based practice'). Given the close involvement of the evaluation researcher with other stakeholders and given, as previously discussed, that evaluation research produces knowledge-as-practice rather than abstract or theoretical knowledge, research findings are more or less immediately fed back into the activity of stakeholders. The grounding of research findings in subsequent practice (praxis) becomes almost simultaneous with the development of that knowledge. While this compressed process of knowledge incorporation is regarded as virtuous by professional evaluators whose own competence is likely to be judged by the immediacy of the results they achieve, it raises important issues for more academically oriented social researchers using evaluation techniques. There is a strong underlying presumption that social-scientific knowledge serves intellectual ends as well as practical ones.

There are also important differences between evaluators and social researchers regarding the artefacts produced at the end of the process. An evaluation report, for example, submitted to the leading stakeholder and funder, and the academic treatment more usually required in scientific reporting, are obviously quite different and serve distinct purposes. Aside from offering participants a further and possibly final opportunity for reflection, formal evaluation reports provide the sponsor with a summation or judgement offering conclusions about whether programme delivery is being achieved and how implementation and delivery might be improved. The aim of the evaluation is to provide the report, and the aim of the report is to aid in the process of programme delivery. For social researchers, in contrast, who have chosen evaluation as the most appropriate means of gathering data necessary for investigating a research question, the evaluation process forms just *one part* of a more complex methodology. To the extent that the expected outcomes of the research process shape the data and determine how the data will be used in producing the final analysis, evaluation research, and 'pure' social research, remain distinct forms of investigation.

From the point of view of social research, evaluation research requires a careful reassessment of:

---

■  the role of research respondents
■  the role of the researcher
■  the constitution of data
■  the linkages between method and outcomes
■  the aims of the evaluation
■  the format in which findings are reported

---

## Conclusion

A key distinction between the role of the professional evaluator and the role of the social researcher is that the evaluator is required to make *judgements* on the basis of the information they have accumulated, whereas the social researcher is required to reach *informed conclusions* derived from a careful consideration of the data they have gathered. Notwithstanding the contextualized nature of the data acquired by using evaluation techniques, the social researcher is conventionally expected to locate this data in the broader context of previous research, a review of literature and some conceptual and theoretical work. The analysis produced by the social researcher, in other words, is not limited by the evaluation phase, but spreads some way beyond it. This is not to say that evaluation and social research are incompatible, but that for the social researcher using evaluation techniques, evaluation is only part of, and not the whole of, the wider process of research. Social research projects are more extensive than the evaluation phases they might contain. Social researchers use evaluation as part of a much broader strategy of investigation, whereas professional evaluators are not required to do this, and may actively discourage reference to exterior conditions and intellectual resources.

Returning to the distinction made at the start of this chapter between evaluators and social researchers, one could argue that evaluation researchers who are fully committed to the immediacy-of-impact model, and who implicitly or explicitly tend to underrate the more general theoretical import of their findings, are no longer conducting social research as this has conventionally been defined by academic social researchers, but have become professional evaluators.

The trend in evaluation research has been towards making the technique more and more comprehensive; towards including a greater number of stakeholders in the process; and towards trying to improve the quality of the data that is brought forward to improve the reliability and validity of the conclusions reached (Rossi and Freeman 1985). Unfortunately, however, although the more comprehensive or inclusive approaches such as realist evaluation attempt to make up for a lack of theoretical sophistication in the earlier experimental and constructivist models of evaluation, it is the practical difficulties of carrying out sophisticated evaluation research that are the most challenging. The trend in evaluation research is towards low-cost and small-scale investigation carried out over a relatively compressed timeframe and offering immediate results. Unless the investigation is conducted in a very simplistic and superficial way, it is difficult to see how the more research-oriented styles of evaluation can be fitted to the current streamlined model. The increased academic and theoretical rigour offered by realist evaluation, for example, is certainly attractive to social researchers who are looking for more robust ways of using evaluation techniques, but such an approach clearly has resource implications. Again, there are a number of parallels here with case-study researchers, who often struggle to attract sufficient support to do their work. Social researchers are certainly supportive of the high standards that realist evaluators set themselves in gathering their data, but the *desire* to do more and better cannot on its own overcome the practical difficulties.

The predominant mode of social research today, research that is often only funded in the most minimal way, is small scale and short term. This creates an expectation that social research no longer needs to be a time-consuming and cumbersome process, but can be a much more immediate kind of undertaking, producing results relatively quickly. Participatory evaluation fits this need for economy, immediacy and urgency of results very well, because it creates the potential for change right from the start. The sponsor, funder and research team do not have to wait until months of painstaking data gathering and data analysis have taken place, but can witness and report on emergent changes straight away. Evaluation is, as we have discussed above, an applied technique that operates with a definition of knowledge as practical outcomes having obvious impacts. This is quite different from the concept of knowledge typically used by social researchers, whose pure, abstract and theoretical interests develop much more glacially. A brief summary of key findings can be produced immediately, but the careful working out of ideas and concepts for discussion at academic conferences or hoped-for publication in specialist academic journals requires many months of additional careful work.

Taking a step back from these important details, one way of reflecting on the usefulness of evaluation techniques for social research is to ask again what the overall purpose of the exercise is. The inclusive and holistic character of participatory evaluation raises the expectation that a number of different purposes can be served simultaneously. The sponsor and funder will be expecting a concise report from the evaluator/researcher giving their best and final opinion of the effectiveness of the programme and how it is being delivered. Stakeholders/participants will be less interested in the final report but, as a result of the mutual learning process through which they have gone, might be expecting to see some practical changes in the operation of the organization at which they work. The evaluator/researcher will be hoping to use the data they have gathered to test a hypothesis or shed empirical light on the research question with which they started out.

The difficulty here for social researchers whose main professional orientation is towards 'research' rather than 'evaluation' is that the outcomes of any systematic investigation inevitably reflect earlier decisions about research design. This is one of the basic insights of social research and explains why so much effort goes into developing methodologies that produce particular kinds of results. The emergent conclusions are a function of the process that gives rise to them. The process of devising a research question, developing a suitable method for gathering the required data and then analysing it is a relatively linear process in which one stage follows logically from the preceding stage. The research is designed to produce particular kinds of results, to answer specific research questions.

This diverges quite sharply form the evaluation model, which is more open about the kinds of outcomes or 'results' that might emerge. The logic of participatory evaluation is that outcomes cannot be known in advance, nor even the exact format of those outcomes, since both of these are factors that mature in the belly of evaluation. The more linear or successionist format of social research, in which outcomes are expected to serve the explicit purpose of helping the researcher answer a specific research question, is not entirely compatible with the open-ended format of evaluation. It may be unrealistic, in other words, to expect to get different outcomes from the exercise *as if there were* no such links between the data and the mode of gathering it.

# Critical Approaches in Social Research: Critical Realism and Value Standpoint Social Research

5

The default position of the social researcher using a positivist scientific approach to developing knowledge of the social world is that the researcher acts as an impartial observer and analyst, who deploys rational judgement in gathering data using recognized techniques in order to arrive at a clear, factual view of a particular social phenomenon. The *validity* and *reliability* of the results depends to a large extent on the robustness of the research process – a process that, without claiming it is infallible, is accepted by a variety of academic and other interested audiences as producing information that is as objective and factual as it can be.

The role of the social researcher is to orchestrate the research process effectively so that the results contribute positively to academic-theoretical understanding of the subject and to practical developments in policy and programmes. The knowledge and experience of the researcher provide integral intellectual support to the process in identifying connections between its various elements. The causative relations between various factors exist in reality (drug addiction *really does* increase the likelihood of criminal activity), but awareness of these relations, how they are co-dependent and what clues they offer about other kinds of causative effects are intellectual constructions in the mind of the observer (which interrelations of social context *might* affect drug addiction?). The social researcher, in other words, does not behave robotically in gathering and analysing data, but exercises creative imagination in teasing out the various threads of cause and effect. Having *imagined* what these might be, further research is devised to test and consolidate these ideas. An accumulation of supportive results further reinforces the scientific status of the knowledge thus produced.

The fact that all participants in social research have value positions was noted in the previous chapter, which explored the question of interests among different stakeholders in evaluation research. The issue we are considering in this chapter is what happens when the social researcher deviates from the basic scientific approach just described in order to put forward a particular *value standpoint*. A value standpoint reflects ideas and beliefs held by the researcher, ideas and beliefs that often express affiliation to a particular ideological or political position. (The broader ideological and political context of researching social and welfare policy is discussed in Chapter 7.)

Clearly, social research being conducted from a particular value standpoint amounts to quite a shift away from traditional principles of scientific social research such as value neutrality, open-mindedness and neutrality. However, we might equally question whether it is actually possible to do research from a neutral position. Many feminist researchers in particular have questioned this view, arguing that objectivity is actually a mask for male domination. This argument could also be connected to other social divisions like class, race or age. These views are held in place by an informed expectation that certain specified aspects of current society could or should be different. Although it is perfectly possible to be an advocate of the status quo (that is, a supporter of leaving things as they are), most political and ideological standpoints argue for social change. The way opposition expresses itself is by being *critical* of other points of view.

## What does it mean to be 'critical'?

Analytical criticism:

- improves the *evidential basis* of the debate
- add to *'the force of the better argument'*
- accepts the possibility of *alternatives*

While criticism sometimes collapses into simple name calling, academic or *analytical criticism*, as we will label it, generally sets out from the idea that alternative views are mistaken because they are based on false premises of one kind or another. Critics of laissez-faire capitalism, for example, argue that it is simply not true that participants enter the market on equal terms or that decisions are based on perfect knowledge. The most intelligent strategy for asserting the correctness of one view, and the corresponding falsity of alternative views, is to highlight deficiencies in those underlying presumptions. Analytical criticism is thus 'positive', in that it attempts genuinely to move the debate forward by gradually shifting the discussion onto firmer ground. A first way in which analytical criticism contributes to the process, therefore, is by improving the *evidential basis* of the debate.

Analytical criticism makes a second key contribution to improving the quality of debate by attempting to apply *'the force of the better argument'*. Once all parties are sufficiently agreed that, on the available evidence, some aspect of the real social world is as it appears to be, the debate shifts to making claims about whether or not attempts should be made to change it, and if so how.

Although much of the debate over practical solutions is concentrated in the political sphere, and is undoubtedly influenced by political ideology, the quality of the arguments over the need for change put forward by academic and other social researchers will certainly have an influence on the decisions made by policy makers. The quality of the argument depends both on the validity of the evidence *and* on the strength of the critical voice with which it is being put forward.

The idea of critical argument and debate illustrates a third key contribution of evidence-based analytical criticism, which is the idea that there are always alternatives to the prevailing situation. Replacing the static and fatalistic perspective of pre-modern society that human life is shaped by fundamental forces that cannot be controlled, the modern concept of progress reflects the basic humanist–Enlightenment social value that social actors are able to affect the direction of their lives and of history. Knowledge and negotiation are thus crucial contributors in the process of practical, intellectual and cultural change (see Chapter 1). These three general principles of analytical criticism (improving the evidential basis, argumentation, accepting alternatives) are used in varying degrees by all social researchers who declare their political and ideological views, and especially by activist social researchers who engage in social research to further the causes in which they believe.

In the second section of this chapter we will look at three such critical approaches to illustrate the intellectual and practical value of social research expressing a critical point of view. The first perspective is *critical realism*, which refines the general idea of critical analysis into a clearly defined methodology. Critical realists claim that their approach offers social researchers an analytical toolkit that, although they reject the familiar positivist notion of linear causality (factor A combined with factor B always produces outcome C), provides a robust factual understanding of the mechanisms that produce real surface events, which also suggests strongly that alternative outcomes are possible.

The second and third critical approaches we will be discussing are Marxist-standpoint social research and feminist-standpoint social research. These latter approaches draw on a variety of methodologies and research techniques in developing their research (sometimes including the techniques of critical realism), but what especially marks them out is their political and ideological opposition to what they regard respectively as the injustices of capitalism and patriarchy in modern society. Although they often have different audiences in mind, they share a desire to increase equality and social justice. Whereas critical realism offers a *critical methodology*, Marxist and feminist approaches (and sometimes Marxist–feminist approaches) apply a *critical ideology* in carrying out their social research.

Before looking at these three examples of critical social science and thinking in more general terms about the impact of value-standpoint or advocacy social research on the research process, we should explore how adopting a critical position in respect of ethics and values affects the methodology of social research. Advocacy and criticism not only play a part in analysing the data later on, they may also be instrumental in formulating questions that are worth asking in the first place.

When the social researcher shifts away from being a detached and independent observer, towards being an advocate for a particular point of view, each of the key stages in the research process will be affected, including:

- attitude towards the research project
- relationships with sponsors, funders, gatekeepers and respondents
- formation of the research question
- choice of methodology
- attitude towards the data
- style of data analysis and mode of discussion
- expectations from the findings
- intended impacts on the audience
- expectations of the audience

## Advocacy, criticism and the research process

As noted in the introduction to this chapter, a value standpoint goes beyond general awareness of an issue or routine sympathy for a cause and takes the form of a focused and deliberate desire to act positively in order to bring about social change of some kind. Once a researcher adopts a particular value standpoint, they can no longer act as an impartial scientific observer but become instead the declared holder of a value standpoint, an advocate for a particular group of social actors, and possibly an active campaigner on its behalf. Part of the motivation for being involved in social research as a committed social reformer is the potential it offers to achieve real social change. Although not all holders of particular informed standpoints become activists, there is a tendency for research audiences not to disregard this possibility. Having *any* declared point of view, in other words, diminishes the possibility of being regarded as an impartial, objective observer in the strict scientific sense of the term. Under circumstances in which the researcher behaves as an advocate for a particular value standpoint, the usual open process of reflecting on the data as it is being analysed and the way it is interpreted are supplemented by a more guided or closed approach, since some outcomes are likely to be more welcome to the researcher than others. This is not so much a question of disregarding or suppressing some results in favour of others, but of tending to be more sensitive towards preferred outcomes. More subtle or obscure possibilities offered by the data might go unobserved or unreported.

### Research method and design

Looking first at research method and design, an important distinction to be made straight away is between the integrity of the *method*, and the integrity of the subsequent *interpretation* put on the findings. In principle, strict scientific methods can be applied by social researchers irrespective of the value position they hold. Having a strong value position or standpoint does not preclude the possibility of developing a robust research design or of applying it rigorously. Marxist or feminist social researchers, for example, are just as capable of designing research projects that adopt the standards of scientific rigour as are researchers who generally support the status quo. Those advocating support for emergent social issues might feel the need to be especially scrupulous in their methods in order to forestall any criticism that their findings are weak on the grounds that they are based on faulty technique (Émile Durkheim's *The Rules of Sociological Method* (1895) attempted to achieve this for the emergent profession of sociology). On the presumption that all social researchers operate within agreed professional-ethical boundaries, and do not set out to deceive their expected audiences (which is not only unethical but risks the credibility and future employment of the researcher), the issue of value positioning raises the more subtle challenge of trying to tease out those strands in the research that, *in practice*, have been affected by the value position of the research team.

First, although the risk of *researcher bias* cannot be eliminated altogether, this is less likely to happen when summing numerical data produced by quantitative techniques. The likelihood of arriving at a preferred reading of the data clearly increases when the researcher is using qualitative methods, especially those that require 'interpretation' of the data as a necessary step in transforming data into results. Taking notes in a focus-group session, for example, or gathering information from respondents in a free-form interview are techniques in which the 'voice' of the respondents is always mediated by the researcher. If there is a real possibility of benign misinterpretation, this can be (partly) offset by including in the research design other techniques as well. Triangulation, for example, in which qualitative and quantitative techniques are combined to improve the quality and depth of the data, also has the added benefit of embedding checks and balances in the data-gathering process. The risk of misinterpretation of qualitative data is restrained by the inclusion of 'factual' evidence from sources that do not depend on the interpretivist imagination of the researcher. Providing a thorough literature review that cites the findings of previous research, and describes clearly the theoretical underpinnings of the analysis, has the same collateral benefit. Peer review of results sent for publication in academic journals provides a final test of methodological rigour. These activities will not make the research 'better', nor compensate for poor research design, but they might reduce the possibility of misunderstandings.

Second, in addition to the practical matter of which techniques to use to gather the required data, advocacy and standpoint also affect the *intellectual parameters* of the research. To the extent that the ideas, interests and enthusiasms of the social researcher are integral to their professional activities *as* social researchers (there can be very few social researchers who remain utterly disengaged from the social subject matter), the process of hypothesizing connections between phenomena, of imagining sequences of cause and consequence, is inevitably affected by the ideas, values and beliefs they hold. This is perhaps the most elusive aspect of the impact of advocacy and value standpoint since, as noted at the start of this chapter, much of the formative stage of social research takes place within the imagination of the researcher. Putative links between cause and effect are made in the imagination of the researcher irrespective of whether it has been demonstrated that these occur in 'real' reality. Even at the most rudimentary level of deciding which topic to study and from which point of view, the researcher expresses a subjective interest in the research process (e.g. Weber 1949 [1903–17]). If part of that value system is the expectation that social research contributes to the wider process of social change, this expectation will inevitably play an important part in selecting and shaping the research topic. Unless we envisage a radically different approach to publicly funded social research, in which researchers are randomly assigned to carry out projects for which funding has been agreed in advance, the subjective link between researcher motivation and research topic cannot be eliminated. Even then, it is highly unlikely that a professionally trained sociologist would begin a piece of research without any pre-understandings, knowledge or more general expectations in relation to the field of enquiry.

Third, researchers also need to remain intellectually sensitive to the fact that the *theoretical suppositions* they make are bound to reflect the value positions they hold. A committed social campaigner, for example, might take it for granted that the main causes of poverty are 'social'. An economist might challenge this basic assumption and argue that poverty results from individual failure. In designing research projects to investigate the causes of poverty, the campaigner and the economist are likely to adopt quite different approaches to the task because of differences in the theoretical positions from which they set out. The campaigner might concentrate on investigating how social structure constrains individual opportunity, thus producing inequality in the labour market and eventually poverty for some. The economist might concentrate instead on the individual failure of some social actors to acquire qualifications and skills that are attractive to employers. A weakness of personal motivation, combined with poor decision making, results in labour-market failure and eventually poverty. Discussing the impact of poverty, the campaigner is likely to argue that poverty is necessarily a bad thing, while the economist might argue that the threat of poverty incentivizes people to engage more positively with the labour market.

Finally, advocacy and standpoint also affect the formation of the *research question*. Although a social research project *appears* to stand alone as a discrete piece of academic activity, it is always part of a more complex universe or meaning. In the case of advocacy and campaigning research, this universe will be the wider political 'whole' that the advocate or campaigner is trying

to affect. This is quite different from the 'whole' in more academically oriented research, which will be the field of specialist scientific knowledge where
the research is located. The research question performs a similar *function* in
providing intellectual coherence and stability to both kinds of research project
(advocacy and non-advocacy both benefit from having a clear research question), but the shape and style of the research question will certainly be affected
by the wider political and academic contexts and by the purposes of the
research. Standpoint and advocacy see the research in the context of, and as
playing a specific role in, the bigger campaigning picture.

### Ethical responsibilities

In addition to its practical implications for research design, value-standpoint
research also raises a number of issues about the *ethical responsibilities* of the
researcher. Although the issue of research ethics generally focuses on the conduct of the research, and especially on how respondents are treated (the principles of avoidance of harm and informed consent are discussed in Chapter 2),
the temptation to provide results that are sympathetic towards, or in keeping
with, the value standpoint of the funding organization is also an important
ethical issue.

A first responsibility, then, of the social researcher is to provide an interpretation of the data that would be corroborated by other researchers if the
study were repeated. However, given that social research almost always falls
short of the strict positivist-empiricist criteria of *replicability* (and sometimes
of reliability and validity as well), it is impossible to know whether a different
researcher with different views and expectations would arrive at different conclusions from the same data. The research community therefore has to rely on
*the researcher* to provide an independent voice, and the possibility of independence is soon lost once the researcher becomes an advocate or campaigner for a
particular point of view. Social researchers mediate between audiences and the
data, and mediation is a creative process. While qualitative techniques invariably run the risk of letting the researcher 'tell the story' the way they want it to
be told, it is important to bear in mind that the audience is unlikely to have any
other way of hearing the story, or a different version of it, from anyone else.

If a researcher is selected by a sponsor to conduct a study because the
researcher is known to hold particular views about the topic being investigated, then there is an acceptance from the beginning that, although the usual
criteria of research integrity are being rigorously applied, the results will not be
wholly 'objective' in the strict scientific sense. The integrity of the researcher
is maintained (and perhaps reinforced if the sponsor or funder is particularly
prestigious) because they express, as it were, 'the courage of their convictions'
in carrying out the research. The situation is more ambiguous, however, if the
researcher either has a particular value standpoint that they do not disclose
or if they claim absolute impartiality. The latter circumstance implies naivety
on the part of the researcher (since complete objectivity in social research is

unattainable) and the former might imply an attempt to deceive (which is unethical).

At a personal and professional level, there is always likely to be a point in the research process at which independent and objective reporting of factual research data crosses the boundary into giving audiences a preferred reading of events. Informal conversations at academic conferences, for example, offer opportunities for researchers to say what they really think in language that is less guarded than the more temperate and circumspect statements made in the formal presentation of findings. The research team might be reluctant, for example, to emphasize findings in their official report that are not in keeping with funders' expectations, as this might reduce the possibility of further research funding from that organization. Ambiguities in the findings, or possible disagreements over interpretations between members of the research team, might also only be revealed 'off the record'. So long as all participants are aware that results are being actively framed by the value standpoints of researchers and/or their audiences, the question of ethical probity might not arise. What is ethically dubious, however, is to present research findings *as if they were* entirely value neutral when researchers and their funders are clear advocates of particular value standpoints.

## The audience

A further complicating factor affecting the design and integrity of social research is that the audience itself may have a preference for *hearing* one story or version of the findings rather than another. Many audiences for social research are themselves stakeholders in the process (perhaps as sponsors, funders or gatekeepers) and so the way they *receive* the information will be tempered by their own value positions, including those framed by underlying political/ideological belief systems. Audiences have expectations that are bound to be influenced in various ways by their own value positions and vested interests.

An interesting example of this, and one that clearly demonstrates how government concern over public opinion directly affects research funding, is Wellings et al.'s research into *Sexual Behaviour in Britain* (1994). The political controversy surrounding this study has subsequently been described in detail by Devine and Heath (1999), who note that 'Almost from day one [the National Survey of Sexual Attitudes and Lifestyles] was hampered by politicking at the highest level with its development, fieldwork and eventual publication taking place alongside national arguments and debates about some of the most controversial moral concerns of successive Conservative governments' (Devine and Heath 1999: 127). These governments were concerned that a survey of sexual attitudes and behaviour might, in the popular imagination, tend to legitimize increasing sexual promiscuity, including a lowering of the age at which young men and women have their first sexual encounter. This was perceived as sending 'the wrong kind of message' at a time when government was funding hard-hitting campaigns warning about the spread of HIV/AIDS in the United Kingdom during the late 1980s. The study, which was eventually funded by the Wellcome Trust in 1990 after the Conservative government withdrew its support, also became embroiled in public discussions over the perceived relationship between HIV/AIDS and homosexual activity. The study revealed an important distinction between men and women who identified themselves a homosexual (i.e. as having only or mostly homosexual sexual activity) and what appeared to be a much higher incidence of same-sex sexual activity (i.e. people engaging in same-sex sexual activity but without necessarily identifying themselves as gay). It is interesting to note further that it was not until 2009, following the Office for National Statistics' *Equality Data Review* in 2007, that the moral imaginations of political and public audiences had softened sufficiently to allow the Integrated Household Survey to include specific questions about sexual orientation (Theodore et al. 2010).

On the positive side, researchers might benefit from, and be attracted to, institutions, research centres and academic departments that declare their collective support for a particular value position. Rather than finding that sources of funding are withheld from researchers with declared value positions and/or that particular avenues of research tend not to receive funding for political or ideological reasons, some sources of targeted finding might be increased. Although space precludes a full discussion of the topic here, the variable and uneven way in which funding is made available for different kinds of social research demonstrates how political ideologies ebb and flow over time. It would have been impossible, for example, to raise funds in the 1960s for social research into the lifestyles of gays or lesbians, but relatively easy to research the orientations to work of the British industrial working class.

Recalling our earlier comment that analytical criticism adds to the research process by helping develop 'the force of the better argument', if research results are criticized or rejected *on the grounds that* they are unacceptably expressive of a particular point of view, the solution would be for those holding a different point of view to conduct their own research to see whether an alternative reading of the situation could be substantiated. This movement back and forth between alternative views is, of course, one of the basic processes by which scientific knowledge proceeds. The established point of view (thesis) is challenged by a rival view (antithesis), hypotheses are developed and experiments take place to see which view holds up under testing. Eventually a new synthesis emerges that becomes the new orthodoxy. The difference in social research, however, is that quite often what is being tested is not the facts or the theory, but the rhetoric of the two sides. It is a dispute over values and ideologies, not a strict scientific disagreement over facts. The resource implications of carrying out social research act against the possibility of continual retesting and so many disputes remain very much in the elusive domain of rival interpretation.

Under circumstances in which the main area of contention is political and ideological rather than scientific, the results of social research tend to provide ammunition for the opposing sides to sling at each other rather than producing unambiguous 'final' results that everyone accepts as 'true'. Under these circumstances, the principal ethical consideration for the social researcher is to be aware that their findings are likely to be drawn into the wider ideological and political debates of the day, and to take account of the sensitivities of those who are likely to be affected by those debates. Ethical responsibility for research findings might extend well beyond the moment when results are published. Findings from the Wellings et al. (1994) study just referred to, for example, have been used both by social reactionaries as evidence of continuing low levels of homosexuality (thus reinforcing heterosexual hegemony) and by social progressives who claim that it demonstrates increasing levels of same-sex sexual interaction (thus undermining heterosexual hegemony).

## Ethical justification for adopting value standpoints in social research

Although expressing a particular value standpoint imposes particular kinds of adjustments on the research process – adjustments that carry the research away from the standard positivist scientific model – it is possible to deploy arguments that offer an ethical justification for so doing.

First, value commitment can be seen as merely an extension of the ordinary problem of researcher bias. There is nothing ethically novel about the idea that social researchers find it difficult to isolate themselves from the topics they are studying and so embracing this reality might offer a more realistic way forward. It could be argued, for example, that personal interest in the topic is a basic requirement of being able to carry out systematic research in the first place. The step from personal interest in a topic to wanting to bring about some kind of social change is a perfectly logical one. Besides, declaring a value standpoint from the outset saves those holding opposing views from wasting resources trying to discredit the argument *on the grounds that* it expresses a particular value standpoint.

> Would it be more ethical for researchers only to carry out research from the point of view of standpoints with which they do not agree?

Second, given the way in which social researchers are themselves participants in the social and cultural milieu they are studying, it can be argued that working from a particular value standpoint is simply another way of acknowledging that everyone hopes to find what they are looking for. The human intellect presupposes the likelihood of particular outcomes when formulating questions that it believes are worth asking and so, inevitably, the outcome of any investigation is shaped by the expectations that gave rise to it in the first place. All social research is, at least in this respect, an exercise in déjà vu: the results already exist, approximately, in the mind of the observer *before* the first piece of data has been gathered.

---

Rather than worrying about the ethical implications of formulating research questions that appear to be independent of the 'interests' of the researcher, would it not be more ethical for social researchers to be more concerned with formulating research questions that will give rise to genuinely unexpected findings?

---

A third ethical justification is that very often one of the core values of the researcher, and of other stakeholders (sponsors, funders and gatekeepers), is to bring about actual social change. The purpose of the research is to enable the researcher and other stakeholders to substantiate claims that a particular policy is required or, in the case of evaluation research, to test whether a policy is achieving hoped-for outcomes. In this context, 'values' are not generally treated as an ethical dilemma that needs to be kept separate from the research, but are part of its underlying rationale. It makes little sense to require stakeholders to suppress their value commitment to achieving social change, since this would merely misrepresent the research context. Firm political commitment, however, and openness about value positions that are enthusiastically held, cannot justify shabby research technique.

---

Unless stakeholders are willing to describe their findings as 'opinion' (i.e. journalism and propaganda) rather than as 'research', should they not do their best to ensure that their audiences are aware of their value position?

---

A fourth ethical justification for the researcher moving away from detachment and towards involvement is that commitment to resolving a particular social problem (rather than simply commitment to producing 'good' science) is a natural corollary of the trend in social research towards using methods that require the active participation of the researcher. In *participatory evaluation* (though not summative evaluation), and to an even greater extent in action research and practitioner-led research (see Chapter 6), the distinction between researcher and research subject, and thus between objective observer and subjective participant, is virtually dissolved away. In these forms of participatory social investigation, the knowledge being sought is intimately connected with, and part of, the *personal experience* of the researcher-practitioner. The context-dependent nature of the investigation makes it difficult to claim that conclusions reached are separable from that personal experience. Researcher-practitioners may or may not have high hopes of achieving social change beyond their own workplace or organization but, within those workplaces, they are *already acting as* advocates and campaigners.

> Facilitation of positive outcomes through the presence of a research-participant is itself a valuable and ethical outcome of social research.

Fifth, the shifting role of the social researcher through participation is accompanied by an *intellectual shift* away from the usual open-ended scientific search for new knowledge in and of itself (dispassionate, value-neutral investigation) and towards a more closed or channelled expectation that practical changes in policy might result. Although policy-oriented social research (discussed in detail in Chapter 7) continues to produce outcomes that are theoretically interesting, this dimension tends to be underplayed, since the emphasis is very much on improving the *evidential basis* for achieving practical outcomes. This is not to say that 'theory' plays no part at all in standpoint-driven social research, since, especially for academic advocates and campaigners, a nice new piece of theory can help legitimate the claims being made just as effectively as a slab of hard data. The point is that theoretical innovation need not be the main or sole reason for carrying out social research. The researcher is driven by the desire for change rather than, or as well as, hoping for intellectual reward. This practical and policy-explicit perspective might also be attractive to sponsors and funders who, although they might be flattered to feel they are supporting the scientific quest for new knowledge (something on which canny researchers might play in approaching sponsors), are mainly concerned with achieving practical outcomes for their own organizations and clients. Adopting a grounded attitude has become a precondition for carrying out funded social research in many fields. One of the key criteria against which the Economic and Social Research Council assesses funding applications is the impact the research will have on improving the economic and social prosperity of the United Kingdom:

> The ESRC expects that all the research it funds will be high quality and of scholarly distinction, but we are also committed to increasing its non academic impact and benefit to the UK in public policy, economic prosperity, culture and quality of life. [The ways in which we will maximize impact are] the close engagements with potential research users before, during and after the research process, and a flow of people between research and the worlds of policy and practice. (ESRC 2009: 3 'Impact')

An alternative way of looking at the methodological dilemmas discussed in this section is to think of the different kinds of impacts social researchers hope to achieve, as a kind of bias:

> Bias is best conceptualised as systematic deviation from what would be the most effective route to one goal because of commitment to another [...] So, what is bias from the point of view of one goal is not necessarily bias from that of another [goal]. (Hammersley 2000: 142)

The possible impacts for the social researcher are:

- expression of intellectual virtuosity
- theoretical knowledge in the topic
- practical impact on policy and practice
- influencing political/ideological discourses

To the extent that social researchers want to achieve a range of different impacts or goals through their research, the tendency to prioritize one goal or impact in preference to another amounts to a kind of intellectual bias. The different impacts are not necessarily incompatible, nor are they mutually exclusive (that is, it is possible to combine intellectual outcomes with practical effects, or political influence with practice), but prioritizing between them does mean making particular kinds of intellectual decisions. Since it is not possible to treat all impacts equally, it would seem ethical to declare where one's intellectual preferences lie.

In the next section of this chapter we narrow our focus and discuss three 'critical' perspectives in social research that have been especially influential: critical realism, Marxist-standpoint social research and feminist-standpoint social research. In addition to learning about these important research perspectives, the purpose of the discussion is to see how they deal with some of the methodological and practical issues we have just been discussing.

## Critical approaches in social research

### Critical realism

*Realism* is the philosophical position that it is possible and reasonable to describe a reality that exists independently of anything we might have to say about it. Non-material phenomena such as ideas, values and beliefs can also be considered part of reality. Realism (and *materialism*) contrast with *idealism*, which is the position that it is the ideas or rational understanding social actors have of actually existing physical matter, the mental and intellectual impressions created in the human mind, which are truly significant. It is only when material things become transformed into ideas that they become meaningful. Ideas make phenomena really real.

Associated in particular with the ideas of Rom Harré (1972), Roy Bhaskar (1975, 1979), Andrew Sayer (1984) and Margaret Archer (1995, 2000), the underlying premise of *critical realism* is that it is possible to explain key aspects of the surface forms of real social phenomena by inferring the existence of underlying mechanisms or processes that have caused these surface events, but that cannot themselves be observed directly. Critical realists claim that when patterns and regularities are found, they provide a 'working hypothesis' for theorizing the *causative relations* between forces, events, parties, persons, institutions and so on. Realist theory operates at the level of the mechanisms that can be inferred as working 'beneath the surface' or 'behind the scenes' to cause various observable effects at the surface. For example, one cannot 'see' the mechanisms that cause unemployment but, through a close examination of their effects, it becomes possible not only to describe which factors (general economic conditions, state of the global labour market, commodity prices, consumer demand) are most likely to be involved in the production of unemployment, but also to begin to speculate about how these factors, or some combination of them, were involved in the incidence of unemployment at a particular time and place (job insecurity resulted in unwillingness to change jobs, thus causing rigidity in the labour market, making it unresponsive to changes in the demand for labour).

Most significantly, the technique recommends a form of *retroductive reasoning* in which analysis or observation of the surface event comes *ahead of*, and provides a platform for, wondering how the event could have come about. (Or, describing the procedure the other way around, theoretical analysis comes after the observation and description of surface phenomena.) Futuristic speculation about what might happen next if, for example, similar factors and contexts were in play tends to fall outside the logic of retroductive reasoning, which fundamentally 'looks back' rather than 'looking forward'. Retroductive reasoning contrasts with inductive and deductive reasoning (hypothetico-deductive reasoning), whose theory-building processes tend to look forward rather than, or as well as, looking back.

The 'critical' aspect of critical realism refers to the claim that the core positivist assumption that identifiable surface events can always be explained *and predicted* with reference to the various underlying laws of cause and effect is false. Critical realists argue that, even if it has some utility when examining natural phenomena, this linear or 'successionist' concept of causation cannot adequately explain social and cultural phenomena. Attempts at explaining such phenomena require a circular and *contingent* notion of causation that posits a much more problematic form of underlying mechanism producing surface events, *and* that is sceptical about being able to predict future outcomes (social phenomena are inherently unpredictable). To further our understanding of social phenomena it is not necessary to assume that particular outcomes must always occur. It is in fact the evident failure of positivism to explain adequately the phenomena of society and of culture, the failure to discover any 'laws of motion of society' despite over 150 years of trying, which shows just how necessary it is to develop a different conception of causality. The determining factor here, from a critical-realist standpoint, is that the successionist concept of cause and effect only applies (imperfectly) to *closed systems* in which a limited range of outcomes is possible. When hydrogen and oxygen are combined under controlled laboratory conditions they *must* produce water. In *open systems* – and especially in society, which is the most contingent open system of all – it is never possible to control conditions and mechanisms entirely (society is not a laboratory) and so outcomes are always uncertain and often unintended by social actors (see Sayer 1984: 94–107).

The retroductive mode of reasoning referred to above is especially significant here, since it reacts against positivist science, which *is* generally comfortable with the idea of predicting, of theorizing in advance, how particular combinations of factors will produce precisely specified outcomes. Critical realism treats prediction and speculation much more problematically because it uses a contingent notion of causality, not a successionist one. It is the *mechanism* of the coming together of forces and contexts that is the focus of critical-realist attention, rather than a forensic analysis of the constitution of each of those factors (or at least only to the point at which this constitution is deemed to affect the way the causative mechanism works). Laboratory science *does* need to know as much as possible about the chemical constitution of phenomena, because it sees causation as being directly and categorically related to knowing precisely of what the contributory elements are made. Knowing *how* oxygen and hydrogen combine to form molecules of water is significant knowledge, *because* it indicates the existence of these separate elements (we already have 'water', what we want to know now are the elements of which it is made). Once we have a complete periodic table of all the elements, it becomes a relatively simple matter to figure out new ways of combing them or of predicting what will happen if they are combined. Synthetic substances like plastics did not exist and could not have been discovered in advance of the chemical experimentation that created them. Social-scientific knowledge can never develop in this way, because there is no such thing as a periodic table of the elements of social phenomena. All the effort therefore has to go into looking at the mechanisms of combination, and the only available data for doing this is how things appear at the surface once they have *already been combined* (in this sense the social universe is entirely made up 'plastics' rather than of discrete elements).

It is important straightaway not to confuse critical realism, which is a *rational analytical approach*, with any of the particular critical political or ideological standpoints (such as Marxism and feminist) that have made use of the analytical procedures of critical realism. Having said this, many critical realists are motivated by the idea that as understanding increases of the kinds of mechanisms that facilitate social relations and social functioning, glimpses appear of how things could be 'better'. This declared desire for greater emancipation is not simply positive intellectual rhetoric (a critical intellectual standpoint), but reflects the underlying methodological proposition that different combinations of causative elements and circumstances *really can* produce different outcomes; there is nothing inevitable or fixed about how things turn out. Critical realism offers social researchers an approach to social research that contains within its own theoretical construction of cause and consequence an openness towards imagining how other outcomes *really are* possible.

**Key ingredients of the critical realist approach**

There are three main elements in the critical realist analytical procedure of analytical induction, as it is sometimes called. First is the 'real'. This is all the stuff in the world of whatever kind, whether observed or not, or indeed whether it is 'observable' in the usual sense of the term. The basic or non-negotiable epistemological assumption of critical realism is simply that the 'real' exists independently of our knowledge of it. The second main element is the 'actual'. This is what actually does happen. It is the actual expression of an outcome of the coming together of various factors. The actual does not exhaust all of the other possibilities that could, potentially, have occurred, but it is the one that *did* occur. Differentiating in this way between the 'real' and the 'actual' makes it possible to emphasize that the real is not limited by, nor is it identical with, that which the social actor has experienced empirically themselves (empirical materialism). Nor is the real limited by that which actually occurs, because there are many other experiences that social actors *could* have had. Third is the 'empirical', which is that which is experienced by the social actor. Direct personal experience of an outcome adds weight to the sense that that particular something is real, but the real is not limited by that which is actually experienced. Other possibilities always exist and the fact that a social actor has not experienced these themselves does not make them any less real.

To illustrate these distinctions in the critical-realist analytical procedure, we can refer to the familiar pastime of forecasting the weather. We know that the weather is contingent on the coming together of geographical, climatic, atmospheric and other factors that combine at particular moments to produce actual 'weather' (highly transient though this might be in temperate climates). The forecast produced by the Meteorological Office by no means exhausts all of the possible weather events that could have occurred; it could have rained instead of being hot and dry. The actual weather that does happen (wind, rain, snow, fog, sunshine etc.) is experienced empirically by those who are affected directly by it. The factors that make weather, the weather events that actually occur, the experience of weather (wet, warmth, draughts, cold etc.) and the weather forecast are all real (that is, part of a reality that we accept as existing even if we ourselves have not experienced it personally). Although, as we have already said, the weather a social actor actually experiences empirically has a more definite or concrete sense of reality than either the forecast, or the weather that is happening to other social actors elsewhere, or the weather that could have occurred but did not, they are all treated analytically as equally real (we will return to this point shortly).

In a broadly similar manner, the critical-realist method relies heavily on the presupposition that real surface events (actualities generating empirical experience) arise as a result of the contingent interaction of underlying factors. Analytically, the challenge is trying to identify, describe or specify the mechanism that, under the particular conditions that are applicable, caused the actual to occur. Referring to our earlier example, unemployment, which really is experienced by those who have lost their job, is a surface effect caused by the coming together at a particular time and place of a range of underlying factors and forces (changes in the national economic situation affecting supply of, and demand for, labour). The critical analytical reasoner sets themselves the tasks (a) of describing the actual empirical experience of unemployment; (b) of identifying which underlying forces and contextual factors are in play; and (c) – and this is the most innovative aspect of the critical-realist procedure – of imagining the mechanisms by which the real underlying factors that have been identified cause actual unemployment to occur. With this information, the social researcher with a special interest in unemployment will then try to figure out which linkages between contributing causes and context gave rise to actual unemployment. The space between the 'actual' and the 'real' opens up an intellectual space for imagining what could have been (and how things *might have been* different).

### Evaluation of the critical-realist approach

Inevitably, critical realism has its intellectual and methodological limitations. First, it is vulnerable to the charge that, despite continuing to insist that actual surface events can only be adequately explained through the existence of underlying causative mechanisms, the closest these alleged mechanisms come to being 'real' in an intellectual sense is in the descriptions of them provided by theorists; a point that idealist researchers would happily endorse. It might turn out to be true that underlying causative mechanisms can be treated as real by inferring their existence from surface effects (there must be some kind of causative mechanism producing unemployment, since it is much more evident at some times rather than at other times), but the 'discovery' of these mechanisms is the outcome of a profoundly rationalist-idealist procedure. It is in fact only by using a contingent notion of causality (rather than a simple cause-and-effect model) that the realness of such underlying mechanisms seems plausible at all since, on critical realism's own admission, there can never be any definitive way of proving *which* mechanism has produced *which* effect (was actual high unemployment in the United Kingdom in 1992 caused by problems of labour supply or by problems of employer demand?).

Second, and despite their criticisms of it, *in practice* the investigative strategy used by critical-realist social researchers is little different from the standard scientific procedure of hypothesizing or speculating the existence of an actual/real/material causative relation between phenomena, and of conducing some kind of controlled investigation to see whether these speculations are well founded. The only substantive methodological difference is how best to infer the underlying mechanism *from* the surface evidence: what *kind* of inference can be drawn, what *style* of inference making is being used? Although, as described above, critical realists adopt a sceptical attitude towards inferring the existence of mechanisms operating in a law-like manner (which is another way of doubting whether such law-like relations exist), it is very difficult to avoid completely the idea that such mechanisms display at least some degree of predictability and regularity. Critical realism thus operates with a concept of what we could call *contingent regularity* rather than having no concept of regularity at all (just like it operates with a notion of contingent causation rather than rejecting the idea of 'causation' entirely).

This points us towards a third paradox for social researchers using a critical-realist perspective, which is the difficulty of generalizing from one situation to another. Having abandoned the idea that universal laws or rules of causation can be discovered (and thus that reliable futuristic predictions can be made), the important question arises of whether critical-realist explanations are always *only applicable* to the specific context that is the subject of the investigation. There is nothing in the epistemology nor in the analytical procedure of critical realism that would enable the researcher to say categorically that the causative relation they have inferred explains anything beyond the particular instance being investigated. The price the critical realist has to pay, therefore, for embracing notions of contingent causality and contingent regularity is that they have to be very modest in their expectation of discovering causative relations whose effects can be generalized to other contexts (the causes of rising unemployment in Kansas might have very little in common with the causes of rising unemployment in London). It is questionable, therefore, whether critical-realist investigations can be anything other than isolated case studies (neither the unemployment situation in Kansas nor that in London *necessarily* indicates the existence of *any* common causal mechanism of unemployment).

One response to this difficulty is to invoke the notion of 'cumulation' and argue that critical-realist knowledge proceeds by means of a continual oscillation between moments of empirical investigation and moments of theoretical speculation. The knowledge that 'cumulates', and that can therefore be generalized from one situation to another, is an increasing knowledge of how causative mechanisms do what they do, rather than necessarily learning more about their actual effects. Jahoda et al.'s (1972) classic study of the experience of unemployment, for example, tells us relatively little about what caused the unemployment in Marienthal, while many studies of unemployment carried out by economists are strong on causes but weak on experience. In applying the critical-realist analytical technique to evaluation research, for example, Pawson and Tilley (1997: 119) invoke the pragmatist principle that the end point of the investigation is not to uncover 'secure transferrable knowledge' but more modestly to achieve a 'continual betterment of practice':

> Generalization is not a matter of understanding the *typicality* of a program in terms of its routine conduct. Rather the process of generalization is essentially one of *abstraction*. We move from one case to another, not because *they* are descriptively similar, but because *we* have ideas that can encompass them both. (Pawson and Tilley 1997: 119, emphasis in original)

Two important issues arise from this. First, this explanation illustrates again the rationalist-idealist element in the critical-realist procedure. However well intentioned critical-realist investigators are in trying to ground their research in actual surface phenomena, their search for underlying causal mechanisms carries them decisively into the realm of abstraction or 'theory'. It seems that the emphasis has shifted entirely away from trying to generalize from one practical situation to another, towards being able to make generalizations only within the theory stage of the procedure.

Second, and since there can be no categorical explanation of any social phenomena (practical or intellectual), the wider acceptance of one explanation of causation rather than another continues to depend on 'the strength of the better argument', *in the sense* that 'the argument' becomes a tussle over how astutely each side has built its case on cumulated knowledge of how mechanisms work. Critical realists become expert in understanding how causative mechanisms *work* (based on the procedure of inferring causative events by looking at their surface effects) and are only secondarily interested in the reverse procedure of seeing how these mechanisms can be used to *predict* the occurrence of particular surface effects. Contingency virtually eliminates the possibility of prediction.

Fourth and finally, although clear analytical differences can be specified between the actual, the real and the empirical, these logical distinctions in the theory might be difficult to disentangle in real-life situations. One example of this is the stratification of the 'real' depending on proximity to the empirical experience. It might be the case, intellectually and analytically, that the 'real' encompasses all things 'equally', but in the domain of actual felt experience, that which is experienced empirically by a social actor is bound to be regarded as the *most real* kind of real. This implies that the concreteness of real reality is stratified in terms of the directness by which social actors are affected by it. Tsunami, earthquake and volcanic eruption, for example, are likely to be more real to those who experience them at first hand than to those watching them on television (although those watching on television are perfectly prepared to accept that the event really did happen and that others are affected by it). At the top of the hierarchy of the real is that part of the real that social actors experience themselves. Below this are arranged other strata or degrees of realness that become less and less immediately real as empirical experience of them becomes more and more mediated and thus remote. To the extent that most topics in social research require awareness of experiential and hermeneutic or meaning-laden features affecting the situation, the fact that different degrees of the real are being experienced tends to upset the apparent logicality of the analytical procedure. At which level of 'the real', one might ask, is the causative mechanism under investigation deemed to operate?

Having looked at critical realism as an example of an analytical strategy that empowers the social researcher, and perhaps especially those wishing to tackle actual social issues in practical ways, to seek novel alternative explanations of phenomena we now turn our attention to two leading examples of political-ideological standpoints. Both Marxism and feminism offer social researchers enticing intellectual frameworks, which can easily be extended into practical intervention and activism, for engaging directly with the process of social change.

## Ideological and political standpoints in social research

One might reasonably observe that the general thrust of all academic social research (broadly defined) carried out in the United Kingdom from the late 1960s until at least the late 1980s was consistently critical of the status quo and often amounted to a series of Marxist- and feminist-inspired critical salvos fired at 'the establishment'. In the academic realm, the orthodoxy if not inherent conservatism of positivist social science, especially that which anchored itself to the functionalist conception of social order popularized by Talcott Parsons in the United States, was criticized by an emergent Left-leaning cadre of activists working in British universities. These radical intellectuals (and to a slightly lesser extent liberal-leaning academics in the United States where Marxism was politically excluded) willingly aligned themselves with the view that the widely accepted characterization of society and of social order in terms of equilibrium and gradual or evolutionary change was untenable. They suggested an alternative characterization of society as existing in a state of perpetual crisis. The real wonder of social order was that such a state of temporary stability could exist at all, given that there are so many forces acting against it.

Within this general critical perspective, and along with other prominent social issues surrounding the civil rights movement, which also found its supporters among academics and intellectuals, Marxism and feminism rapidly became the leading providers of a critical/political ideology centred on the ideals of equality and emancipation. Without underplaying areas of potential conflict between these two ideologies (many feminists argue that Marx disregarded the effects of patriarchy in his analysis of the production and reproduction of capitalist society; see Charles 2000), these approaches offered social researchers a 'working hypothesis' for explaining both how society had reached its current state and what solutions might be at hand for changing it. These trends towards social critique also matched the aspirations of a growing proportion of undergraduates entering university wanting to study disciplines in the social sciences and especially in sociology. Many of those involved in disciplines that emerged a little later (cultural studies, social policy, development studies) took seriously the idea that practical social change depended heavily on the knowledge they were producing about social and cultural phenomena. As political ideologies that strongly advocate social change, Marxism and feminism were not only closely in step with the general mood for change, but also provided robust templates for how change could be achieved. They both also had high levels of 'street credibility', in the sense that Marxist and feminist activists were already actively recruiting among the wider population.

## Marxist-standpoint social research

Marxism provides an overarching political ideology premised on the belief that the next stage in human economic and social progress, the next great leap forward in the history of humankind, depends on the transformation of capitalism into socialism. Marxists of the late nineteenth and early twentieth centuries claimed that this simple statement of historical truth was 'scientific', in the sense that Marx's detailed account of capitalist economic relations in *Das Capital* (1954 [1867]) provided a clear evidential basis for rejecting the classical political economy of Adam Smith and David Ricardo. Focusing particularly on the way in which value is added to commodities by the efforts of the worker rather than of the employer (the 'labour theory of value'), Marx argued that the orthodox representation of capitalism as a fundamentally benign and somehow 'natural' economic system that produced benefits for everyone in society was fundamentally mistaken. Having no means of income of their own, workers are forced into paid employment through the fear of starvation, and once there are compelled to produce far more surplus value or profit for the capitalist then they ever receive back in the form of wages. Even allowing for the technological dynamism of capitalist enterprises (innovation in the means of production), the capitalist division of labour is inherently exploitative and divisive, because of the way it manipulates people's participation in the labour process (the relations of production).

Having described the fundamental failings of capitalism as an economic system, Marx and his followers went on to describe how tensions within the division of labour would be expressed politically in the form of increasingly urgent demands from among the working class of the need for radical social change. The basis of their claim is that, given the enormous wealth-generating capacity of capitalism, it must be possible to find a better way of distributing both the effort that is required to generate wealth and the economic and social benefits it produces. Although many nineteenth-century Marxists believed that industrial society was on the brink of full-blown revolutionary upheaval in which the working class would simply take control away from the capitalist class (revolution was both imm*anent* and imm*inent*), history took a different turn. During the twentieth century, demands for social change were redirected towards a reformist rather than a revolutionary strategy. Although social change is still seen as an immanent feature of capitalism (it contains within itself the seeds of its own destruction), rather than envisaging a single decisive moment of change, a more gradual process of change has developed in which economic and political pressure is brought to bear to resolve exploitation and inequality a piece at a time.

The practical benefit of this scenario for social researchers adopting a Marxist standpoint is that their social research produces evidence of the form and degree of exploitation and inequality in specified parts of the social system. Marxist-standpoint social research thus improves the evidential basis of the debate about the need for social reform. Intellectually, Marxism provides social researchers with a broader narrative into which the individual bits or fragments of knowledge about the need for social change can be fitted. In formulating research questions, for example, it offers a sophisticated theoretical paradigm in which one instance or type of inequality or exploitation can be understood in terms of social inequality in general. Its basic model of causality is that the different forms and levels of actual inequality are invariably rooted in the capitalist labour process.

The narrative framework of Marxism thus increases the intellectual coherence of the critical view of society, both in terms of the concepts and vocabulary it supplies (for example, the concepts of exploitation and alienation) and in terms of the arguments that are put forward. Depending on whether the research is exploratory, whether it is designed to test or retest previous findings, or whether it is designed to evaluate policies that have already been put in place, Marxist-standpoint social research increases and consolidates our knowledge of the social world under capitalism. It helps substantiate 'the force of the better argument' in terms of the need for social change and what form that change should take. By adopting a generally 'critical' approach, Marxist-standpoint social research energetically pursues the idea that alternatives to the current system can and must be found. Taking measures to ensure that people from all backgrounds have opportunities for adequate participation in the labour market is key to achieving social equality and progress.

## Feminist-standpoint social research

The second 'critical' approach we want to consider briefly in this chapter is feminist-standpoint social research. In terms of the role it plays in supporting the ideals and objectives of social researchers who wish to increase levels of equality in society, the feminist standpoint offers a range of characterizations and explanations of the often socially unequal positions occupied by women and men. Feminist-standpoint social researchers have successfully demonstrated that modern society is gendered in significant ways and that one of the effects of this gendering process is to produce inequality between women and men. *Gender*, in other words, is not simply an attitude of mind or a superficial feature of the cultural milieu, but is fundamental to all aspects of social relationships between women and men, relationships that are often characterized by inequality. Interestingly, the pervasiveness of gender is such that it also affects relations between men, and between women, in the sense that gender provides a template for all kinds of social relationships.

Treating 'gender' as a social construct (which is not to deny that gender derives *to some extent* from biological distinctions between the two sexes), feminists argue that, even though the practical means men use to exclude women from positions of power and independence might appear to be attributable, for example, to the operation of the labour market or the alleged practical advantages to the family of the traditional domestic division of labour, many men are motivated to dominate women as an end in itself. This is why gender discrimination persists in societies that have the highest standards of living and in which, therefore, it might be expected that men have little to gain from excluding women from positions of economic strength (Walby 1997). Gender also expresses itself in the form of entrenched social and cultural attitudes that strongly inhibit the development of non-traditional or alternative ways of understanding social relations between women and men. Part of the role of social researchers adopting a feminist standpoint is to try to penetrate these misconceptions by continuing to provide research findings demonstrating the inequalities that gender causes.

In the theoretical domain, and not underestimating differences between the various strands within feminist thought, the feminist standpoint offers social researchers a way of conceiving the inter-relationships between the various manifestations and consequences of gender inequality as they are played out in various social contexts and social practices, and of how one manifestation of the effects of gender can be understood in terms of, and in relation to, other gendered social practices. In this sense, and without suggesting that all feminists adopt the methods of critical realism, the concept of gender can be understood intellectually as operating as a kind of society-wide generative mechanism.

The feminist standpoint also provides social researchers who have a practical interest in achieving greater social equality with useful knowledge of the particular pinch points or 'moments' when gender inequality might arise. It has been found, for example, that the success of a particular policy initiative depends on overcoming gendered attitudes towards childcare (e.g. Gatrell 2007). Developing a realistic procedure for promotion within organizations requires members of selection panels to adopt a more gender-neutral conception of styles of leadership and decision making (e.g. Lewis et al., 2007). Successful restructuring within employing organizations might require managers to confront stereotypical ideas about the suitability of men and women for different kinds of work roles (e.g. Tomlinson 2007). In each of these examples, and irrespective of whether the key players involved are themselves advocates of a feminist ideology, dispelling the popular misconception that women and men occupy different positions in the social hierarchy is key to achieving genuine progress.

## Conclusion

This chapter has provided an account of how social researchers often adopt a critical orientation in carrying out their research. Developing the concept of analytical criticism, we have argued that social research contributes significantly to our knowledge of social phenomena by:

- improving the evidential basis of the debate
- adding to 'the force of the better argument'
- always considering alternatives

In adopting a critical orientation, social researchers make particular decisions both about the methods they select to carry out their research and about the various value commitments that are embedded in that research. Critical realists, for example, deploy the technique of analytical induction in order to develop knowledge of the underlying causes of surface phenomena, but in a way emphasizing that other kinds of surface phenomena could occur. Being critical in social research means accepting the highly contingent, and often unpredictable, nature of social phenomena. Although methods requiring the active participation of the researcher, such as participant evaluation and action research, do not always describe themselves as critical methods, by emphasizing process and context the kind of knowledge they produce can be described as critical knowledge.

We have also spent some time reflecting on the ethical implications for social researchers who adopt particular value positions or standpoints in their research. Accepting that questions of value always are embedded in social research, the dilemma for the social researcher is how explicitly they should declare their own value standpoint, and how strongly they should allow it to influence their research. A value standpoint goes beyond general awareness of an issue or routine sympathy for a particular cause, and takes the form of a focused and deliberate desire to act positively in order to bring about social change of some kind. As a value position becomes a value standpoint, the researcher becomes an advocate and possibly an active campaigner. The more strongly a value standpoint is held, the greater is its impact on research design.

Value standpoints have implications for each of the following stages of the research:

- the choice of research topic
- the formation of the research question
- the choice of research methodology
- the style of data analysis
- the way research results are framed
- how results are presented to various audiences

The ethical dilemma for standpoint researchers is tied both to their personal honesty and integrity and to the reliability and validity of the research. At a personal level, consideration has to be given to whether the researcher is being sufficiently open and honest about the value standpoint they take. Being aware of one's own value position is a necessary first step in being able to make other stakeholders sufficiently aware of it as well. Enabling other stakeholders to recognize *their* value standpoint can be one of the most important research outcomes; an outcome, moreover, that is unique to social research.

In terms of the impact on research design, being aware of the value standpoints in play is also necessary in order to improve the validity and reliability of the research. The research question asked, for example, can hardly be relied on to produce coherent data if it fails to take into account of, or, worse still, attempts to disguise, the value standpoint from which it has arisen. Value standpoints can also affect the way in which the data are analysed, the kinds of interpretations put upon them and how they are represented to various audiences. *Ostensibly*, research into job insecurity in a local labour market is about developing better knowledge of differences between employment sectors and variations in the experiences of women and men, but *actually* it is about providing evidence of gender inequality to support a particular *political view* about the position of women in society. Each of these practical moments in the research is also an ethical moment, in the sense that the social researcher has to take responsibility for maintaining a distinction between well-founded factual knowledge and ideology.

# Making It Personal: Action Research, Practitioner Research and Self-Reflexive Practice

This chapter discusses *action research*, another increasingly influential approach to social investigation that, like participatory evaluation discussed in Chapter 4, offers the social researcher increased opportunity to be directly involved in research where the emphasis is very much on practical outcomes. As Coghlan and Brannick (2005: 13) helpfully point out, 'the term action research is a generic one used to refer to a bewildering array of activities and methods'. In their own summary (2005: 14–20) they offer descriptions of traditional action research, participatory action research, action learning, action science, developmental action inquiry, cooperative inquiry, clinical inquiry, appreciative inquiry, learning history, reflective practice and evaluative inquiry.

In similar vein, McIntyre suggests that participatory action research (often referred to as PAR) emerges from 'a cross-fertilization of research traditions' including 'critical action research', 'community-based participatory research' and 'participatory community research'. She adds that 'all variants of PAR traditionally focus on systemic investigations that lead to a reconfiguration of power structures, however those structures are organized in a particular community' (McIntyre 2008: 4). Not surprisingly, given the diversity of approaches included under the generic heading 'action research', the fields of social inquiry in which action researchers have applied themselves is also wide and varied, ranging from research into community programmes, rural development, business and commercial organization, developing socio-technical solutions to industrial restructuring, and studies in education, healthcare and social welfare.

A summary of the key dimensions of community-based action research is provided by Stringer:

> Community-based action research works on the assumption, therefore, that all stakeholders – those whose lives are affected by the problem under study – should be engaged in the process of investigation. Stakeholders participate in a process of rigorous inquiry, acquiring information (collecting data) and reflecting on that information (analyzing) to transform their understanding about the nature of the problem under investigation (theorizing). This new set of understandings is then applied to plans for resolution

of the problem (action), which, in turn, provides the context for testing hypotheses derived from group theorizing (evaluation). (Stringer 2007: 11)

Given the heterogeneous constitution of action research, we need to consider how best to organize our discussion of it. This is by no means an arbitrary decision since, as McNiff and Whitehead have pointed out, 'action research is not a thing in itself; the term always implies a process of people interacting with one another' (McNiff and Whitehead 2002: 16). Defining action research as a 'process' rather than as a fixed set of methodical steps means that separating out the various parts of action research in order to analyse those parts transgresses the holistic intent of this approach. A first principle of action research is precisely to move beyond the analysis of the whole in terms of its parts and to accept that the essence of understanding the whole is to see it as a continual unfolding of relations and interconnections *between* its various parts – 'parts', moreover, whose constitution is continually altering in light of how those relationships unfold. Action research cannot be adequately understood as a number of discrete individual methodological steps that can be conveniently fitted back together in order to define what action research is.

Nevertheless, and acknowledging the holistic, organic and experiential dimensions of the action perspective, our strategy in this chapter is to look critically at action research under three headings. These are:

- the *procedure* of carrying out an investigation using action principles
- the *role* of the action researcher
- the kinds of practical and intellectual *outcomes* produced

Adopting this thematic approach enables us to offer an intellectual synthesis of the key characteristics of the action perspective, but without disregarding the wide variety of applications and contexts in which it can be applied. Action researchers reject the imposition of any compulsory methodological template for their work, but universally endorse the benefits of participants' learning experiences. We can usefully approach the content of this chapter in the same positive spirit of enquiry.

## The procedures of action research

Action research can be described as an *inside-out* technique, in the sense that the issues to be resolved, and the selection of who should be involved in the process of investigating them, often emerge from within the research context itself. The problem being investigated and the likely parameters of its resolution tend to be predetermined by the circumstances from which they originate. As William Foote Whyte and his colleagues point out in their account of participatory action research (PAR), the standard academic technique, in which the professional researcher controls the entire research process (and it is deemed to be primarily a *research* process), is set aside in favour of a participatory process of change resulting in what they call 'organizational learning' (Whyte et al. 1991: 9). Rather than being preoccupied with data or theoretical insight, the focus of action research is to identify and achieve what Whyte et al. (1991: 9) usefully call 'action objectives'.

For research to be defined as action research, it needs to be driven not by abstract theory and data gathering, but by 'action objectives'; necessarily, these must come from within the organizational context in which the investigation is to take place. As Whyte et al. put it: 'In [participatory action research] the researcher is constantly challenged by events and by ideas, information, and arguments posed by the project participants' (Whyte et al. 1991: 42). The need for the process is therefore determined by the organization, which sees itself as in some state of reorganizational need, rather than by the incoming researcher having 'selfish' academic interests of their own.

In organizational settings, action objectives include such things as redesign of the structures of the organization, changes in the bases of working relationships and new forms of consensual thinking regarding outcomes and objectives. Formulating what the final action objectives *are* is itself part of the participation process. The perceived legitimacy of action objectives for those taking part depends on those objectives being adequately negotiated from the outset. Action objectives cannot be imposed either by the professional researcher or by personnel in the upper echelons of the hierarchy: 'Only as we work with members of the organization, diagnosing those problems [people in the firm are already facing], do we draw upon the research literature as well as our own past experience' (Whyte et al. 1991: 40).

This view is reiterated by Coghlan and Brannick who, also working within an organizational perspective, agree that action research should aim primarily at 'solving real organizational problems'. They emphasize the *circular*, rather than linear, procedure of action research. They suggest that action research

> Incorporates a collaborative enactment of action research cycles [planning, taking action, evaluating action, further planning] whereby the intended research outcome is the construction of actionable knowledge [...] [A]t the same time as you are engaging in the project or core action research cycles, you need to be diagnosing, planning, taking action and evaluating about how the action research project itself is going and what you are learning. (Coghlan and Brannick 2005: 14, 25)

It is the real-time, problem-oriented and problem-solving nature of the investigation that gives action research its 'action' perspective. Action research thus adopts a *pragmatic* attitude towards the aims of the research. As Stringer puts it: 'action research is a systematic approach to investigation that enables people to find effective solutions to problems they confront in their everyday lives' (Stringer 2007: 1).

Although most social researchers expect to achieve outcomes that can contribute both to the development of new theory *and* to the solution of practical problems, the emphasis in action research is very much on the latter. Action researchers are often less concerned with gathering data objectively in order to tackle some abstract theoretical point of interest to other members of the academic community than with achieving more immediate resolution of a perceived operational difficulty and/or with trying to implement changes to create improved outcomes for practitioners and stakeholders. Action research therefore tends to be problem centred and problem oriented rather than taking its direction from theoretical reasoning. In this respect, an action approach might be especially appropriate in those investigative contexts in which the situation is likely to be flexible and in which outcomes have to be seen as an *emergent property* of the research process. One of the advantages of the action approach is that it might offer the only way forward in studying some varieties of social phenomena that lie beyond the reach of conventional data-gathering techniques. Adopting a more detached attitude towards theoretical commitments means that action research often has an exploratory or innovative character.

The circular nature of action research, in which intermediate or transitory outcomes are continually being fed back into the process by participants (we discuss the concept of reflexivity shortly), combined with its problem-solving orientation, tends to result in a considerable foreshortening of the usual research process. In contrast with conventional forms of social research in which the planning, data-gathering, analysis and results phases are clearly organized as a series of steps, often occupying an extended timeframe (three or more years in the case of doctoral research), action research 'declares' its results as it goes along. Even as early as the first meeting of participants, positive outcomes might be discernible, outcomes that need not be held back until subsequent presentation or publication of the findings. Results become coterminous with, and in some instances inseparable from, the investigative procedure as a whole.

### Pure and applied social research

Circularity, pragmatism and a foreshortening of the research cycle all indicate the marked difference between action research and the more conventional forms of academic social research. Whyte describes this in terms of the familiar contrast between the 'pure' and the 'applied' aspects of social investigation: 'the prevailing view – supported by common practice – is to assume that it is up to the behavioural scientist to discover the facts and relationships, and it is up to others to somehow make use of what social researchers discover' (Whyte et al. 1991: 8). Argyris and Schon (1991: 85) draw the familiar distinction between rigor and relevance:

In our view, social scientists are faced with a fundamental *choice* that hinges on a dilemma of rigor or relevance. If social scientists tilt toward the rigor of normal science that currently dominates departments of social science in American universities, they risk becoming irrelevant to practitioners' demands for usable knowledge. If they tilt towards the relevance of action research, they risk falling short of prevailing disciplinary standards of rigor. (Argyris and Schon 1991: 85)

The emphasis on application rather than on pure 'data' or pure 'theory' places action research in the same methodological (epistemological) family as evaluation research, which we discussed in Chapter 4. They share an applied and problem-centred orientation and both advocate some innovative reconfigurations of the usual research process. 'Data', 'theory', 'research question' and 'outcomes' are all redefined in order to accommodate the shift away from the theoretical predetermination of the research topic, and its replacement by the action objectives being sought by the organization. Whyte is critical, for example, of indirect evidence (such as that provided by metrics or survey-type data), which only provides a proxy measure for understanding the actual situation. He strongly favours an action-oriented definition of 'data' as grounded information that is obtained though actual participation in the research context. Pure research proceeds using a combination of direct and indirect data. Action research always presumes that direct data are more reliable and insightful.

One clear example of how action research breaks with conventional procedure is the tendency of working backwards from the findings and analysis stages in the process, towards the retrospective identification of research questions. To the extent that a process of action research is often instigated by members of a particular organization, the process of accumulating information, of seeking opinion from potential or actual participants and of sketching out an initial picture of the issue or situation that needs attention, often gets underway *before* a specific 'research question' has been identified. Whyte et al. observe, for example: 'It was not until we encountered the dramatic results of participation in Xerox that we were driven to the rethinking of the underlying research question. That in turn led us to see the need for a radical paradigm shift for research on one of the most studied topics in organizational behaviour' (Whyte et al. 1991: 49). The key methodological innovation here is that the research process goes into reverse as incoming information requires a reformulation of the problem under investigation. Action research requires a continual redefinition of the problem under investigation.

This is not to say, however, that action researchers cannot contribute to academic-theoretical debates. In discussing the procedure of devising some general conclusions from the Xerox and Mondragón studies, for example, Whyte et al. (1991: 53) refer to 'retrospective theoretical analysis of materials', which aims at 'highlighting certain key phenomena and relationships that either explain what happened or suggest new hypotheses about key relationships'. The clear admission here is that the studies in question were not designed in advance to test some pre-existing hypothesis in the manner of a controlled experiment, but that, once completed, the findings can be aligned with some pre-existing debates about organizational behaviour. The Xerox and Mondragón studies, for example, added to already existing and well-known debates about 'theories of cooperatives within a capitalist economy, conflict managements within a cooperative system, and the limits of adaptability of cooperatives to economic crisis situations' (Whyte et al. 1991: 34):

> Our experience places PAR in the middle of a research process which begins with a combination of theoretical and practical concerns, an extended PAR process in organizations, and the subsequent reformulation of existing explanations (e.g. about the participation–productivity relationship) [...] It is not, therefore, an alternative to existing social science but a way of dramatically enhancing our achievement of the goals of theoretical understanding and social betterment by widening the range of strategies at our disposal. Active involvement with practitioners struggling to solve practical problems is highly likely to open up researchers' minds to new information and new ideas, leading to advances in theory as well as in practice. (Whyte et al. 1991: 53–4)

## The role of the action researcher

The second organizing theme in this chapter is the role of the action researcher in action research. The researcher or investigator will very often already be a member of the organization at which the investigation takes place. Such an investigator will be taking on *the role of* researcher within a particular organizational context or investigative situation. They are very likely to be combining the role of 'researcher' with some position that they already occupy in the organization. Whether they refer to what they are doing as 'action research' will depend on their personal familiarity with social research methodology. The notion that researchers emerge from within organizations clearly supersedes the more conventional situation in which the researcher is separate from the organization and will have little personal knowledge of, or previous personal contact with, members of the organization. The obvious loss of objectivity and distancing this involves is offset by the advantage that 'researchers' emerging from within organizations are already likely to be very familiar with the issues to be resolved. The person taking on the role of social researcher for the duration of the study might be familiar with the kinds of activities in which social researchers are involved (they might have received instruction as part of a Master's qualification), but this need not be a condition for taking on or being offered the role of participatory action researcher within their own organization. More important are the requirements that they are thoroughly familiar with the question, issue or topic being studied; that they are motivated to help bring about necessary change; and that they occupy a position of trust in respect of other participants in the organization or process. The terms on which an internally appointed action researcher enters or instigates the research process, and the precise duties and responsibilities of the role, might also be matters for negotiation.

The second type of action researcher is typically somebody who comes into the research context or the organization at which the research is to take place from outside. This person is likely to have an academic interest about which they hope to increase their knowledge and understanding by developing a piece of action research. They will either be an established professional researcher (like Whyte and his colleagues) or will be in the process of acquiring higher-level academic qualifications by, for example, undertaking doctoral research. These researchers might be invited to join an organization for the purposes of carrying out a study (possibly as an employee or in the capacity of consultant), or they might have approached the organization themselves seeking permission to carry out a period of study to gather data for some academic purpose of their own.

In both cases, and depending on the precise levels of involvement the process requires the researcher to have, they will act as a *facilitator* within the process. Facilitation might be constructed in relatively formal terms, if for example the researcher is an academic investigator entering the research context in their capacity as an expert adviser or consultant during the action research process. In other instances where the researcher is researching their own organization they might take on a less formal coordinating or organizing role. As facilitators, researchers might simply provide a point of contact for participants, perhaps taking responsibility for recording information. If the research results in the producing of a written report for the organization, and/or of academic outputs such as a PhD thesis, conference paper or article for a specialist journal, then it is probable that responsibility for this will rest with the action researcher. Being responsible for writing up the activity and for communicating and disseminating the results is clearly one of the most significant aspects of the action researcher's role in the process and is also a key part of their ethical responsibility towards other participants. The degree of direct involvement of the researcher in the research process is geared to the depth and intimacy of the facilitation they are required to provide.

Although there are clear differences between these two modes of entry into or initiating action research (as an insider or as an outsider), once the process is underway the question of who initiated it may become largely unimportant, at least in terms of how the process develops. Such differences as do remain between participants are likely to focus on the question of the kinds of outputs they are hoping to achieve through participation. The insider will usually hope that the process will resolve an evident organizational problem. The academic outsider will be hoping to generate reliable and useful data as part of their wider academic interests. These differences are not entirely clear-cut, however, since a positive outcome for one might very well coincide with a positive outcome for the other. Besides, as we discussed in the previous section of this chapter, 'outcomes' are subject to negotiation and change in action research, so the finishing point might be quite different to that which the organization member or researcher envisaged at the outset. Outcomes at the level of personal development and learning will necessarily affect participants whatever their objective or professional interest in the process.

The role of the action researcher therefore remains somewhat ambiguous, since the researcher has become a participant in a process of which previously the researcher would have been in control. Loss of control, even if this has been negotiated away, inevitably relieves the researcher of many of their previous positivist responsibilities (and loss of control of what used to be treated as a scientific process). The removal of these aids, however, and the spirit of the action perspective also make it necessary for the researcher to renegotiate their own role in the process. Action researchers might find themselves operating in similar mode to participatory evaluators.

As the reader might reasonably have inferred from the foregoing discussion, whereas in conventional positivist social research the researcher takes on the role of an objective observer who attempts to remain separate from the research process, in action research the researcher becomes what Coghlan and Brannick call 'an agent of change'. The distinction between researcher and research subject is dissolved away as the researcher becomes actively incorporated into the research process. Participation gives way to *incorporation*, in the sense that all participants, *including researchers*, become an indivisible part of an overall learning process. By closing and eventually by eliminating the separation of researcher and researched, the whole 'research' process moves decisively away from a relatively remote data-gathering exercise towards becoming an integrative personal experience for the researcher and all those involved in the process. The usual linear or sequential model of investigation is displaced by a circular or integrative one in which the researcher/research subject distinction is largely dissolved away.

Recalling our discussion in the previous chapter of role of the researcher in value-standpoint research, the action perspective can be seen as an example of how the commitment of the researcher to the issues being studied becomes a feature of the overall research process. In the same way that 'knowledge' is redefined to permit the inclusion of information derived from subjective experience (see below), so also the usual separation of the researcher from the subject matter is set aside in favour of a more integrative approach.

## Ethical responsibility

These changes in the position of the researcher in the research process and, within that process, merging the experiences and contributions of the researcher and the researched clearly raise some important ethical issues. In what ways, we might reasonably ask, are action researchers bound by the professional codes of research ethics used by the academic research community? Coghlan and Brannick define ethics and values in action research very much in terms of the quality of the relationship between the researcher and other stakeholders:

> In action research ethics involves authentic relationships between the action researcher and the members of the client system as to how they understand the process and take significant action. Values and norms that flow from such ethical principles typically focus on how the action researcher works with members of the organization. (Coghlan and Brannick 2005: 12)

The question, of course is how the notion of 'authenticity' is to be judged and by whom. Action researchers coming into the situation from the outside will be expected to be properly aware of, and to comply with, standards of professional and ethical conduct in the usual way. The situation is less clear-cut for those acting as action researchers who are already members of the organization, who are might be unaware of the existence of such codes and/or uncertain whether they apply in what might be deemed a private situation. It seems clear enough, however, in practical terms that those filling the role of researcher within an organization will necessarily have to conduct themselves professionally and with ethical probity or they will simply not be able to carry out the study, let alone bring it to a satisfactory conclusion. As previously noted, action research is characterized by an inclusive research design and therefore relies very heavily on the commitment and willing participation of all of those involved. Such commitment is unlikely to be forthcoming if the trustworthiness of the person who has been tasked with organizing the investigation is questioned by other participants. The issue of the perceived trustworthiness of the professional researcher who comes into the organization from outside might be less of an issue, at least for members of the organization who are participating. Participants within organizations might reasonably assume that assurances of ethical probity have been provided by the incoming researcher as a condition of taking part in the first place. Whatever assumptions have been made, however, and although it might not be reasonable for incoming researchers to take ethical responsibility for the entire process, researchers must continue to have ethical responsibility for their own actions.

It is less clear how the principle of informed consent operates in the context of action research. The basic principle of action research is that it tries to overcome the boundaries between researcher and research subject or respondent. It is an extension of evaluation research in the sense that it adopts, or at least tries to adopt, a non-hierarchical approach in assuming that all those participating in the research process do so on an equal footing. The assumption that the researcher is in a more privileged or better-informed position than respondents or research subjects is actively suppressed. This does, however, raise questions about the relative 'knowledgeabilities' of the various participants. While it is relatively straightforward for social researchers to explain the purposes of the research, and its likely outcomes and outputs, in a way other participants can understand, it might be impossible to say for certain that all participants are equally well informed. Whereas consent forms used in researcher-led methods, such as surveying and interviewing, constitute a kind of informal contract between researcher and researched, in action research consensual agreement is more widely disbursed across the various relationships between participants. The ethical principle of informed consent thus becomes manifest *qualitatively* through the trust, empathy and sensitivity with which participants conduct themselves. To the extent that participants act ethically, their behaviour can be read as a form of informed consent. Furthermore, we also need to remember that the use of forms is not always and in every circumstance appropriate.

## The kinds of practical and intellectual outcomes produced

An inevitable consequence of the methodological liberalism of action research is that it is also *heterogeneous* in terms of the variety of outcomes it produces.

### Practical outcomes

First are *practical outcomes* for organizations seeking solutions to practical problems. Assuming that the initial negotiating phase of the investigation enabled participants to reach agreement over the issues requiring attention, the delivery of practical outcomes should be largely self-evident. Such solutions should be beneficial to all those who participated and, depending on the scope of the study, to others working in the same organization or organizational framework. These might be fellow employees, service users or clients, other stakeholder agencies and personnel. An associated practical outcome might the development of further internal action-type projects to deliver additional benefit within the organization. Although practical outcomes are especially significant for 'internal' action researchers who have been appointed to the task from within the organization, practical results are also significant for professional and academic action researchers appointed from outside, as they reinforce the positive practical aspects of action research, and perhaps serve to attract other academic researchers to the action perspective. Other external stakeholders (for example funders and sponsors who have supported the academic researcher in their activities and/or those who may have been involved in negotiating access to the research context) might also benefit collaterally by being associated with positive practical outcomes.

### Personal outcomes

Second are the *personal outcomes* for participants in terms of what is frequently referred to as the 'learning process' of action research. As McNiff and Whitehead put it:

> Action research is an enquiry by the self into the self, undertaken in company with others acting as research participants and critical learning partners [...] [Action research] is a way of researching one's own practice and generating personal theories of practice which show the process of self-monitoring, evaluation of practice, and purposeful action to improve the practice for social benefit [...] The process of influencing social change begins with the process of personal change. (McNiff and Whitehead 2002: 15,21, 25)

A similar description of action as learning is offered by McIntyre, who describes her action approach as

> The active participation of researchers and participants in the coconstruction of knowledge; the promotion of self- and critical awareness that leads to individual, collective, and/or social change; and an emphasis on a colearning process where researchers and participants plan, implement, and establish a process for disseminating information gathered in the research project. (McIntyre 2008: 5)

If, as this pedagogically oriented characterization of the purposes and outcomes of action research maintains, action research is mainly a process of personal development leading to enlightenment and even liberation for those taking part, then outcomes at the personal level might outweigh the importance of finding practical solutions for the organization.

## Reflexivity

Third, and looking at the *knowledge outcomes* of action research, there is an obvious association between the learning-process outcomes just mentioned and intellectual outcomes. These can both be characterized as manifestations of the concept of *reflexivity*. We have noted a number of times that there is a very strong association between action research and the idea of 'reflection'. Action research is often characterized as a process of self-reflection that encourages all participants in the investigation to become much more aware of how they can alter their behaviour by reflecting on what they do. Reflecting on a particular experience routinely causes changes in subsequent choices of action. In this sense, 'reflection' is a perfectly ordinary activity in which social actors are continually engaging. As the social theorist Anthony Giddens (1990: 38) puts it: 'thought and action are constantly refracted back upon one another'. This ordinary idea of reflection has been refined by social scientists into the more technical concept of reflexivity, which refers to particular features of social behaviour and to some fundamental properties of social-scientific knowledge. Giddens describes the technical concept of reflexivity as follows:

> The reflexivity of modern social life consists in the fact that social practices are constantly examined and reformed in the light of incoming information

about those very practices, thus constitutively altering their character. (Giddens 1990: 38)

What Giddens wishes to emphasize here is that knowledge of social phenomena is perpetually under review, because no sooner have social scientists declared their findings than this information swiftly becomes part of the phenomena they have been studying. Reflexivity, then, suggests that research is necessarily interpretive. Further knowledge statements *about* social phenomena cannot easily be held separate *from* those phenomena. Studies of unemployment become part of the phenomenon 'unemployment'.

In addition to the important practical effects of reflexivity on subsequent behaviour, Giddens also wants to draw attention to the implications of reflexivity for the kind of knowledge that can be produced by social researchers. Unlike positivist empirical knowledge, which presumes that factual statements can be made about concrete natural phenomena, social-scientific understanding of events and phenomena is multilayered at the level of meaning and interpretation (what Giddens (1974) has described as the *double hermeneutic* of social-scientific knowledge). In this perspective, knowledge is available simultaneously at the level of the *researcher's* understanding of the situation and at the level of how *respondents* understand what is going on. Depending on the degree of involvement of the researcher in the data-gathering procedure, respondents' interpretations are inevitably and already affected by the presence of the researcher (the researcher becomes a contributory factor in the situation respondents are experiencing). As Giddens puts it:

> The development of sociological knowledge is parasitical upon lay agents' concepts [i.e. on what ordinary people think is happening]; on the other hand, notions coined in the meta-languages of the social sciences [the technical jargon of scientific reporting] routinely reenter the universe of actions where they were initially formulated to describe or account for. (Giddens 1990: 15)

Terms like 'alienation', 'social mobility' and 'globalization', for example, which developed as part of the specialist conceptual vocabulary of social scientists, have since become incorporated into common usage. Located somewhere between the common-sense notion of reflection and the more abstracted notion of reflexively formed knowledge is the operational or methodological notion of reflexivity, which is often applied by social researchers in describing their impact on research outcomes. For example, a researcher engaged on a project about the global mobility of capital in the financial sector may find that the people being researched also use these terms, and in ways that may have different (and no less complex) understandings attached to them.

In action research, reflexivity is understood as 'the constant analysis of one's own theoretical and methodological presuppositions which helps with retaining an awareness of the importance of other people's definitions and understandings of theirs' (Coghlan and Brannick 2005: 6, following Lynch 1999). Furthermore, Johnson and Duberley (2000) offer a distinction between 'epistemic' and 'methodological' reflexivity. These are defined as follows:

> Epistemic reflexivity focuses on the researcher's belief system and is the process for analysing and challenging our meta-theoretical assumptions. Methodological reflexivity is concerned with the monitoring of our own behavioural impact upon the research setting as a result of carrying out the research. This requires us to follow the research procedure and protocols identified and demanded by the different research traditions [positivism, hermeneutics and critical realism]. (Coghlan and Brannick 2005: 6, following Johnson and Buberley 2000)

A similarly practical definition of reflexivity is offered by Davies (2008). In her book *Reflexive Ethnography*, she defines methodological reflexivity as follows:

> In the context of social research, reflexivity at its most immediately obvious level refers to the ways in which the products of research are affected by the personnel and process of doing research [...] [Reflexivity] expresses researchers' awareness of their necessary connection to the research situation and hence their effects upon it, what is sometimes called reactivity. (Davies 2008: 4–7)

Looked at positively, and bearing in mind the powerfully reflexive nature character of the information ('knowledge') produced during the action research process, action research can be seen as an attempt to overcome the epistemological difficulties raised by the double hermeneutic (the multilayered constitution of social-scientific knowledge) by treating 'knowledge' very much as a combined product of the research situation, rather than persisting with the largely futile effort of trying to hold the researcher's understanding *separate from* those of other participants.

Drawing on procedures developed by critical realist social researchers, for example (discussed in detail in Chapter 5), Coghlan and Brannick describe their own approach as 'pragmatic critical realism', which they define as follows:

> This approach follows a subjectivist epistemology similar to the hermeneutic tradition [i.e. one which emphasized qualities of meaning and interpretation] but an objectivist ontology like the positivists [i.e. presuming the existence of real material stuff]. This approach concentrates on epistemic reflexivity [in contrast with methodological reflexivity] which looks at exposing interests and enabling emancipation through self-reflexivity. (Coghlan and Brannick 2005: 6–7)

The object of analysis is taken to be external, substantive and real (objective), while the *means of understanding it*, of making intelligible and meaningful knowledge statements about that external reality, is taken to be a matter of subjective interpretation. Positivism and interpretivism are brought together by cross-matching the more usual pairing of positivism with objectivism/realism (factual knowledge about real stuff), and of interpretivism with relativism/subjectivism (that knowledge, and the products of knowledge, are entirely socially constructed). In the context of action research this approach has the advantage that, while all participants might be happy to agree to a shared factual account of the opening situation, they can still, legitimately, express different interpretations of what this situation means to them. The learning process of action research can be described as a series of negotiations between participants to see whether they can also come to an agreement over, or develop a shared sense of, what the situation 'means'.

## Different kinds of knowledge outcomes

Fourth, applying the concept of reflexivity to action research in this way helps us understand how the action process produces different kinds of knowledge outcomes for different kinds of participants:

---

■ practical knowledge outcomes for organizations
■ personal knowledge outcomes for participants
■ intellectual knowledge outcomes for academics, which could be theoretical or methodological

---

Coghlan and Brannick put it thus:

> As the name suggests, action research is an approach to research which aims at both taking action and creating knowledge or theory about that action. The outcomes are both an action and a research outcome, unlike traditional research approaches which aim at creating knowledge only. (Coghlan and Brannick 2005: xii)

The reflexive production of 'knowledge' through action procedures can be described as a *multiple process of knowledge production* in which practical and personal outcomes run alongside interpretations of a more abstract or theoretical kind. The process can yield practical outcomes for the organization, personal gains for individuals *and* knowledge outcomes for academics.

An interesting example of the redefinition of theory outcomes in action research can be found in Whyte el al. (1991), who refer to 'theory' very much in terms of what the *organization* has learnt. It is practical understanding of what they need to do to change the situation, which constitutes a primary theoretical strand in the research. The theory of organizations, which is the common intellectual property of society, might also benefit, but theory has not been treated as if 'developing organizational theory' was a distinct and deliberate aim of the research: 'Rethinking past practice leads to theoretical reformulation that in turn leads to improved practice. The processes of rethinking both theory and practice thus strengthen both theory and practice' (Whyte et al. 1991: 44). 'Theory' here refers to the firm's own thoughts about how it operates, not to a separate body of theory in the sense that academic 'pure' researchers would think of it.

While the conventional academic researcher might dismiss information from action research as being seriously compromised by the subjective involvement of the researcher (and in fact by the liberalism of its research design), action researchers often regard their information as deeply enriched by that self-same subjectivity. What is required is that those wishing to adopt an action perspective need to develop a different attitude towards, use alternative criteria for judging, 'data', 'knowledge', 'outcome' and 'theory'. In action research, the closely circumscribed body of objective data typical of conventional approaches is replaced by a new kind of 'data', which includes subjectively informed experience and involvement. As we have just been discussing, one of the dark arts of action research, so to speak, is to redefine 'outcomes' so as to treat the participatory learning process *as* a key outcome – an outcome that cannot be judged against external, objective criteria of scientific plausibility or significance.

Although it might not always be possible to treat the information produced during action research as if it were hard data of the conventional kind, it can still be treated as a useful and valuable variety of knowledge that is in fact much closer to the ordinary kind of practical understanding that social actors habitually use in living their lives. The theory of knowledge (epistemology) used by action researchers treats knowledge as an 'emergent property' of a necessarily fluid and dynamic situation, rather than as a stable external something waiting to be 'discovered' by scientists. It is foolish, so action researchers might argue, to discount all of the less formal varieties of knowledge simply in order to support artificially the strictly positivist variety. Action research also challenges the researcher to reflect on whether the 'hard' data of empirical investigation might not be so hard after all. The fallibility of research data in social research is a problem for everyone, not just for action researchers.

Under circumstances, like the one described by Whyte et al., in which 'knowledge' needs to be defined as practical solutions to a practical problems, such a definition is necessarily pragmatic. 'Knowledge' is defined in terms of the agreed and stated action objectives of the exercise. Achieving the desired outcomes in terms of individual and organizational change is the final test of the 'truth' or 'validity' of the process. It is not necessary to judge outcomes against external, universal criteria, as the criteria are integral to the learning process itself. Academic researchers wishing to adopt an action perspective will need to reflect on whether it is appropriate for them to treat the outcomes of an action research exercise *as if* they can be judged against the usual scientific criteria of validity and reliability. Is it appropriate to continue to apply external/universal criteria of knowledge in the context of action research?

### Refining action research techniques

Fifth and finally, action research can produce outcomes in terms of refining the *techniques* of initiating, organizing and reporting an action research project. To the extent that 'theory' and 'method' are linked together, such that the results of a research project are inevitably a product of the techniques used to gather the data, the practical and intellectual outcomes of the action research process shed light on *the means of their production*. Much of the effort for methodological improvement focuses on the role of the action researcher as facilitator of the process, since the usefulness to an organization both of an internal researcher and of a professional coming in from outside is likely to increase as that researcher becomes more experienced. This is clearly one of the practical benefits to the researcher of the learning process of action research: she or he becomes a better action facilitator as a result of the previous involvement in such processes (by the same token, participants within organizations become better at negotiating change). If the researcher is an experienced academic action researcher, then their accumulated experience can be used to mentor the development of other potential action researchers, thus increasing the pool of action resources available to carry out action research. Besides refining the technique and thus competence of the action researcher *and* of the action research community, more specific improvements can be made in terms of protocols for arranging and conducting initial meetings with participants, techniques in understanding the dynamics of the process once it is underway, and skills in recording and documenting information arising from the action research process.

## Criticisms of the action perspective

As we have begun to see, action research is *methodologically liberal* in term of the design and conduct of the process and the role of the researcher. It is also *heterogeneous* in terms of the kinds of practical and intellectual outcomes it produces. Action research does not reject the orthodoxy of positivist social research entirely, but it does seek to increase the depth and reach of social investigation. The benefits of this alternative procedure do, however, come at a cost. In this final section we will explore some of the limitations of action research from the point of view of an academic social researcher who might be thinking of using the action perspective to gather their research data.

Some of the limitations of action research in terms of its practical application are relatively easy to identify. Action research would not be an appropriate method if the research intends partly withholding, even in a benign way and in respect of academic outcomes, the objectives of the research from participants. Action research and any form of covert research design are therefore incompatible. Action research is also fairly limited in terms of the size of the project, since the principle of active participation breaks down as the size of the group increases. Size also has implications for the continuity of the data-gathering process since, although quite wide discretion is currently adopted by ethnographic researchers to allow the research conditions to vary between one respondent and another, and between one subgroup of respondents/participants and another, there are limits beyond which participants can be regarded as sharing in the same experience. If researchers approach organizations with the promise of achieving valuable practical outcomes, they are also likely to have to commit themselves to a research process that is intensive but short term.

From their perspective as strong advocates of action research as a pedagogic process of self-enlightenment, McNiff and Whitehead come close to suggesting that the action perspective is largely incompatible with the orthodox approach:

> It is important to bear in mind which areas do and do not lend themselves to action research questions. Generally speaking, action research approaches are appropriate for issues to do with values and how these values can be realised in practice. They are not appropriate for issues which aim, for example, to show the relationship between variables. (McNiff and Whitehead 2002: 93)

Although the term 'variables' is being used here to distance participatory, community-centred action research from the positivist experimental approach, most social researchers are searching for information that might further the understanding of causality, and causality necessarily requires the concept that there are certain key factors or 'variables' that are correlated in various ways.

### Radical involvement

One way out of these difficulties is to recognize that action research is itself a multilayered undertaking. Pulling back from the brink, so to speak, certain limits can be built into the action research process from the outset. One such limiting factor is the degree of *involvement* of the researcher in the process. All social researchers are aware of the likely impact of the researcher as a contaminating factor in the production of data, but in stepping decisively outside the usual confines of the conventional role, action research raises some challenging ethical and epistemological issues. Most obvious is the impossibility of separating out the different experiences of those taking part. Assuming that the action researcher is one of the main beneficiaries of the action learning process (possibly also gaining valuable data and intellectual outputs as well), then it becomes very difficult to disentangle the effects on them of the learning process they experienced from the impacts on other participants. Multiple outcomes and experiences are in play simultaneously, thus rendering attempts to treat such outputs as if they were separable somewhat futile. Asking each participant to provide a report of their own individual learning experiences is both cumbersome and, to the extent that the learning process is the main event, redundant.

Action research thus raises the problem of chronic contextual relativity, in which each set of findings has to be seen as nesting within a never-ending series of contexts, each lying behind another. Chronic reflexivity can cause the research to become trapped in a perpetual loop of self-reflection. Each moment of enlightenment becomes the point of departure for a further self-examination, leading to further moments of enlightenment and so on. Participants can reach the point of no longer remembering that the process was intended to produce outcomes other than their own self-enlightenment. The 'generative transformational process' (McNiff and Whitehead 2002: 24) of action learning never does reach a 'final' conclusion. As Davies puts it:

> This turning back, or self-examination, both individual and collective, clearly can lead to a form of self-absorption that is also part of the definition of reflexivity in which boundaries between subject and object disappear, the one becomes the other, a process that effectively denies the possibility of social research. (Davies 2008: 5)

This highlights one of the key ethical challenges of action research, which is that if knowledge is treated as an emergent property of a cooperative undertaking, then knowledge has to be seen as a joint production of all those involved, *including* input from the researcher. The democracy of the action procedure serves to democrat*ize* the knowledge produced. By highlighting this mutual definition of knowledge, however, it becomes impossible for the researcher to disentangle their personal contribution from the collective outcome. They have not merely affected the outcome by their own actions, they have become *part of* one of its most important outcomes. This raises the difficulty of the double hermeneutic in a slightly different form, which is that the researcher is forced into the position of having to provide an informed interpretation of what has been going on, an interpretation that attempts to include not only some appreciation of the interpretations of other participants, but also a form of collective consciousness that they have helped to produce.

### Motivations and expectations

Researcher involvement is also implicated in important variations in the motivations and expectations of participants and, referring back to the notion of authenticity, of their ethical responsibilities. Although initial discussions between participants about the kinds of objectives they hope to achieve might produce a level of working agreement, it remains the case that different participants will still pursue agendas of their own. All participants can be described as having a shared interest in the process of arriving at positive outcomes, but this is likely to be especially so for the action researcher whose reputation and status within an organization, or their personal academic career, depend on the quality of the results. Researchers who are committed to a particular value standpoint, for example, will find it impossible to prevent their ideas and value commitments from having some influence over the experience of other participants. Indeed, given the transformation of ethical responsibility into issues such as trust, empathy and sensitivity noted above, it would be somewhat disingenuous of researchers *not* to declare their personal value interests. Furthermore, conflict of interest might arise owing to the different kinds and qualities of outputs from the action research process. For example, high levels of positive practical outcome for the organization might yield relatively poor intellectual outcomes for the researcher. The action researcher might then be tempted to try to 'pull the analysis around' to improve the chances of achieving the outcomes that matter most to them.

## States of knowledge

Perhaps the most pressing difficulty for those considering adopting an action perspective is the status of the knowledge it produces. For academic researchers in particular, the challenge is how or whether it is realistic for them to continue to hope for 'objective' or 'scientific' theoretical insight from a process that produces subjective forms of knowledge. How, in other words, at the level of knowledge outcomes, can the distinctions we noted at the start of the chapter between 'pure' and 'applied' research and between 'rigor' and 'relevance' be reconciled? Reflecting on the theoretical import of a study of the Mondragón cooperative movement in the Basque country in Northern Spain, for example, Whyte et al. (1991: 34) describe the tension that arose between participants and academics:

> [S]o much staff effort and time had been put into the projects that the cooperative members and their colleagues and supervisors were becoming very impatient to see some practical results. This created a complex research dilemma in which the search for truth [academic intellectual interests] and the demand for action [interests of the organizations] were intertwined, much as many academic social researchers fear. The results, however, show that these goals not only can be combined but can complement each other. (Whyte et al. 1991: 37)

This example shows how the different kinds of knowledge outcomes come into conflict. Ultimately, and reflecting on how the studies at Mondragón and at the Xerox Corporation contribute to wider academic/intellectual theoretical understanding of 'theories of cooperatives within a capitalist economy', 'conflict managements within a cooperative system' and 'the limits of adaptability of cooperatives to economic crisis situations' (Whyte et al. 1991: 34), these academic authors have to treat the completed studies *as a whole* as data. This is not dissimilar to case-study research, or to evaluation research, where, because of the highly contextualized nature of the work (the context dependency of participatory methodologies), wide-ranging generalizations cannot be made. It is a moot point whether the broad theoretical debates identified by Whyte et al. could have been determined *in advance* of undertaking the research. Trying to incorporate these broader theoretical concerns into a research question seems to have become an exercise in *retro-fitting* a research question to bodies of data that have already been collected.

To the extent that action research projects are justified primarily on the grounds that they will help resolve practical problems, it becomes difficult afterwards to claim high levels of theoretical insight and innovation, or that the research contributes significantly to the general fund of human knowledge. In many cases, action research adds very little to theoretical knowledge, since no reference has been made to the theoretical or methodological restraints that conventionally form an essential part in the design of academic social research. It is not reasonable to claim retrospectively that the findings of an action-research study shed important light on particular theoretical issues (even if one adopts a very broad definition of these matters) if these played little part in the original research design. Action research thus represents a decisive step away from the conventional hypothetico-deductive method, in the sense that the search for solutions to theoretical issues and debates takes a back seat.

Although it is useful to think about the outcomes of action research in terms of a multiple process of personal discovery and learning, of finding practical solutions to practical problems, and of producing 'data' that are useful for wider academic analysis, it is unrealistic after the fact to assert the objective status of these outcomes. In terms of the kind of knowledge produced, for example, it is very difficult to argue persuasively that action research offers any possibility of meaningful reconciliation between the applied and pure forms of social research. The method is heavily interpretivist and, certainly at the level of the personal learning experience involved, infused with a quality of experiential subjectivity and reflexivity that is a world away from the detached and objective analysis of material phenomena. To the extent that the means of relating information to the wider academic community is inseparably tied in with what is being constituted as *information*, attempts to combine an interpretivist epistemology with a realist or objectivist conception (ontology) of the kind of material about which it claims to be making knowledge statements seems hardly sustainable. Rather than attempting to produce a 'unified theory' of epistemology and ontology, it might be simpler to accept that reality comprises different kinds of matter and that there are different modes of describing it.

Another way of saying this is that the action researcher has to manage a distinction between 'knowledge' and 'experience'. Experience could be defined in this context as having the property of a residual fund of reflexively acquired awareness; an awareness that might include awareness of the process of reflexivity itself. The underlying aim of action research is to make people aware of the reflexive nature of their own leaning process. Knowledge, in contrast, is of an intellectual quantum that can be transferred from one person to another. It may subsequently be the case that this 'public' knowledge (as distinct from subjective knowledge) is experienced personally by the person becoming aware of it, and that their understanding will not be identical with that of all the other delegates at the conference – the inputs have to be separable from the recipients. I can become increasingly aware of my capacity to learn and become more sensitive to the process of being a learner, but this 'intellectual experience' is *not the same thing* as my having a reasonable 'objective' or 'factual' knowledge of the principle of action research, *and* of being able to make sensible knowledge statements about it that other social actors can understand *irrespective* of how they feel about their own learning processes.

The positivist definition of knowledge is of something that goes beyond the ideas of any particular individual and their personal experience, and is essentially transferable between persons. Knowledge is treated as *separable from* the experience of the knower. Actually existing factual reality provides a testing ground for the feasibility and reliability of factual knowledge. The action researcher on their way to an international convention must trust the technical knowledge of the airplane designer *even though* this knowledge is not part of their own experience.

Looking finally at the wider academic credibility of action research, the quandary of posing experiential learning against the rigorous and scientific accumulation of knowledge has been recognized by McNiff and Whitehead. These authors seem rather confused when they suggest that since 'the Academy is still the highest authority in what counts as legitimate knowledge', action research reports have 'to stand in terms of [their] academic rigour' and 'action research accounts need to demonstrate internal methodological consistency, so that work cannot be rejected on technical grounds' (McNiff and Whitehead 2002: 106). Yet the whole emphasis in action research as described by these and other influential campaigners for the action approach is that action research stands on its own terms as a legitimate learning experience. It seems somewhat paradoxical to expect to be taken seriously by 'the Academy' and yet seek to reject the model of knowledge on which it typically relies. Action research is either inside or outside – it cannot reasonably be both. To be taken at their word, it should not matter at any of those involved in the learning processes of action research what the Academy or any other outside authority thinks about it.

Perhaps the most pressing question, then, in deciding whether or not to deploy an action perspective is *what kind of knowledge* the researcher is interested in, and therefore *what kind of data* or information they require to work on the issues they have identified. Those who are attracted by the dynamic problem-centred nature of action research need to accept that action research produces a variety of knowledge-as-experience that is not the same as, and in many ways not comparable with, positivist definitions of knowledge. How the action researcher community might respond to these criticisms depends on whereabouts in the broad spectrum of action approaches one enters the discussion. The organizational behaviour approach, which Whyte (1991) describes as one of the foundations of PAR, sees the learning process as affecting and improving working relations within organizations. By the time we get to McNiff and Whitehead (e.g. 2002), the action perspective has become transformed by its enthusiastic supports into a mutual learning process affecting the researcher as much as, if not more than, the other participants. Positive organizational change is now supplemented in the full action model by the positive individual self-transformation of all participants. The learning organization is supplemented by the learning individual. And the individual who appears to learn the most is the action researcher!

# Social Research and Social Policy

7

This final substantive chapter discusses the important topic of the relationship between social research and the policy-making process. In order to do this, it focuses on the role of social policy research and social policy analysis in the field of social and welfare policy. Although many social researchers tend to highlight the academic and theoretical dimensions of their work, the plain reality is that intellectual curiosity is unlikely to be the only driver of funded social research. The intellectual and theoretical context of asking research questions is crucial, but so too is the political and policy context. A key purpose of this chapter, then, is to think about the role social researchers play in the political and ideological discourse about social and welfare policy.

The basic argument in this chapter is that although social policy research and analysis struggle to meet the strict standards of objectivity demanded by positivist definitions of scientific evidence, they do have the virtue of contributing positively to the general ethical and moral discourse *about* social and welfare policy. Social and welfare policy is certainly a very *practical* matter, but it is also *discursive*, in the sense that substantive decisions about the ultimate aims of policy are profoundly affected by the political and ideological context. Social policy research does provide evidence to help improve policy management and administration but, perhaps more importantly, it also improves the general discourse about social and welfare policy. What is really challenging about the role of social policy research and analysis is how the practical and the discursive aspects of its role become combined.

We also need to consider how the ethical and value framework of social research is similarly shaped by the political and ideological context. This is an especially tangled issue since, in the case of research in the field of social and welfare policy, broader social values of the kind identified in Chapter 1 (the collective good, individual freedom, the pursuit of Reason) are also likely to form part of the underlying philosophical basis of the policy framework itself. Notwithstanding the distribution of views across the political spectrum, academic researchers and policy makers are all fishing from the same pool of ethics and social values in order to legitimate their activities. If social policy researchers *do* have the capability to produce changes in the personal and policy outlook of other stakeholders in the policy-making community, then this constitutes an important aspect of their *ethical responsibility* towards that community.

## Social welfare policy and the political context

To begin with, we must clarify what we mean by social and welfare policy. Space precludes a comprehensive narrative of the emergence of social and welfare policy in modern industrialized societies since the nineteenth century, but we should note a number of key moments in its development. At its simplest, 'policy' refers to attempts by governments to control or regulate various aspects of economic and social behaviour and, where a regulatory need has been identified, to attempt to take measures to produce some kind of significant change in that behaviour. The policy-making process is central to the exercise of political power in democratic social systems. The philosophy of the political Right is to regulate as little as possible and to intervene even less, while the political philosophy of the Left sees regulation much more positively as an opportunity to implement beneficial changes. Policy-generating governments thus tend to be those that adopt an interventionist approach to governance, and policy measures provide one of the main levers for realizing these ambitions.

Social and welfare policy, which is the main focus of our interest here, refers to the development and implementation of measures and programmes whose primary purpose is to address the social and welfare needs of the population. Originating from widespread public concern in the late nineteenth century in industrialized societies such as the United States and the United Kingdom with urban problems like poverty, health, housing, sanitation and conditions of industrial work, social welfare policy is most readily associated with Franklin D. Roosevelt's New Deal programme in the United States in the 1930s, and with the emergence of the welfare state during the mid-twentieth century in the United Kingdom. The New Deal emerged as a national government response to the widespread social and economic hardship experienced by a significant proportion of the US population during the Great Depression, which began in 1929 and reached its lowest point in 1933. At the outset of the depression in 1929, nearly 25 per cent of the US population was unemployed. It was not until late 1935 that the US economy recovered the 28 per cent fall in gross domestic product (GDP) it had experienced since 1929. The New Deal comprised a complex package of measures designed to provide basic welfare payments to the unemployed, while at the same time attempting to stimulate the national economy through national government funding of ambitious construction projects (Galbraith 2009 [1954]; Shaffer 1999;, Hanes and Hanes 2003). This interventionist approach to finding solutions to social and welfare problems has remained a characteristic of Democrat administrations in the United States ever since and includes notable policy initiatives such as Lyndon B. Johnson's 'War on Poverty' during the 1960s, and especially the introduction of Medicare as an amendment to the Social Security Act in

1965, and the Clinton Administration's social and welfare policies of the 1990s (Godwin 2009).

Looking briefly at developments in the United Kingdom, the first majority Labour government of 1945 adopted the interventionist view that it had received a firm mandate from an electorate who had very recent experience of the national war effort against Germany and Japan, and that the state had a clear responsibility to develop social policies aimed at raising the general level of health, education, housing and social welfare across the population. Along with established responsibilities for economic and foreign policy, the social welfare of the general population had also become a key responsibility of the state. The interventionist philosophy of the Labour government of 1945 drew directly on the principles of the Beveridge Report of 1942. The report proposed a 'Plan for Social Security', or National Insurance Scheme, which 'embodies six fundamental principles':

> flat rate of subsistence benefit; flat rate of contribution; unification of administrative responsibility; adequacy of benefit; comprehensiveness; and classification [...] Based on them and in combination with national assistance and voluntary insurance as subsidiary methods, the aim of the Plan for Social Security is to make want under any circumstances unnecessary. (Beveridge 1942)

It was assumed that everyone would pay into the scheme, but even if they could not afford to do so, they were still entitled to receive health and welfare benefits. The funding principle here is that if the costs of a national welfare programme are spread widely enough across a population, then the potential risk to public finances is dissipated. Those in need at any given moment will always be outnumbered significantly by those who are making little or no claim against their national insurance. The lower rates of contribution paid by some are offset by the higher contributions of others. The principle of universality together with the sheer scale of these challenges meant that social welfare had to be dealt with at a national level.

The economic rationale for central funding of large-scale public projects, both in the United States and the United Kingdom, came from the demand-side economic theory of John Maynard Keynes. Keynes argued that since government is already a major player in the national economy (a reality that again had been amply demonstrated by the highly centralized administration of the national war effort in 1914–18 and 1939–45), it makes good economic sense for the government to use its own capacity for creating employment to stimulate general demand in the overall economy. Private firms benefit directly from public expenditure first because of increasing demand for the goods and services they supply to public projects, and second because high employment creates buoyant demand for consumer goods and services. Profitable production depends on a reliable supply of raw materials and labour, but just as surely it relies on a continuous supply of consumers to buy its products.

Beginning in 1945 in the United Kingdom, large volumes of public funds were directed into new programmes in education, a National Health Service, major house-building and other infrastructure projects and social welfare programmes. With the exception of public expenditure on housing and infrastructure projects, the proportion of public funds spent on social and welfare programmes in the United Kingdom has remained consistently high ever since. In 2010–11, for example, UK public expenditure reached £697 billion, which was 47.3 per cent of GDP (the comparable figure in 2000–01 was £364 billion, which was 36.8 per cent, and in 1990–91 £227.5 billion, which was 39.4 per cent of GDP). Of total expenditure in 2011, 35 per cent (or £244 billion) was spent on health and welfare (HM Treasury). From the 1960s onwards, in both the United States and the United Kingdom, publicly funded social welfare has remained one of the obligatory features of government policy. Political differences between left and right, democrat and conservative, and often differences *within* parties between those who advocate more or less intervention, have tended to be over how to pay for it and how much can be afforded, rather than whether there is any such social need.

### Whizzkids, think tanks, policy units, 'the best and the brightest'

The national provision of social welfare necessarily required both the emergence of large and complex government bureaucracies to deliver the new public services *and* the development of a new discourse *about* social and welfare policy. Dryzek describes the discursive aspect of policy analysis as follows: 'Policy analysis encompasses a variety of activities concerned with the creation, compilation, and application of evidence, *testimony, argument, and interpretation* in order to examine, evaluate, and improve the content and process of public policy' (Dryzek 2006: 190, emphasis added).

In the United Kingdom, the role of social researchers in the field of social welfare, originally concerned with monitoring and auditing the activities of government departments and civil servants having responsibility for devising and managing the public administration of social welfare programmes, gradually expanded during the 1960s as government departments increasingly required 'expert opinion' and 'original research' to develop and manage their welfare programmes. It became impossible for policy makers to depend on general advice from civil servants and senior bureaucrats, who themselves relied heavily on their personal experience of being involved in public administration, and governments turned instead towards expert opinion. In true Keynesian manner, increasing government intervention through social and welfare programmes stimulated public interest in the role of welfare policy, and created a demand for increasing numbers of experts and academic researchers to provide the required intellectual labour. In the United States, for example, expert opinion could be sought from the National Science Foundation (1950), the Brookings Institution (1927), the RAND Corporation (1948) and the Ford Foundation (1936). Government-funded and charitable foundations prominent in the United Kingdom include the Joseph Rowntree Foundation (1904) and the Wellcome Trust (1936). Government funding for social research is channelled primarily through the Economic and Social Research Council.

These organizations had the capacity to provide government policy makers with the concentrated advice they needed, not only to understand, administer and manage policy implementation (i.e. the practical steps that had to be taken to implement and manage social and welfare programmes), but also to develop and refine new *ideas about* social and welfare policy (i.e. to develop a new field of policy discourse). Increasing demand for expert opinion was accompanied by the emergence of specialist university departments in public administration and later in policy development. In the United Kingdom, for example, there was a substantial expansion of social-science faculty and students during the 1970s and 1980s, and increasing subdivision of those disciplines from public administration into social policy, applied social studies, critical social policy and criminology.

If analytical policy research, provided largely by government-employed research analysts, and avowedly 'independent' research institutes was the default setting of social policy analysis in the United States, a slightly different balance between policy discourse (theory) and policy intervention (practice) has characterized social policy research in the United Kingdom. Here, and alongside the growth in official research taking place inside government departments and think tanks and policy units such as those set up to advise the Conservative governments of Margaret Thatcher and John Major during the 1980s and 1990s, and later of the Labour prime minister Tony Blair, a research tradition has developed that has added a distinctly critical dimension to the general discourse on social policy. Academic researchers tend to use research findings described in official policy announcements *as part of* the context and background of their own critical research (e.g. Sklair and Miller 2010). This critical attitude is summarized in the leading academic policy journal's statement of editorial policy:

> *Critical Social Policy* has, since its launch in 1981, provided a forum to develop an understanding of welfare from socialist, feminist, anti-racist and radical perspectives within the British and international context. The only collective editorial policy is a common opposition to the radical right and an awareness of the failures of the Fabian and other orthodox models to meet its challenges.

Historically, then, and moving in step with the expansion of state provision of social welfare systems, social policy research and analysis have evolved from public administration to public policy research and to critical policy analysis. These developments have culminated in the development of an increasingly pragmatic orientation towards social and welfare policy research and analysis. The pragmatic orientation arises from a combination of:

- increasing complexity characterized by the greater interdependency of different social and welfare policy domains
- a shift towards action-oriented and participatory forms of social research
- a concomitant shift towards context-dependent rather than linear notions of causality

We will discuss each in turn.

### The new pragmatic orientation: Pure and applied understanding

The first, and perhaps the most decisive, step change in the development of a pragmatic orientation in social policy research and analysis has been the task of coping with increasing *complexity*. Compared with the situation in the earlier decades of the twentieth century, when new policies could be introduced on the grounds of political commitment alone ('the force of the better argument') and without reference to the effects of previous policies since there were none (the evidential basis), from mid-century onwards any new intervention had to take account of an *already existing* policy context. Furthermore, policy analysis also had to take account of the activities of very large government bureaucracies such as the National Health Service in the United Kingdom, whose task is to deliver those policy interventions. This resulted in what we could call a layering of the policy context, in which the various individual domains of social and welfare policy have become overlaid to such an extent that it is increasingly difficult to analyse them as if they are separable. Complexity means analysing not only waves of policy in a single domain, for example in education policy or housing policy, but of how policy interventions in one domain affected outcomes in *other* policy domains, for example the impact of housing policy *on* poverty or of education policy *on* employment.

Policy changes in one domain might actually be geared towards, or are expected to have a collateral benefit for, meeting social needs in other domains. At the aggregate level, for example, the underlying rationale of much government economic policy is to raise tax revenue explicitly to pay for national programmes in social welfare: programs for which the poor must rely on the state to pay and which the state has an obligation to provide. Similarly, foreign, defence and immigration policies all have implications for the general welfare of the population, because such policies tend to affect patterns of trade and commerce and levels of production and employment. Higher education policy is similarly multifarious in its effects, providing advanced-level skills and research that stimulate private enterprise and thus the national economy, while at the same time providing individuals with valuable opportunities for upward economic and social mobility. The benefits of higher education are often described *in terms of* the improved social and welfare situation of graduates (DfES 2004: 6–7).

An instructive example of the difficulty of disentangling cause and consequence in the policy domain at the aggregate level comes from the analysis of the welfare reforms introduced by the Clinton Administration in the US between 1992 and 1999. These required an additional welfare expenditure of over $30 billion, much of which was used to enhance the earnings potential of welfare recipients, thus encouraging them to choose work rather than welfare. Van Den Bosch and Cantillon ask, however:

> What was the impact of [the Clinton welfare reforms]? Perhaps surprisingly, given the scale and size of the reforms, this question is not easy to answer. Certainly, at the end of Clinton's second term, the number of people on welfare had more than halved compared with the start of his first term. Labor force participation amongst single women with children increased by more than 10 percentage points in this period. Poverty fell significantly. However, at the same time the US economy went through a period of strong growth and labour force expansion. It turns out to be quite difficult to disentangle the impact of policies from the effects of the booming economy. (Van Den Bosch and Cantillon 2006: 309)

A little like the shift in systems theory away from functions viewed separately towards an analysis of modes of communication *between functions* (e.g. Luhmann 1995 [1984]), social and welfare policy research increasingly has to account for the nature of connectedness *between* policy domains.

### Action and participation

Complexity in respect of the practical inseparability of policy domains has prompted a second important shift towards a pragmatic orientation, this time at the level of *research design*. Recalling our discussion of evaluation research and action research in Chapters 4 and 6, it was noted that as social context is acknowledged as having a decisive impact on the kinds of evidence, findings and knowledge produced by social researchers, social researchers have become much more circumspect in attributing specific outcomes to specific causes. They have also given greater acknowledgement to their own active role as participants in, and indeed often as leading architects of, the research process. The very nature of social research means that it is difficult for social researchers to avoid playing a leading role in the process of social construction that characterizes much social research. Under these changed conditions, and especially following the shift away from positivist-style survey and field experiments towards evaluation and action-oriented forms of participatory social research, the positivist model of researcher impartiality and objectivity, which takes as its core principle that the researcher can remain entirely separate from that which she or he is studying, has become increasingly marginalized.

Although it can be argued that the shift towards action research and other participatory modes of social analysis has sometimes been a matter of intellectual choice (small-scale ethnographic participation is simply more fashionable than large-scale social surveying), it can also be suggested that the general trend in this direction is a necessary response to trying to conduct meaningful research in the context of an increasingly complex and multilayered policy-making domain. If, as noted above, it is no longer feasible to separate one policy domain from another, nor to believe that one outcome can be related unambiguously to a particular policy input, it becomes necessary to abandon the orthodox linear (positivist) notion of causality as cause and effect, in favour of a much more contingent and dynamic notion of causality. The hypodermic model of policy implementation, where a clear-cut intervention is assumed to produce a clear-cut effect, has to be abandoned in favour of a model of contingent/multiple and sometimes uncertain outcomes.

### Towards a dynamic concept of causality

As discussed in relation to critical realist approaches to social research in Chapter 5, positivist notions of causality remain useful when applied to research in the context of closed systems (where the range of variables can be controlled), but are of diminishing utility in the context of open systems (where they cannot). One thing critical realist approaches have in common with the action and participation models of social research is that they try to embrace complexity and make allowances for the highly contingent and often unpredictable nature of social phenomena. It makes little sense to talk of 'final outcomes' in the context of evaluation and action research, since they are very much about *knowledge-as-process* rather than about knowledge-as-fact or knowledge-as-end-product. The kind of knowledge produced by action researchers is always provisional, depending as it does on further practical outcomes and consequences. The shift from orthodox to participatory evaluation research, for example, was a necessary methodological response to the realization that replicating positive programme outcomes in different contexts means analysing *the processes that produce positive change*, rather than simply measuring inputs and outputs.

A further interesting characteristic of the dynamic-pragmatic definition of knowledge used in action and participatory approaches is its attitude towards future events. Whereas the more orthodox empiricist-positivist model generally stops short of speculating about the likely future shape and direction of the phenomenon under investigation (although it does attempt to discover universal laws whose effects are presumed to be timeless), the dynamic attitude towards causality used by participatory and action researchers makes those who use this approach much more willing to treat hoped-for future outcomes or effects as if they were *already part of*, or somehow coterminous with, the research findings. This makes good sense in the context of research into social and welfare policy, where pragmatism demands that some form of policy intervention needs to be made *despite the fact* that the knowledge base remains incomplete.

While such an intellectually liberal approach might have little place in laboratory science, it can be extremely helpful in the policy domain, where the emphasis is firmly on applications rather than on theory. Practical benefit to end users takes precedence over the intellectual-theoretical preoccupations of academics. 'Good policy' is that which works in practice and not that which happens to have the most elegant theoretical anatomy. If it is not feasible, in the context of applied social policy research, to isolate variables sufficiently to be able to make decisive statements about cause and consequence, then other grounds have to be invoked for supporting the legitimacy of the research. And what better grounds can there be than evidence of positive and beneficial outcomes for the recipients of social and welfare programmes? Results are justified and legitimated against the political necessity of producing positive policy outcomes rather than against positiv*ist* notions of empirical factuality.

To the extent that the pragmatic orientation just described has proved to be influential among social policy researchers and analysts, the question arises of whether the shift towards policy applicability and away from strict scientific rigour undermines not only the academic but also the political credibility of policy-oriented social research. What is at stake here is not so much social researchers' self-perceptions of the integrity of their work, but the role and function that they hope to have in the policy-making process. This is the topic for discussion in the following section.

## The role of social researchers in the policy-making process

In Chapter 5 we posited the notion of analytical criticism, which social researchers use in order to make three kinds of positive contributions to knowledge of social phenomena:

> ■  it improves the *evidential basis* of the debate
> ■  it adds to '*the force of the better argument*'
> ■  it promotes the possibility of *alternatives*

Using the notion of analytical criticism, it can be suggested that while social and welfare policy researchers continue to make contributions of empirical value (i.e. improving the evidential basis), their role has tended to shift towards contributing to the discursive aspect of the policy debate (i.e. adding to 'the force of the better argument' and the consideration of alternatives). They have an increasingly necessary role to play in the political and ideological aspects of the policy debate.

In his detailed analysis of bias and partisanship in social research, for example, Hammersley (2000) has emphasized the importance of the ideological-political aspect of the policy discourse:

> There is a general rejection of the idea that social research should be concerned simply with producing value-relevant, objective knowledge. The emphasis, instead, is on the need for research to serve, perhaps even to be integrated into, other kinds of practice, whether these are concerned with improving economic productivity or with *challenging the political status quo*. (Hammersley 2000: 1–2, emphasis added)

> This, in turn, often leads to the conclusion that the task of research goes beyond producing accounts of how and why things are to making clear what is wrong and what must be done to remedy it. Indeed, the fact of reflexivity is often seen as implying that the role of the researcher properly includes collaboration in *the political activity necessary to bring about social change*. (Hammersley 2000: 3, emphasis added)

Although Hammersley continues to support the claim that social researchers are capable of producing empirically robust research, his own observations about the potential for bias and partisanship can be traced back at least as far as the important interventions made by Becker (1967) and Gouldner (1973). These influential social researchers initiated a discussion about the 'natural' or 'inevitable' political partisanship of social researchers, in the sense that social researchers tend to investigate social phenomena (and thus participate in the social and welfare policy debate) from *the point of view of*, and often *in the interests of*, those individuals and social groups who will benefit from a particular policy intervention. Gouldner referred to this as 'underdog sociology' or 'committed sociology'.

In this respect, and notwithstanding continuing attempts by social policy researchers to maintain some degree of methodological objectivity, social policy research is undertaken *on behalf of* individuals and groups who benefit least from participation in capitalist society. There is no research into the social and welfare challenges faced by wealthy members of society since, by definition, such challenges are rarely experienced by people in this category: there is no such thing as 'top-dog sociology'. Actual occurrences of social disadvantage and inequality, together with their conceptual counterparts deployed in research projects, already presuppose the existence in society of a distinct category of social actors whose needs are not being met and whose interests, therefore, need protecting and supporting.

### Value neutrality and ethical responsibility

Looking at these developments in terms of the personal ethical responsibility of social researchers towards other stakeholders in the policy-making process, one of the costs of shifting the emphasis in social research away from the 'pure' and towards the 'applied' end of the spectrum (from evidence to argument) is that it becomes increasingly difficult to rebut the criticism that the whole process of social research can no longer be treated as if it is offering an 'outsider's view' of the phenomenon under investigation, but has itself become an element within the social construction of the reality it purports to represent. In becoming more policy oriented, social researchers have to address the receding possibility of value neutrality in their work. The objective, dispassionate and 'scientific' status of the knowledge social researchers strive to produce must come into serious question once researchers avow the policy-relatedness of their research.

Indeed, this is not merely a matter of scientific or methodological nicety but, since an important part of the motivation of social researchers is a desire to 'make a positive difference' to the social situation under investigation, an issue that strikes deep into the very personality of social research. The desire to publicize the extent of social and welfare needs in society, and to represent those who experience those needs, constitutes a form or methodological bias, in the sense that social researchers are predisposed to emphasize research findings that most clearly justify the continuing need for intervention. To the extent that it is unlikely that researchers will recommend policy changes that are expected to have *negative* outcomes (and accepting that some unexpected outcomes might turn out to be so), there is an in-built intellectual prejudice within the research team who want to find a positive – that is, policy-relevant and policy-effective – outcome. While it would be disingenuous to criticize social researchers for having good intentions, they are, nonetheless, predisposed towards preferring some research outcomes more than others. Indeed, this predisposition is likely to have a bearing throughout the research process, from the initial formulation of the funding application to decisions about research method and analysis, to choices over how findings can best be presented and to which audiences (ethical responsibility towards audiences is discussed in more detail below).

The tendency towards intervention is likely to be especially prominent among researchers in the policy field, since intervention is part and parcel of the applied nature of this kind of social research; it is research with an in-built potential for bringing about policy change. Recalling our references to Max Weber's notion of value neutrality in Chapter 4, social and welfare policy researchers have to make a special effort to avoid the temptation of letting their general desire to intervene affect their particular research findings. The extent to which the audiences for social policy research treat the findings and opinions of social researchers as expert knowledge that, as non-experts, they are unlikely to feel able to challenge is also the extent to which such researchers have to be aware of their own agenda, and to take responsibility for it.

It is in this respect that social policy research can be treated as a form of advocacy or value-standpoint research in which the declared or acknowledged interests of the researcher form *part of* the research question and the research process. It is not just a question of participating in the general tendency for social researchers to believe in the value of their work, and to hope for practical benefits arising from it, but of needing to be involved in this kind of research activity in order to meet a personal ethical and moral need to do so. Social policy researchers and analysts, in other words, must not only be aware of the value content of their research in a professional sense, but must also reflect on whether being a social researcher is part of their own personal path to righteousness.

As noted in Chapter 5, advocacy need not constitute a form of deceit or ethical misconduct *as long as* the researcher makes their view explicit in both the conduct and the reporting of their research. Standpoint researchers may be able to turn their advocacy of a particular standpoint into a virtue by claiming that, in putting their arguments forward from a declared political and ideological standpoint, they are saving the wasted effort their critics would otherwise put into identifying that this is the point of view for which they are arguing. It is taken as read that standpoint research is partisan, but partisanship need not be a bad thing (nor can it be avoided) in social research, and especially in such an ideologically and politically infused field like applied social policy research.

More difficult to control is the possible subliminal impact of personal beliefs, including the personal belief that one has a *moral duty* to change people's minds on particular issues. For example, although social reformers and philanthropists of the nineteenth century might not have declared explicitly that their intervention in the policy domain resulted from a sense of Christian duty, it is nonetheless clear that their desire to bring about social reform was very much in line with the altruistic intent of much of the Christian belief system with which they identified. 'Charity' strongly expresses both a personal and a professional policy ethic. Both the Red Cross and the Red Crescent are charitable organizations sharing the same altruistic desire to help people who cannot help themselves, but they remain separate organizations *because of* their different religious and value traditions.

This raises an important ethical consideration for social researchers attempting to alter the general direction of the policy paradigm, which is the impact their research might have on the ethical and moral outlook of sponsors and funders and ultimately on the social conscience of the policy-making community. Although in its most applied dimension social policy research tends to focus specifically on the details of programme development, implementation and administration, it is also likely to have an impact on the broader ideological and political underpinnings of that policy domain. Social researchers might therefore have some capacity to convert other stakeholders in the policy-making community to their own point of view and/or to encourage them to develop a *different attitude* towards a particular social issue.

If social policy researchers *do* have the capability to produce changes in the personal and policy outlook of other stakeholders in the policy-making community, then this constitutes a further important aspect of their ethical responsibilities. Unlike ordinary conversation, in which participants assess the merits or otherwise of different points of view on the basis of personal judgement, the discourse of the policy-making community constitutes a different kind of conversation in which the 'expert' or 'specialist' status of their opinion allows social researchers to have more influence over the attitudes of their audience. Once social researchers become willing participants in the political and ideological discourse surrounding the research topic or policy domain in which they are interested, the 'rules of engagement' between stakeholders are not quite the same as they are in the more controlled and reserved world of academic conversation. Social researchers need to be aware of this 'change of code' in order to protect themselves, and their audiences, from misunderstanding and possible deceit.

For example, a social researcher who is a committed feminist who *personally* supports the need for policy intervention to protect the pension rights of married women is likely to find it difficult to prevent this attitude from affecting their *professional* conclusions. They *already believe* that such intervention is legitimate and necessary and might continue to believe so even if other empirical evidence is available supporting an alternative view. An example of this is the tension that arose between feminist social researchers who believed that a majority of women find themselves in household and labour-market situations in which, were it not for the determining influence of the social structure, they would choose not to be, and other female researchers who suggested that women do exercise a fair degree of choice in the matter (Hakim 1995 and 1998; Crompton and Harris 1998; Brannen et al. 2005). There is unlikely to be any 'scientific' resolution of this tension because of the political and ideological commitments at stake.

Adopting a radically positivist methodological position, it could be argued that feminists (or Marxists or environmentalists or members of any other standpoint group) should automatically *exclude themselves* from carrying out research into policy domains in which they have a declared, personal and professional value interest. Who is to say whether the level of insight into a particular policy issue born of personal knowledge and commitment is sufficient to offset the possible negative effects that such insight might have on undermining the scientific credibility of their findings? Taken to *its* logical conclusion, the insight-is-essential argument implies that social research should *only* be undertaken by those who do have personal experience of the situation being investigated. The social and welfare needs of single mothers, for example, can only be properly understood by people in this situation, so all social research into single-motherhood should be undertaken by single mothers. Even more disturbingly, it could be suggested that the ability to appreciate and understand fully the *results* of such a study *is also limited* to those having personal experience of that situation. Full knowledge can only ever be insider knowledge. However, while these comments are mostly designed to provoke reflection on the part of different research communities, we need perhaps to think a bit more deeply than we currently do about how our inevitable attachments to particular political agendas both inform as well as undermine our capacity to act as researchers serving the public good. While we are perhaps inevitably drawn to particular research due to personal factors, this can prove both enabling as well as disabling.

### Policy discourse in practice: The short game and the long game

Adapting a distinction that has been used by feminist standpoint researchers between the short-term and long-term objectives of political campaigning, and especially in respect of promoting 'the equal opportunities agenda' (e.g. Cockburn 1991; Charles 2000), the immediate details of policy change might feed into a more glacial process of shifting the political agenda. If a series of research outcomes all tend to point in a similar direction, this might constitute a policy trend with sufficient momentum to alter the general trajectory of the policy agenda. Bodies of social research can help establish the hegemony of a new policy orientation, and provide a bulwark against challenges to the ideological and political status quo. This is similar to the process by which trends develop in styles of research methodology, for example the shift away from quantitative and towards qualitative method since the 1980s and, at a more general level still, the 'revolution' in the underlying epistemological or scientific paradigm described by Thomas Kuhn (1962).

There is an echo here of the concept of cumulation used by some evaluation researchers (e.g. Pawson and Tilley 1997), which characterizes social research into a particular phenomenon or policy domain very much as a composite entity that is gradually built up from multiple pieces of research and analysis. No single investigation in the policy domain can be regarded as conclusive, but it might be possible to accumulate a reasonably coherent and persuasive body of findings on the basis of which a recognizable process of contingent causality can be identified. A similar analysis of the role of social policy research in policy development has been offered by Hammersley (e.g. 1992). While emphasizing the difference between 'specialist research' and 'practitioner ethnography' (1992: 145), this commentator argues not only that the relevance of social policy researcher to policy practice is 'usually indirect and general rather than direct and specific' (1992: 138), but that its contribution rarely takes the form of a single specific demonstration of causality. Social research is a collective form of knowledge produced by, and in the first instance for, a particular research community:

> It is often not possible to answer questions that are directly relevant to practical problems adequately [...] through a single piece of research. It will often require a research programme, a set of coordinated studies dealing with various elements of the problem [...] Indeed, I think there is a strong argument that reports of particular research projects should always be addressed to other researchers, and that communications directed towards practitioners should draw on a wide range of studies, not just one. Only then can the benefits of the collective assessment of findings by the research community be obtained. (Hammersley, 1992: 138–9)

In the policy domain in the 1980s, for example, the emergence of a body of research into the negative effects on patients with identifiable mental health issues, who had hitherto been managed through long-term residential institutional care, produced a new policy based on 'care in the community'. This amounted to a complete change in the general orientation of policy towards mental health care (the emergence of a new policy paradigm) that included a much more proactive conception of the ability of people with chronic mental health difficulties to live their lives in largely conventional household settings. Individuals were treated *as* individuals rather than being required to surrender their autonomy to the collectivizing norms of residential institutions (Robbins 1993; Titterton 1994; Hadley and Clough 1996).

A more recent example is the abandonment of a broadly liberal-humanist conception of higher education (HE) as a vital learning experience that enables participants to develop their general intellectual capabilities, in favour of a much more instrumentalist view. Such features are especially evident in the United States and the United Kingdom. The current preoccupation with 'employability' rather than 'learning' demonstrates a policy shift in HE policy that sees the primary purpose of the HE sector as providing a steady supply of employment-ready graduates for industry, rather than as providing individuals with life-transforming educational development (Ransome 2011).

### Public opinion

Finally, we need to consider briefly the more dissipated aspects of the policy discourse (rather, that is, than concentrating only on its more concentrated academic ones), which can be broadly defined as 'public opinion'. To the extent that successful policy development and implementation depend on making adequate political judgements about how the electorate perceives the need for a particular policy intervention, and on what kind of popular response it is likely to receive, public opinion becomes part of the policy-making mix. Policy makers are likely to be sceptical about even the most robust research information if the political challenges it raises are too great. This places social policy researchers in a difficult position, since there is no guarantee that the most evidentially robust findings, and apparently clear-cut policy recommendations, will become a reality if they do not receive a positive reception in the popular imagination. The need to 'sell' new social and welfare policy interventions to the electorate shows once again that policy research and analysis are implicated in, and must engage with, wider political and ideological debates.

In the United Kingdom in 2011, for example, the Conservative–Liberal coalition government proposed radical and controversial changes to the delivery of primary healthcare at the local level. Whereas strategic health authorities and local health managers working for primary care trusts had made decisions over the purchasing and delivery of services, these responsibilities were to be taken over by general practitioners. It was also expected that increasing areas of healthcare work would be contracted out to private providers. Public concern, as well as concern among members of parliament, even from ministers within the coalition over the feasibility and desirability of the changes, resulted in a substantial delay before implementation pending the outcome of a comprehensive 'listening exercise'. While arguments over administrative and management procedures were important (and there were expected costs of £1 billion in likely redundancy payments), the most significant issue under discussion, and the reason why the Prime Minister David Cameron had to agree to a complete review, centred around a defence of the basic ideological principle of protecting public funding of the National Health Service in the United Kingdom, and of guaranteeing services 'free at the point of delivery'.

In summary, then, the thrust of the argument in this section has been that rather than closing the door on social and welfare policy research on the grounds that it lacks empirical rigour, the new pragmatism increases the need for discourse about social policy. And it is in respect of the political and ideological dimensions of the policy debate that social and welfare policy research and analysis are making their most significant contribution. It makes little difference, in other words, that social researchers no longer make such robust contributions to the evidential basis of the policy debate, because that aspect of the debate *has itself* been superseded by an equivalent increase in the need for discourse about social and welfare policy. The most valuable contribution that social policy researchers make to the current discourse is to add a distinctly *critical voice* to the general policy discourse.

## Conclusion

In this chapter we have described the emergence of an increasingly pragmatic orientation among researchers and analysts working in the field of social and welfare policy, characterized by a shift away from the quest for pure knowledge more or less for its own sake, towards the delivery of applied practical outcomes. Among the most persuasive kinds of practical outcomes are those that inform the policy-making process. Indeed, it can be argued that the primary justification for publicly funded social research is precisely that social research is relevant to policy development. If no such relevance can be discerned, then policy researchers and analysts will struggle to claim legitimacy for their work even if, from an academic point of view, the science behind it is exemplary.

We suggested that this pragmatic orientation arose in response to increasing complexity in terms of multilayering in policy contexts, a shift towards participatory forms of evaluation and action research, and the deployment by social researchers of non-linear, non-positivist (although not necessarily anti-positivist) notions of causality. Changes in the way that social researchers do their work, and the consequences these have for the kind of knowledge they are able to produce, have the unexpected virtue of enabling social policy research to contribute something useful both to improving the evidential basis of the policy discourse and, by virtue of its tendency towards standpoint, to the political-ideological discourse that provides much of the context within which the policy debate takes place. While it might do neither of these things perfectly, it can make a valuable contribution to both.

Social policy research and analysis thus turn their vices into virtues by contributing both to the empirical aspects of the policy debate (the evidential base) and to the ideological-political aspect (the force of the better argument). Even if they are unable to produce policy directly, critical social and welfare policy researchers can provide policy makers with a clearer understanding of the basis on which they ought to take their decisions, together with helpful indications of the key points of comparison, and difference, between the available policy options. The substantive evidence and rhetorical commentary they provide can help test the extent to which the winning side in the debate really is exercising 'the force of the better argument'. Within the ideological-political policy discourse, social policy researchers and analysts are able to offer an important critical voice to clarify broader ethical and moral aspects of the debate. These are value aspects that cannot easily be resolved by recourse to empirical evidence.

This positive interpretation of the valuable contribution of critical and value-standpoint social policy research might also help to explain the broad difference between policy advisers in the United States, who are asked by government only to comment on the administrative and managerial challenges of policy development, and those in the United Kingdom, where there has been more emphasis on appraising the desirability of particular policy outcomes *with or without* invitations from government to do so. In Weber's more technical vocabulary, in the United Kingdom and in Europe more generally there has continued to be more of an emphasis on the (substantive) rationality of ends (the value framework of policy intervention) rather than on the (formal) rationality of means (the management and administration of programmes).

## Ethical responsibilities

We also noted the important ethical responsibilities that social policy researchers and analysts have in contributing to the policy-making discourse. Two kinds of ethical responsibilities are involved here. First is the responsibility of being honest in respect of the true scientific status of the evidence social policy researchers seek to contribute to the evidential basis of policy debates. To the extent that divisions within and between political parties over social welfare policy are increasingly to do with relatively fine-grained differences over practical issues of *funding and implementation*, social researchers are required to help provide evidence to help settle some of these debates. Empirical evidence, and even less academic theory about social policy, cannot provide *solutions* to policy issues, but it does provide an important source of 'expert opinion' that is, in principle at least, less immediately contaminated by the prejudices or ideology of one side of the debate or the other. Funded academic and professional research into social and welfare policy also has the potential for reducing public expenditure on welfare programmes if the research increases the likelihood that a particular policy intervention will be successful in its aims. Increased emphasis on 'value for money' as a criterion of policy development is a case in point.

Second, social researchers have an ethical responsibility to take seriously the impact that their research, and especially the way they explain and interpret their findings, can have on the broader political and ideological discourse. Actual policy emerges at the intersection of evidence and argument and social policy researchers have an ethical responsibility towards both. Moreover, the interventions in the policy debate made by professional and academic commentators constitute a distinct layer or value position of their own within the debate. Just as the cross-domain effects of policy interventions have to be taken into account, so also do the impacts of politics and ideology and, in its academic aspect particularly, the impact of conceptual work.

We are touching here on one of the essential features of the social research process, which is that both theory and evidence are necessary in order to develop a properly informed view of a particular policy context, intervention, appraisal and evaluation. Social research thus both provides an *interpretive framework* for organizing one's thoughts about actually occurring events and at the same time helps formulate the *kinds of research questions* that need to be posed in order to gather evidence of cause and effect. Asserting the essential connectedness of 'theory' with 'evidence' in this way helps us fathom one of the apparent paradoxes of social policy research, which is the false requirement to keep these two distinct elements or phases apart from one another. The need for social policy research to be, and to be seen to be, helpful in improving the evidential basis, while at the same time maintaining high levels of academic and theoretical (or simply scientific) rigour, demonstrates quite well the circularity of the relationship between pure and applied social research.

# Conclusion

## Theoretical consciousness

At the beginning of our discussion we stressed the importance of seeing the theoretical aspects of social research not as a separate and sometimes inconvenient peripheral to research design, but as playing a necessary and often central part in it. Notwithstanding the intellectual and abstract constitution of theoretical and epistemological issues that sometimes makes them challenging to grasp, they are, we have argued, very practical, in the sense that they provide clarification of the intentions of the researcher and the purposes of the research. We introduced the idea of theoretical consciousness as a way of describing a general willingness on the part of the social researcher to integrate theoretical and epistemological issues more fully into the basic design of the research. Theoretical consciousness provides a valuable resource that, on a par with literature searching and knowledge of different data-gathering techniques, increases the range of choices available to the social researcher.

An additional advantage of deploying theoretical consciousness is that it adds dynamism to research design by encouraging social researchers to see their initial choices in terms of, and in comparison with, alternative theoretical and epistemological approaches. A decision, for example, not to treat social phenomena as if they were broadly the same as phenomena in the physical and natural environments does not mean that social research cannot be 'positivist' in the broader intellectual sense of trying to identify patterns of cause and consequence. Acknowledging the particular constitution of social phenomena, however, not least the fact that they are often socially constructed, does require careful reflection on the difference between one kind of causality and another kind. If it is envisaged that the research needs to elicit depthful information from respondents about particular experiences they have had, careful consideration needs to be given to the status of the information they provide. If the data are entirely subjective, which is to say they are only truly meaningful or intelligible from within the consciousness of the person describing them, the evident lack of objectivity raises important questions about the reliability and validity of the data. It is not reasonable to infer that conclusions from a small-scale ethnographic study relying on personal information can be applied to the general population. Similarly, if the research emphasizes the contingent nature of respondents' experience and the importance of context, it is improbable that the findings can be generalized, either to broader theoretical debates or as a basis for wider substantive claims.

Being secure in the decisions taken also means understanding *the nature of* that decision-making process. At a minimum there needs to be consistency between the researcher's definition of what constitutes knowledge, their understanding of the nature of the phenomena being investigated, the kind of data thatwill provide the most effective analysis of those phenomena and, finally, what the purpose of the investigation is. Is it to test or develop concepts and theory? Is it to add to the fund of descriptive material? Is the research purely academic or does it have practical or policy implications? Theoretical consciousness means making 'positive' and consistent choices between one approach and another, rather than making 'negative' decisions against the alternatives.

## Analytical criticism

Theoretical consciousness is linked to a second term we introduced, which is the idea of analytical criticism. Embracing the idea of reflexivity, we must accept that from the very moment the research process begins in the imagination of the researcher, social research is, in a truly experiential sense, a learning process *for the social researcher*. Analytical criticism refers to the way in which the decisions social researchers make at each stage of the process require active and critical assessment of alternatives. None of the stages or phases of social research takes place in isolation but is a consequence of, and is itself implied in, the stages that preceded it and come after. Furthermore, each decision is embedded within a range of theoretical and methodological contexts. For the research to be intellectually valid *in terms of* the wider debates with which it seeks to engage (in addition, that is, to operational questions of the validity and reliability of the data), the researcher needs to be aware of those wider contexts. It might not be feasible for the social researcher to have a detailed knowledge of how each and every piece of each and every theoretical and methodological puzzle can be fitted together, but having a working understanding of their general contours will certainly improve the quality of research design.

Decision making is one of the essential skills of the critical analyst, and this process of reasoning provides a number of tests for the social researcher. First, in what ways does the research improve the evidential basis of the field of debate with which it is engaging? Second, how does the researcher envisage their work being used by others to reinforce and strengthen 'the force of the better argument'? Third, and assuming that the research is able to meet the first two tests, what kinds of alternatives to the prevailing situation does it offer? Analytical criticism acts against the forces of reaction and inertia by challenging the basis on which current knowledge stands, by engaging with debates about it, and by promoting the principle that the search for alternatives is always worthwhile. Theoretical consciousness and analytical criticism are about becoming confident in being able to pose and answer these questions robustly.

## Value neutrality

A third focus for the book has been how social researchers manage their own value positions. Social research is itself an exercise in social construction. Social researchers have a remarkably free hand in selecting the topics they wish to investigate, in applying linguistic labels and abstract concepts to facilitate their description and analysis, and in offering their preferred interpretations of those social phenomena. The activities of selection, abstraction and interpretation offer the social researcher multiple opportunities to produce results that reflect their own value position. Up to a point, value neutrality in social research is inevitable (some might say desirable), since the character of many social phenomena is determined in fairly precise and direct ways by their value content. Studying unemployment, for example, or the exploitation of children or neglect of the elderly becomes a meaningful thing to do *because of* the prior value assumption that a more systematic understanding of such phenomena will significantly improve the real lived experience of social actors who are adversely affected by them.

In accepting this argument, however, social researchers are not absolved from the basic responsibility not only of reaching their own better understanding of values, and of explaining to their audiences which value positions are in play, but of trying to develop a research design that positively accepts the challenge of value neutrality. To the extent that the academic community endorses as valid and legitimate research that does not seek to deceive or misinform its audiences, and condemns as illegitimate and false research that does, the issue of values underpins the question of research ethics. The various guides, statements and protocols contained in professional codes of research ethics are an attempt to transpose underlying value positions (and, in the context especially of social research, social values) into practical guides for action. Following the agreed rules on legitimate purpose, avoidance of harm, informed consent, security of data and truthful rendering of results makes the research ethical. More than this, however, we have argued that in the same way that 'following the rules' of ethical research increases the possibility that the research is 'value worthy' or 'value virtuous' in terms of how, in strictly practical terms, the research process has been conducted, social researchers should also strive to make their research value worthy and value virtuous *in intellectual terms*. The ethical probity of social research, in other words, is not just a matter of what the researcher *does*, but of what they *think*. And it is in the theoretical domain that much of this thinking takes place.

## Relationships

Ethics and values in social research, together with the underlying value positions they represent, enter the research process most decisively at the moment the researcher initiates the various professional relationships on which social research depends. Some of these relationships, such as that between a researcher and the organization by which they are employed, or with a sponsor or funder, are relatively formal and are regulated legally by contracts of one kind or another. However, other relations between members of the research team, but especially between the researcher and research respondents or subjects, require a much more personal form of regulation based on a degree of personal commitment and trust. Professional codes of ethics describe the general parameters of these relationships, specify the terms on which the various parties enter research relationships, and offer guidance as to how social researchers should try to manage these relationships. As noted a number of times in the foregoing discussion, and notwithstanding the diligence with which the professional codes are being observed, the final judge of whether the research is or is not ethical is the good conscience of social researchers themselves.

One of the most difficult relationships to manage ethically is that between the social researcher and the wider academic and other audiences to which they will be reporting their findings. Although this might appear to be quite an anonymous or formal kind of research relationship, the moment a social researcher declares their results is a moment of trust between researcher and audience. Audiences, and especially the non-academic audiences that social researchers often address, trust researchers to provide them with a fair and reasonable summary of findings based on an honest and robust interpretation of their data. To the extent that social research explores topics that are inherently unstable, and embedded within wider political and ideological debates, social researchers have to be especially skilled in managing the value content of their work. The temptation to lapse into a preferred value position at the very moment that audience interest is most intense, and levels of trust are at their highest, is a temptation that can only be resisted if researchers are honest with *themselves* about *their own* values and ideals.

# Glossary

*Action research* A variety of participatory social research in which positive outcomes occur during the research process. Often defined as a learning process, action researchers focus on developing practical outcomes for individuals and organizations. See *participatory evaluation* and *self-reflexive practice*.

*Alienation* A term developed by Karl Marx to describe the loss of well-being experienced by workers in capitalist society. Alienation is associated with forms of working in which the products of work, working relationships and any sense of self-worth and self-esteem become debased. Marx argued that the compulsion to work in this way would eventually result in revolution.

*Analytical criticism* A form of academic reasoning in social research that, in adopting a critical orientation to the evidence and subject matter, aims to improve the evidential basis, add to 'the force of the better argument' and reflect positively on alternatives to the status quo.

*Causality, causation* The logical assumption that consequences arise from particular causes that can be isolated and described. *Positivist* scientists usually operate with a simple input–output or linear notion of causation in which A+B=C or, more rigorously still, if A and B are combined in the way specified, *they must produce C*. Social scientists usually operate with a circular or contingent notion of causality, in which outcomes arise from complex combinations of factors such that A+B might, but does not inevitably nor necessarily, produce consequence C. Social research often focuses on trying to identify the causes of a particular social phenomenon, which inevitably involves a notion of causality.

*Collectivist* A perspective that treats phenomena in terms of, or from the perspective of, the whole rather than its divisible parts. Collectivists usually assume that the sum is greater than its parts, and that the whole has properties that are not found in its individual parts. A term used to describe the perspective of social theorists and sociologists, like Karl Marx and Émile Durkheim, who often take the collectivity, rather than the individual, as the focus of their analysis. Contrasts with *individualist*.

*Communal* Relating to the shared or common experience of social actors who form collectivities. Also refers to the shared interests and expectations of members of social groups.

*Comparative method* Especially in sociology and anthropology, an approach in which social phenomena are compared with other social phenomena rather than being measured against some absolute standard or scale. Comparisons are made in the same society at different points in historical time, or between different societies at the same point in historical time.

*Constructivist/constructivism* See *social construction*.

*Covert research* Social research in which those being studied are unaware of the fact. Sometimes refers to social research in which respondents or subjects are aware they are taking part in a study but are unaware of its true purpose.

*Critical realism* An influential perspective in social theory associated with the ideas of Roy Bhaskar (1979, 2002) and Margaret Archer (1988, 2000). The underlying realist premise of critical realism is that it is possible to explain key aspects of the surface forms of social phenomena by inferring the existence of underlying mechanisms that cannot themselves be observed. Its critical aspect is that it is not logically necessary to assume that particular outcomes must always occur. It embraces the possibility of alternative outcomes. Contrasts with *deductive* and *inductive* reasoning.

*Deductive reasoning* A basic type of methodology in which general propositions and hypotheses are tested by examining whether they are supported by specific instances. An analytical procedure that goes from the general towards the particular. Contrasts with *inductive reasoning*. Most reasoning in the human and social sciences involves a combination of deductive and inductive reasoning. See also *critical realism*.

*Empirical/empiricist* A philosophical attitude towards the nature of human knowledge stating that knowledge is based on experiencing phenomena through the physical senses. Following John Locke (1632–1704), regards the human mind as a 'blank slate' that only becomes knowledgeable through experience. A scientific methodology that seeks to arrive at objective descriptions and measurements of phenomena as facts. The empiricist laboratory method involving detailed experimentation is the stereotype of 'hard' science, as distinct from the 'soft' science used in the arts, humanities and social sciences. Opposed to *idealism* and some forms of *rationalism*.

*Enlightenment* The period from the late seventeenth and eighteenth centuries in Europe dominated by a series of new ideas in philosophy, politics, the arts and intellectual life generally that promoted a progressive and liberal attitude based on Reason rather than on tradition or religious faith alone. Advocates the idea that human beings do not occupy a special place in the universe ordained by God, but that *Homo sapiens* is part of nature and that knowledge of nature and of life can be gained through observation, experiment and rational judgement. Growing awareness of individuality and the human capacity to affect the conditions of its own existence provided a foundation for modern ideas about social development and progress, political representation and social organization.

*Epistemology* A branch of philosophy concerned with understanding what knowledge is. *Empiricists* argue that knowledge comes only through experience, while *rationalists* argue that ideas and cognitive reasoning are the basis of knowledge. Distinct from *ontology*, which is concerned with the nature of matter, and teleology, which, in respect of human subjects, tackles the question of the nature and direction of development.

*Ethics* Rules or conventions that render actions legitimate in terms of the moral beliefs and values of the society in which they take place. Unethical behaviour is behaviour that does not reflect those underlying values.

*Evaluation research* A variety of social research that seeks to test whether desired outcomes, usually in the form of programme or policy interventions, are being achieved. Includes a range of techniques from external audit to *participatory evaluation*, and looks at outcomes as well as processes.

*Existentialism* Originating in the thought of the Danish theologian Søren Kierkegaard (1813–55) but developed by the French philosopher J.-P. Sartre (1905–80) during the 1940s and 1950s, existentialism is a philosophical position claiming that the personal experience of being is much more important than the orderly quest for objective knowledge. Knowledge of self is inaccessible to all but the self that is being experienced. Existentialism generally rejects the *rationalist* and *realist* perspectives that there is an independent world 'out there' that can be studied separately from the experiences of any particular individual. All knowledge is in fact experiential.

*Fact* A statement about an object or phenomenon that, on the basis of the current state of knowledge or level of scientific expertise, is taken to be irrefutable.

*Formal rationality* In relation especially to the work of Max Weber, refers to the decision-making process in respect of the best technical means of achieving particular ends. Distinct from *substantive rationality*, which refers to the desirability of the ends that social actors are trying to achieve.

*Functionalism* An abstract approach in social theory and sociology that describes the various institutions and practices of society in terms of how they function to the benefit of the 'social system' as a whole. Notions of 'purpose' and 'function' are seen as largely identical. The leading functionalist social theorists are Talcott Parsons (1902–79) and R.K. Merton (1910–2003).

*Gatekeepers* Individuals who control points of entry into organizations. Gatekeepers might also be responsible for devising the terms and conditions of entry.

*Gender* A term referring to socially constructed social and cultural beliefs about the respective roles of men and women in society. Related to, but distinct from, the biological notion of physical sex. Gender includes important assumptions about patterns of sexuality and identity, and of maleness and femaleness.

*Hegemony* A concept used especially by the Marxist theorist Antonio Gramsci (1891–1937) to describe modern forms of economic and political power that are based less on physical force and more on consent. A hegemonic society is one in which the general population agree to be governed in a particular way. Gramsci criticized some forms of political hegemony on the grounds that 'consent' might be based on a false or ideological understanding of the real situation. Actors agree to be ruled under false pretences.

*Humanism, humanist* A philosophical and political perspective that explores reality from the point of view of the human subject. The humanist perspective, especially in its liberal and Marxist formulations, tends to assume that social action is driven by a benign and sympathetic regard for the needs of others. Humanists tend to see individual experience through the lens of a *collectivist*, rather than *individualist*, perspective.

*Idealism, idealist* The philosophical position that the highest attainments of human activity are ideas rather than material objects. Material developments are seen as a means to a higher end, usually conceived in terms of reaching advanced forms of consciousness or of intellectual/spiritual accomplishment. Idealist philosophers differ over whether there is a single point of ultimate attainment to which all human endeavour is converging and which provides a measure of how far civilization has progressed, or whether there are separate end points in different fields of effort and between cultures. Distinct from *materialism*.

*Individualism, individualist* A philosophical and political attitude that sees the quest for individuality, acting independently of the collective will, not being dominated by authority, as a positive expectation. Individual*ists* can be distinguished from *collectivists* on the grounds that the former see the benefits of acting separately from others as likely to be greater than the benefits of acting together.

*Inductive reasoning* A basic type of reasoning in which general propositions and suppositions are developed on the basis of one or two specific instances or observations. An analytical procedure that goes from the particular towards the general. Contrasts with *deductive reasoning*. Most reasoning in the human and social sciences involves a combination of deductive and inductive reasoning. See also *critical realism*.

*Informed consent* An essential and non-negotiable ethical principle in social research that requires social researchers to make sure that research subjects and respondents are properly aware of, and are willing participants in, social research.

*Interpretivism* A methodology in the social sciences associated particularly with Max Weber and his method *verstehen*, which means literally 'to interpret' social action in terms of what social action means to those performing it. See also *methodological individualism*.

*Lived experience* Refers to social action in terms of, or from the point of view of, personal experience that has actually taken place, rather than in terms of hypothetical or imagined happenings.

*Materialism* An approach in social theory and philosophy that asserts the importance of actual material phenomena over metaphysical representations of them in the form of ideas. Distinct from *idealism*.

*Methodological individualism* Associated particularly with Max Weber, a method in social research that attempts to explore social phenomena from the point of view of the individual social actor. Distinct from the *collectivist* approaches of Émile Durkheim and Karl Marx, Weber's approach is that the basic unit of analysis in social research is the individual social actor and not collectivized entities such as 'class' or 'society'.

*Methodology* A general term for the way in which social researchers design their investigations. Different *epistemological* or philosophical positions, for example *empiricism* and *interpretivism*, tend to require the use of one methodology rather than another. Different methodologies use different combinations of methods or techniques in gathering and analysing data.

*Morals* A special category of beliefs based on underlying ideals and *values*, which are taken to provide the best guide for social action. Some morals, and the rules of *ethical* behaviour to which they give rise, are based on religious beliefs and the exercise of faith. Morals can also be based on *humanist* and scientific forms of reasoning.

*Objective, objectivism* Looking at phenomena factually and dispassionately in terms of their external physical properties and characteristics. Contrasts with *subjective/subjectivism*.

*Ontology* From the Greek word for 'being', a branch of philosophy concerned with understanding the nature of matter. The basic distinction is between matter that has an observable material form, the stuff of the physical universe studied by the physical and natural sciences, and *non*-material *meta*physical matter like thoughts and ideas, which have no directly observable form and are studied by philosophers and social scientists. See *materialism* and *idealism*.

*Over-determined, over-determination* In social theory and psychoanalysis, referring to the way in which a phenomenon might be determined in advance, or is overshadowed in its surface form, by some previously occurring or underlying force.

*Paradigm* A set or collection of ideas and beliefs. The philosopher of science Thomas Kuhn adopted the term in describing how one 'scientific paradigm', or collection of scientific beliefs and associated modes of reasoning, could be replaced by an alternative scientific paradigm.

*Participatory evaluation* A variety of *evaluation research* in which the social researcher, or member of the organization who is conducing the evaluation, is an active participant in the evaluation process rather than acting only as an observer. Similar to some forms of *action research*.

*Patient confidentiality* A term used in the medical professions, and heavily reinforced by professional codes of ethics and sometimes legal requirements, that personal and sensitive information provided by patients during a medical consultation cannot be passed to a third party without the explicit consent of the patient. An underlying assumption is that patients, and in the context of social research subjects and respondents, *will only* provide information *on condition that* it is not passed on.

*Positivism, positivist* Based on the *realist* presumption of an actual exterior reality existing separately from human knowledge of it, a term introduced by the French social philosopher Auguste Comte (1798–1857) to describe the most rigorous form of scientific investigation aimed at the discovery of 'facts' and 'laws'. Metaphysical speculation is rejected as incapable of producing factual knowledge. As a form of methodology, proceeds by way of systematic, often *empirical* investigation of phenomena and attempts to describe the laws that govern them.

*Practitioner research* Research carried out by members of an organization. Often involves *reflexivity*, in the sense that the practitioner/researcher investigates their own actions. See *action research* and *evaluation research*. Practitioner researchers take on the role of social researchers while conducting their study.

*Rationalism, rationalist* The philosophical position that reality only becomes accessible to human consciousness because of the human capacity for intellectual reasoning. Resists the alternative empirical view that things can only be known as a result of having direct physical experience of them, because these sensations still have to be interpreted or made sense of by the human mind. Some rationalists, such as Immanuel Kant (1724–1804), argue that even if knowledge is limited by experience, the capacity for intellectual reasoning presupposes the prior existence within the human mind of various capacities for rational thought that exist independently of the sensations and experiences that people have of the world around them. In order to make sense of the very first sense experiences it encounters, the human mind must *already* be equipped with 'synthetic knowledge' or the capacity for processing sense data. See *idealism* and *materialism*.

*Realism, realist* The philosophical position that it is possible and reasonable to describe an actually existing reality that exists independently of anything we might have to say about it. Non-material phenomena such as ideas, values and beliefs might also be considered part of reality. The method of description is usually *empirical*. See also *idealism* and *rationalism*.

*Reflexivity* An influential concept developed by the sociologist Anthony Giddens to describe a leading characteristic of modern *lived experience*, which is that social actors continually monitor their own behaviour and adjust their future actions accordingly. It is a characteristic of late-modern society that organizations also continually monitor and revise their procedures, possibly through the intervention of *practitioner researchers*. Personal reflexivity is also taken to be a leading characteristic of *action research*.

*Reliability* A technical term that poses the question of whether the research design actually is able to measure what it claims to measure. Is face-to-face interviewing a reliable method for finding out about whether respondents drive within the national speed limit? See also *validity*.

*Replicability* In the context of *empirical* scientific experimentation, the requirement that the same procedure, if repeated exactly, will produce exactly the same result. Sometimes used more casually in social research to refer to the possibility of repeating a study in the expectation of arriving at similar conclusions.

*Self-reflexive practice* Using the concept of *reflexivity*, and associated particularly with participatory forms of *action research*, describes a process in which researchers undergo a process of self-change and self-renewal as a result of their participation in the research process. Self-renewal can become the main objective of the action research process.

*Social construction* A social or cultural phenomenon or practice that does not occur in nature but has been actively created by human beings. Because socially constructed phenomena originate through deliberate human action, it is a mistake to regard them as having essential, natural or universal properties. Socially constructed phenomena can be discontinued, changed or reconstructed as the situation demands. To have real impact on social behaviour, social constructions often require social actors to interpret them in a particular way. For example, biological sex is a factual anatomical type, whereas notions of gender and identity are socially constructed.

*Social value* A special category of *socially constructed* values that promote the well-being of society and/or arise out of the *lived experience* of social actors.

*Socialization* A common sociological name for the process by which social actors assimilate the norms and values, the general conventions and expectations, of the society in which they live. The influential *functionalist* theorist Talcott Parsons argued that the stability of the social system (society) depends to a very large extent on the successful socialization of individuals. He further argued that the family is the primary site of socialization both for children and for adults. The education system, peer groups, youth cultural groups and the mass media are also acknowledged as contributing to the socialization process in modern society.

*Solidarity* Social solidarity refers to the property of cohesion characteristic of social groups or societies that exhibit high levels of social order and stability. Political solidarity refers to the expression of shared beliefs, values and objectives that bind social collectivities together.

*Stakeholder* In social research, a person, group or organization that has a stake or vested interest in the research process. Stakeholders might have something to lose as well as to gain through their participation. Stakeholders might seek to influence or control the research process. Stakeholders are not equal in terms of the power they exercise.

*Standpoint research* A variety of social research in which the researcher conducts the research from a particular political or ideological point of view. Standpoint researchers might also be advocates or campaigners for particular social or political causes.

*Structuralism* A mode of systematic academic investigation that originated in the analysis of how the verbal and written utterances of social actors (language) are produced by the operation of the underlying structuring properties of grammar and syntax. The key implication is that surface phenomena, whether in the form of language, art, personality politics, can be explained in terms of, or as an effect of, invisible underlying structures.

*Subjective, subjectivism* Referring to the personal or interior thoughts and feelings of social actors. Acknowledges the emotional and personalized nature of social experience. Looking at meaning from the social actor's own point of view. Distinct from *objective/objectivism*.

**Substantive rationality** See *formal rationality*.

**Theoretical consciousness** An attitude towards social research that acknowledges the theoretical dimensions of the research process, and recognizes that the theoretical dimension has important practical implications for research design. Sees theory as having a necessary and positive influence over the investigation of social phenomena.

**Universal social values** A set of *social values* that are claimed to be universally applicable to all social actors and actions in a particular society, and possibly to all societies.

**Validity** A technical term for the truthfulness or plausibility of research findings. Internal validity poses the question of whether a research procedure measures something that *can be* measured and/or *is worth* measuring. External validity poses the question of 'generalizability', or whether that which is being measured might also be characteristic of other similar cases. See also *reliability*.

**Value neutrality** A principle of method in social research highlighted by Max Weber, which is that although all research is infused with value positions of various kinds (social research is very often precisely *about* the values that social actors hold), researchers must strive not to allow their own values to invalidate the conclusions they reach.

**Value standpoint** Research conducted explicitly from the point of view of a particular set of expressed values.

**Values** Ideas that provide a source of motivation. Values might be based on religious beliefs or on ideas about desirable economic, political and ideological objectives and how to achieve them. For example, acting rationally in pursuit of individual economic advantage is part of the Western capitalist value system. See *social value* and *universal social values*.

**Verstehen** Associated with Max Weber, a German word meaning 'understanding'. Weber develops the term to describe the particular *methodology* of the social sciences, which is concerned with understanding and interpreting social action, if possible from the point of view of the social actor. The *interpretive* approach and the style of *inductive reasoning* associated with it are defining characteristics of the social-scientific technique. Distinguished from *deductive reasoning*, which is associated with the physical and biological sciences.

# Bibliography

American Sociological Association (1997) *Code of Ethics*. Washington, DC: American Sociological Association.

Archer, M. (1995) *Realist Social Theory: The Morphogenic Approach*. Cambridge: Cambridge University Press.

Archer (1988) *Culture and Agency*. Cambridge: Cambridge University Press.

Archer, M. (2000) *Being Human: The Problem of Agency*. Cambridge: Cambridge University Press.

Arendt, H. (1963) *Eichmann in Jerusalem: A Report on the Banality of Evil*. New York: Viking Press.

Argyris, C. and Schon, D.A. (1991) 'Participatory action research and action science compared', in W.F. Whyte (ed.), *Participatory Action Research*. London: Sage, pp. 85–96.

Barthes, R. (1973 [1957]) *Mythologies*. London: Paladin Books. Originally published in French.

Bauman, Z. (1992) *Intimations of Postmodernity*. London: Routledge.

Baumrind, D. (1964) 'Some thoughts on the ethics of research: After reading Milgram's "behavioural study of obedience"', *American Psychologist* 19: 421–3.

Becker, H.S. (1967) 'Whose side are we on?', *Social Problems* 14: 239–47.

Beveridge, W. (1942) *Social Insurance and Allied Services: A Report Presented to Parliament by Command of His Majesty*. November, CMND 6404. London: HMSO.

Bhaskar, R. (1975) *A Realist Theory of Science*. Brighton: Harvester Press.

Bhaskar, R. (1979) *The Possibility of Naturalism: A Philosophical Critique of the Contemporary Human Sciences*. London: Harvester Press.

Bhaskar (2002) *From Science to Emancipation*. London: Sage.

Blackaby, D., Charles, N., Davies, C., Murphy, P., O'Leary, N. and Ransome, P. (1999) *Women in Senior Management in Wales*. Manchester: Equal Opportunities Commission.

British Sociological Association (2002) *Statement of Ethical Practice*. Durham: British Sociological Association.

Brubaker, R. (1984) *The Limits of Rationality*. London: Allen and Unwin.

Cesarani, D. (2004) *Eichmann: His Life and Crimes*. London: Heinemann.

Charles, N. (2000) *Feminism, the State and Social Policy*. London: Macmillan.

Charles, N., Davies, C., Blackaby, D., Murphy, P., O'Leary, N. and Ransome, P. (2000) 'It's still there! Maintaining the glass ceiling in Wales, *Contemporary Wales*, 13: 116–37.

Chelimsky, E. (1995), 'Where we stand today in the practice of evaluation', *Knowledge and Policy*, 8: 8–19.

Chun Wei Choo (1998) *The Knowing Organization: How Organizations Use Information to Construct Meaning, Create Knowledge and Make Decisions*. Oxford: Oxford University Press.

Clarke, A. (1999) *Evaluation Research*. London: Sage.

Cockburn, C. (1991) *In the Way of Women*. Basingstoke: Macmillan.

Coghlan, D. and Brannick, T. (2005) *Doing Action Research in Your Own Organization*. London: Sage.

Comte, A. (1974 [1830]), *The Positive Philosophy*. New York: AMS Press. Originally published in French.

Council of Europe (1950) *European Convention for the Protection of Human Rights and Fundamental Freedoms* (last amended by Protocol 14 effective June 2010). Strasbourg: Council of Europe.

Crompton & Harris (1998) 'Exploring women's employment patterns: Orientations to work revisited', *The British Journal of Sociology* 49(1): 118–36.

Davies, C.A. (2008) *Reflexive Ethnography*, 2nd edn. London: Routledge.

Department for Constitutional Affairs (2007) *Mental Capacity Act 2005, Code of Practice*. London: HMSO.

Department for Education and Skills (DfES) (2004) 'Student loans and the question of debt', Department for Education and Skills Discussion Paper. Norwich: HMSO.

Department of Health (2006) *National Health Service Act 2006*. London: HMSO.

Devine, F. and Heath, S. (1999) *Sociological Research Methods in Context*. London: Macmillan.

Dryzek, J.S. (2006) 'Policy analysis as critique', in M. Moran, M. Rein and R.E. Goodin (eds), *The Oxford Handbook of Public Policy*. Oxford: Oxford University Press, pp. 190–203.

Durkheim, E. (1964 [1895]) *The Rules of Sociological Method*. New York: Free Press. Originally published in French.

Durkheim, E. (1968 [1897]) *Suicide*. London: Routledge. Originally published in French.

Economic and Social Research Council (2005) *ESRC Strategic Plan 2005–2010*. Swindon: ESRC.

Economic and Social Research Council (2009) *ESRC Strategic Plan 2009–2015*. Swindon: ESRC.

Economic and Social Research Council (2010) *ESRC Research Data Policy*. Swindon: ESRC.

Economic and Social Research Council (2011) *ESRC Framework for Research Ethics*. Swindon: ESRC.

Fetterman, D.M. (2001) *Foundations of Empowerment Evaluation*. Thousand Oaks, CA: Sage.

Freire, P. (1974) *Education for Critical Consciousness*. London: Sheed and Ward.

Galbraith, J.K. (2009 [1954]) *The Great Crash 1929*. London: Penguin.

Gatrell, C. (2007) 'A fractional commitment? Part-time work and the maternal body', *International Journal of Human Resource Management*, 18(3): 462–75.

General Assembly of the United Nations (1948) *Universal Declaration of Human Rights*. http://www.un.org/en/documents/udhr/index.shtml, accessed 16 August 2012.

General Assembly of the World Medical Association (1964) *Declaration of Helsinki*. Latest revision 2008. Helsinki: 18th WMA General Assembly.

Giddens, A. (1974) *The New Rules of Sociological Method*. London: Hutchinson.

Giddens, A. (1990) *The Consequences of Modernity*. Cambridge: Polity Press.

Godwin, J. (2009) *Clintonomics: How Bill Clinton Reengineered the Reagan Revolution*. New York: American Management Association.

Gouldner, A. (1973) *For Sociology*. Harmondsworth: Penguin.

Gramsci, A. (1971) *Selections from the Prison Notebooks*, ed. and trans. Q. Hoare and G. Nowell Smith. London: Lawrence and Wishart.

Guba, F.G. and Lincoln, Y.S. (1989) *Fourth Generation Evaluation*. Newbury Park, CA: Sage.

Habermas, J. (1984 [1981]) *The Theory of Communicative Action, Volume 1: Reason and the Rationalization of Society*, rrans. T. McCarthy. London: Heinemann. Originally published in German.

Hadley, R. and Clough, R. (1996) *Care in Chaos: Frustration and Challenge in Community Care*. London: Cassell.

Hakim (1995) *Key Issues in Women's Work*. London: Althore.

Hakim (1998) *Social Change and Innovation in the Labour Market*. Oxford: Oxford University Press.

Hall, I. and Hall D. (2004) *Evaluation Research: Introducing Small-Scale Practice*. Basingstoke: Palgrave Macmillan.

Hammersley, M. (1992) *What's Wrong with Ethnography? Methodological Explorations*. London: Routledge.

Hammersley, M. (2000) *Taking Sides in Social Research: Essays on Partisanship and Bias*. London: Routledge.

Hammersley, M. (ed.) (2008) *Questioning Qualitative Enquiry: Critical Essays*. London: Sage.

Hammersley, M. and Gomm, R. (2008) 'Assessing the radical critique of interviews', in M. Hammersley (ed.), *Questioning Qualitative Enquiry: Critical Essays*. London: Sage, pp. 89–100.

Hanes, S. and Hanes, R.C. (2003) *Great Depression and New Deal*. Detroit: UXL.

Harré, R. (1972) *The Philosophies of Science*. Oxford: Oxford University Press.

HMSO (2006) *Health and Social Care Act 2006*. London: HMSO.

Hobbs, D. (1988) *Doing the Business: Entrepreneurship, the Working Class and Detectives in the East End of London*. Oxford: Oxford University Press.

Hood, C. (1991) 'A public management for all seasons', *Public Administration* 69(1): 3–19.

House of Lords Report (2009) *Surveillance: Citizens and the State*, Constitutional Committee Second Report, January 21 2002. London: HMSO.

Humphries, L. (1970) *Tearoom Trade: A Study of Homosexual Encounters in Public Places*. London: Duckworth.

Jahoda, M., Lazarsfeld, P.F. and Zeisel, H. (1972 [1933]) *Marienthal: The Sociography of an Unemployed Community*. Trans. from the German by the authors with J. Reginall and T. Elsaesser. London: Tavistock Publications.

Johnson, P. and Duberley, J. (2000) *Understanding Management Research*. London: Sage.

Joseph, J. (2003) *Social Theory: Conflict, Cohesion and Consent*. Edinburgh: Edinburgh University Press.

Kalling, T. and Styhre, A. (2003) *Knowledge Sharing Organizations*. Malmo: Copenhagen Business School Press.

Kren, G.M. and Rappaport, L. (1994) *The Holocaust and the Crisis of Human Behaviour*, 2nd edn. New York: Holmes and Meier.

Kuhn, T.S. (1970 [1962]) *The Structure of Scientific Revolutions*. Chicago: University of Chicago Press.

Lewis, S., Gambles, R. and Rapoport, R. (2007) 'The constraints of a "work-life balance" approach: An international perspective', *International Journal of Human Resource Management*, 18(3): 360–73.

Luhmann, N. (1995 [1984]) *Social Systems*. Stanford: Stanford University Press. Originally published in German.

Lynch, K. (1999) 'Equality studies, the academy and the role of research in emancipatory social change', *Economic and Social Review*, 30(1): 41–69.

Macintyre, A. (1985) *After Virtue*. London, Duckworth.

Marx, K. (1954 [1867]) *Capital*. Vol. 1. London: Lawrence and Wishart. Originally published in German.

McIntyre, A. (2008) *Participatory Action Research*. London: Sage.

McNiff, J., and Whitehead, J. (2002) *Action Research: Principles and Practice*, 2nd edn. Abingdon: Routledge-Falmer.

Merton, R.K (1949) *Social Theory and Social Structure*. New York: Free Press.

Milgram, S. (1963) 'Behavioural study of obedience', *Journal of Abnormal and Social Psychology*, 67: 371–8.

Milgram, S. (1973) *Obedience to Authority: An Experimental View*. New York: Harper and Row.

Miller, A.G. (1986) *The Obedience Experiments: A Case Study of Controversy in Social Science*. New York: Praeger.

Mills, C.W. (1959) *The Sociological Imagination*. New York: Oxford University Press.

Moran, M., Rein, M. and Goodin, R.E. (eds) (2006) *The Oxford Handbook of Public Policy*. Oxford: Oxford University Press.

Mouzelis, N. (1995) *Sociological Theory: What Went Wrong?* London: Routledge.

Orne, M.T. and Holland, C.H. (1968) 'On the ecological validity of laboratory deception', *International Journal of Psychiatry*, 6: 282–93.

Parsons, T. (1951) *The Social System*. London: Routledge & Kegan Paul.

Pawson, R. and Tilley, N. (1997) *Realistic Evaluation*. London: Sage.

Pitts, M. and Smith, A. (eds) (2007) *Researching the Margins: Strategies for Ethical and Rigorous Research with Marginalised Communities*. Palgrave: Macmillan.

Pollitt, C. (2003) *The Essential Public Manager*. Buckingham: Open University Press.

Pollitt, C. (2005) 'Decentralization: A central concept in contemporary public management', in E. Ferlie, L.E. Lynn and C. Pollitt (eds), *The Oxford Handbook of Public Management*. Oxford: Oxford University Press.

Popper, K.R. (1957) *The Poverty of Historicism*. London: Routledge & Kegan Paul.

Popper, K.R. (1968 [1934]) *The Logic of Scientific Discovery*, revd edn. London: Hutchinson.

Ransome, P.E. (1992) *Antonio Gramsci: A New Introduction*. Hemel Hempstead: Harvester Wheatsheaf.

Ransome, P.E. (2011) 'Qualitative pedagogy versus instrumentalism: The antinomies of higher education learning and teaching in the United Kingdom', *Higher Education Quarterly* 65: 2: 206–23.

Rickert, H. (1986 [1896]) *The Limits of Concept Formation in the Natural Sciences: A Logical Introduction to Historical Sciences*. New York: Cambridge University Press.

Robbins, D. (ed.) (1993) *Community Care: Findings from Department of Health-Funded Research 1988–1992*. London: HMSO.

Roberts, B. (2002) *Biographical Research*. Buckingham: Open University Press.

Rorty, R. (1989) *Contingency, Irony and Solidarity*. Cambridge, Cambridge University Press.

Rossi, P. and Freeman, H. (1985) *Evaluation: A Systematic Approach*. Beverly Hills, CA: Sage.

Saussure, F. de. (1916 [1915]) *Course in General Linguistics*. London: Peter Owen. Originally published in French.

Sayer, A. (1984) *Method in Social Science: A Realist Approach*. London: Hutchinson.

Scriven, M. (1997) 'Truth and objectivity in evaluation', in E. Chelimsky and W.R. Shadish (eds), *Evaluation for the 21st Century: A Handbook*. Thousand Oaks, CA: Sage.

Seale, C. (ed.) (1998) *Researching Society and Culture*. London: Sage.

Seale, C. (1999) *The Quality of Qualitative Research*. London: Sage.

Shaffer, H.G. (1999) *American Capitalism and the Changing Role of Government*. London: Praeger.

Silverman, D. (2007) *A Very Short, Fairly Interesting and Reasonably Cheap Book about Qualitative Research*. London: Sage.

Sklair, L. and Miller, D. (2010) 'Capitalist globalization, corporate social responsibility and social policy', *Critical Social Policy*, 30: 472.

Smyth, M. and Robinson, G. (eds) (2001) *Researching Violently Divided Societies; Ethical and Methodological Issues*. New York: United Nations University Press.

Social Policy Association (2009) *Guidelines on Research Ethics*. London: Social Policy Association.

Spencer, H. (1969 [1873]) *The Study of Sociology*. Ann Arbor: University of Michigan Press.

Stringer, E.T. (2007) *Action Research*, 3rd edn. London: Sage.

Swansea University (2008) 'Policy Statement for Ethical Research'. Swansea: Swansea University.

Tapper, T. and Salter, B. (2004) 'Governance of higher education in Britain: The significance of the Research Assessment Exercise for the Funding Council model', *Higher Education Quarterly*, 58(1): 4–30.

Theodore, J., Evans, J. and O'Brien, R. (2010) *Measuring Sexual Identity: An Evaluation Report*. London: Office for National Statistics.

Titterton, M. (ed.) (1994) *Caring for People in the Community: The New Welfare*. London: Jessica Kingsley.

Tomlinson, J. (2007) 'Employment regulation, welfare and gender regimes: A comparative analysis of women's working-time patterns and work–life balance in the UK and the US', *International Journal of Human Resource Management*, 18(3): 401–15.

US Government Printing Office (n.d.) *Permissible Medical Experiments. Trials of War Criminals before the Nuremberg Military Tribunals under Control Council Law No. 10: Nuremberg October 1946–April 1949* (Nuremburg Code), vol. 2: 181–2. Washington: US Government Printing Office (n.d.), vol. 2, pp. 181-182.

Van Den Bosch, K. and Cantillon, B. (2006) 'Policy impact', in M. Moran, M. Rein and R.E. Goodin (eds), *The Oxford Handbook of Public Policy*. Oxford: Oxford University Press, pp. 296–318.

Walby, S. (1997) *Gender Transformations*. London: Routledge.

Weber, M. (1949 [1903–17]), *The Methodology of the Social Sciences*, trans. and ed. E.A. Shils and H.N. Finch. New York: Free Press.

Weber, M. (1976) *The Protestant Ethic and the Spirit of Capitalism*, trans. T. Parsons. London: Allen and Unwin. This translation originally published in 1930; Weber's original text 1904–05.

Weber, M. (1978 [1921]) *Economy and Society*, Vols. 1 and 2, ed. G. Roth and C. Wittich. Berkeley, CA: University of California Press.

Weber, M. (1983) *Max Weber on Capitalism, Bureaucracy and Religion: A Selection of Texts*, ed. and part trans. Stanislav Andreski. London: Allen and Unwin.

Weiss, C.H. (1998) *Evaluation: Methods for Studying Programs and Policies*, 2nd edn. Upper Saddle River, NJ: Prentice Hall.

Wellings, K., Field, J., Johnson, A. and Wadsworth J. (1994) *Sexual Behaviour in Britain: The National Survey of Sexual Attitudes and Lifestyles*. Harmondsworth: Penguin.

Whyte, W.F. (ed.) (1991) *Participatory Action Research*. London: Sage.

Whyte, W.F. (1993) *Street Corner Society: The Social Structure of an Italian Slum*, 4th edn. Chicago: University of Chicago Press. First published 1943.

Whyte, W.F., Greenwood, D. and Lazes, P. (1991) 'Participatory action research: Through practice to science in social research', in W.F. Whyte (ed.), *Participatory Action Research*. London: Sage, pp 9–55.

Windleband, W. (1901 [1898]) *A History of Philosophy: With Especial Reference to the Formation and Development of Its Problems and Conceptions*. New York: Macmillan. Originally published in German.

Wittgenstein, L. (1961) *Tractatus Logico-Philosophicus*. London: Routledge & Kegan Paul. Originally published in German.

# Index

Note: Page numbers in *italics* refers to glossary references.